Not Alone

New Directions in the History of Education

Series editor, Benjamin Justice

The New Directions in the History of Education series seeks to publish innovative books that push the traditional boundaries of the history of education. Topics may include social movements in education; the history of cultural representations of schools and schooling; the role of public schools in the social production of space; and the perspectives and experiences of African Americans, Latinx Americans, women, queer folk, and others. The series will take a broad, inclusive look at American education in formal settings, from prekindergarten to higher education, as well as in out-of-school and informal settings. We also invite historical scholarship that informs and challenges popular conceptions of educational policy and policy making and that addresses questions of social justice, equality, democracy, and the formation of popular knowledge.

Dionne Danns, *Crossing Segregated Boundaries: Remembering Chicago School Desegregation*

Sharon S. Lee, *An Unseen Unheard Minority: Asian American Students at the University of Illinois*

Jason Mayernick, *Not Alone: LGB Teachers Organizations from 1970 to 1985*

Margaret A. Nash and Karen Graves, *Mad River, Marjorie Rowland, and the Quest for LGBTQ Teachers' Rights*

Diana D'Amico Pawlewicz, *Blaming Teachers: Professionalization Policies and the Failure of Reform in American History*

John L. Rury, *An Age of Accountability: How Standardized Testing Came to Dominate American Schools and Compromise Education*

Kyle P. Steele, *Making a Mass Institution: Indianapolis and the American High School*

Not Alone

LGB Teachers Organizations from 1970 to 1985

JASON MAYERNICK

Rutgers University Press
New Brunswick, Camden, and Newark, New Jersey
Oxford and London

Rutgers University Press is a department of Rutgers, The State University of New Jersey, one of the leading public research universities in the nation. By publishing worldwide, it furthers the University's mission of dedication to excellence in teaching, scholarship, research, and clinical care.

Library of Congress Cataloging-in-Publication Data
Names: Mayernick, Jason, author.
Title: Not alone : LGB teachers organizations from 1970–1985 / Jason Mayernick.
Other titles: Lesbian, gay, bisexual teachers' groups from 1970–1985
Description: First edition. | New Brunswick : Rutgers University Press, [2023] | Series: New directions in the history of education | Includes bibliographical references and index.
Identifiers: LCCN 2023016180 | ISBN 9781978825895 (paperback : acid-free paper) | ISBN 9781978825932 (hardcover : acid-free paper) | ISBN 9781978825901 (epub) | ISBN 9781978825925 (pdf)
Subjects: LCSH: Teachers' unions—United States—History—20th century. | Homosexuality and education—United States—History—20th century. | Sexual minorities—Civil rights—United States—History—20th century.
Classification: LCC LB2844.53.U6 M39 2023 | DDC 331.88/113711—dc23/eng/20230715
LC record available at https://lccn.loc.gov/2023016180

A British Cataloging-in-Publication record for this book is available from the British Library.

Copyright © 2024 by Jason Mayernick
All rights reserved

No part of this book may be reproduced or utilized in any form or by any means, electronic or mechanical, or by any information storage and retrieval system, without written permission from the publisher. Please contact Rutgers University Press, 106 Somerset Street, New Brunswick, NJ 08901. The only exception to this prohibition is "fair use" as defined by U.S. copyright law.

References to internet websites (URLs) were accurate at the time of writing. Neither the author nor Rutgers University Press is responsible for URLs that may have expired or changed since the manuscript was prepared.

♾ The paper used in this publication meets the requirements of the American National Standard for Information Sciences—Permanence of Paper for Printed Library Materials, ANSI Z39.48–1992.

www.rutgersuniversitypress.org

Manufactured in the United States of America

To Fred, who told me to get out of the Coal Region, get an education, and made sure I was able to do just that.

Contents

	List of Abbreviations	ix
	Introduction: The Value of Teachers	1
1	The National Education Association: Teacher Sexuality and Professionalism	21
2	The American Federation of Teachers: Negotiating National Union Policy	60
3	The Gay Teachers Association of New York: Community and Relationships	92
4	California and the Image of LGB Teachers	126
	Conclusion: Recurring Themes	165
	Acknowledgments	179
	Notes	181
	Bibliography	213
	Index	223

Abbreviations

ACLU	American Civil Liberties Union
AFL-CIO	American Federation of Labor and Congress of Industrial Organizations
AFT	American Federation of Teachers
ATA	American Teachers Association
BAGL	Bay Area Gay Liberation
GAA	Gay Activists Alliance
GLSEN	Gay, Lesbian, Straight, Education, Network
GTA	Gay Teachers Association of New York City
GTLA	Gay Teachers of Los Angeles
GTSWC	Gay Teachers and School Workers Coalition
LGB	Lesbian, Gay, and Bisexual
LGBT	Lesbian, Gay, Bisexual, and Transgender
LGBTQ	Lesbian, Gay, Bisexual, Transgender, and Queer
LGTA	Lesbian and Gay Teachers Association
LSW	Lesbian School Workers
NEA	National Education Association
NGLTF	National Gay and Lesbian Task Force
NGTF	National Gay Task Force

PFLAG	Parents and Friends of Lesbians and Gays
UFT	United Federation of Teachers
UTLA	United Teachers of Los Angeles

Not Alone

Introduction

The Value of Teachers

> There I was marching down Market
> Street carrying a giant red apple, and a
> "Support Gay Teachers" banner while
> hundreds of people clapped and shouted
> their support! It would be impossible to
> describe the feeling that filled my
> insides as I walked that one mile but I
> knew that it was entirely new.
> —Sarah Tuttle on marching in the 1977
> San Francisco gay liberation parade

Between 1970 and 1985, lesbian, gay, and bisexual teachers (LGB) publicly left their classroom closets, formed communities, and began advocating for a place of openness and safety for LGB people in America's schools. This book examines the formation, activities, goals, and impact of six LGB teacher groups active in American cities and unions. LGB K-12 teachers came out in large numbers for the first time during this period, and this was the first time they successfully resisted being forced out of America's schools. Through these groups, LGB teachers successfully protected themselves and

LGB students from an educational system that was openly hostile to anyone who did not appear heterosexual.

When we discuss the value of teachers and their importance to a community or society, we are talking about at least two distinct values: one value that is tangible and one that is symbolic. Teachers create tangible value for a community by doing the necessary job of education. We can see this tangible value by observing how educators teach their classes, interact with their colleagues, and perform throughout their careers. This tangible value is ostensibly measured today by countless teacher assessment strategies, the compilation of standardized test scores, and other points of data generated by the actions of K-12 educators, which seek to determine how well a teacher performs.

How teachers are portrayed, what they are perceived to be, and the moral impact they are assumed to have on their students determines their symbolic value. This symbolic value often contrasts, and sometimes contradicts, the tangible value of teachers. Communities measure a teacher's symbolic value not through tests and statistics but by determining how closely an individual educator, or a group of educators, is perceived to conform to the dominant moral norms of a place. The act of excluding a class of individuals from being teachers, the ultimate form of community disapproval, says a tremendous amount about the values and culture of a community. Moral judgments of educators, and the negotiation that surrounds them, profoundly influence what is taught in American schools by determining who has been allowed to teach at specific times and in particular spaces.

The collective judgments of communities form a spectrum of acceptability over time. Individual educator's actions and person are ultimately measured against an idealized assertion of what a teacher "should be." This process often applies to types of teachers, with individuals receiving praise or censure based on the groups they belong to. A "good teacher" reinforces and is part of the ideal education that a community desires for its children and youth. A "bad teacher" threatens that same set of ideals and desires. The degrees of gradation on this spectrum are as varied and numerous as the number of schools and school districts in the United States, changing based on geography and over time as specific behaviors become more or less acceptable. The success of LGB teachers' groups rested on their ability to convince other educational stakeholders that LGB teachers were not a threat to the symbolic value of education and should be afforded the same rights and protections as any other educator. In short that they were "good teachers" and deserved respect for their work.

This study explores collective LGB teacher agency in its earliest manifestations across the United States. It examines some of the first successful efforts to shift the boundaries of acceptability for K-12 teachers beyond the heterosexual and discusses the first places where groups of LGB teachers convinced their colleagues and communities that they were "good teachers." This shift in acceptability occurred not only because of the broader change occurring in American society during the 1970s and 1980s, which lessened the systemic discrimination faced by LGB people, but also through the organizing and activism of LGB teachers. LGB teachers were not merely along for the ride as society around them changed but were an active part of that change.

This study shows how LGB teachers and their allies broadened the boundaries of professionalism, created communities of support for themselves, negotiated for employment protections, and fought against political opponents who wanted them pushed back into their classroom closets or out of America's schools altogether. After gaining the support of their colleagues and the protection of their unions, they refused to be put back or pushed out, and instead continued pursuing their equality as professionals. These successes created a space of relative professional security. LGB teachers could then be more vigorous in making schools safe for LGB students because their livelihoods had some protections.

Oral histories play an integral role in detailing the goals and accomplishments of the LGB teachers' groups in the following chapters. It would have been challenging, if not impossible, to conduct this study utilizing only archival sources. The archival sources available for LGB teachers' groups, while extensive, represent only one dimension of the narratives examined in this book. Primary archival sources allow us to see what was occurring at the moment, but oral histories collected decades later allow us to explore the voices of the activists involved from another angle. These oral histories provide context for the primary sources and broaden the overall narrative to include what teacher activists thought their contributions were. Historians can easily oversimplify or even exclude the accomplishments and motivations of individual activists and small groups from a historical narrative by not considering oral histories in their works. Minoritized groups are especially susceptible to being overlooked in this way because of the scarcity of primary sources they leave for analysis.[1]

The size of the LGB teachers' groups examined in this study varies; some of the groups had dozens of members, while the membership of other groups was much smaller. In some of the events detailed in this study, the identities of LGB teachers and their allies are unclear. Like following tracks without knowing who made them, it is only through an examination of the changes their activism produced that the existence of these activists becomes clear. Despite the small size of early LGB teachers' groups, their value as subjects of historical inquiry remains intact because, again, this is a study of beginnings and exceptions that showed what was possible. These LGB teachers' groups broke through a historic oppression and created the first cracks through which the light of a better day could be seen.

All teachers balance their public and professional personas with their private lives. This tension between private and public lies at the heart of any discussion about teacher professionalism. We expect teachers to be government bureaucrats who provide the mandated service of education while simultaneously being nurturing caregivers who value the accomplishments of individual students. Local communities employ teachers to convey the values of a specific place, but teachers always have the possibility of subverting those values; what they teach and what they believe are not necessarily the same. This disconnect contains the potential for teachers to clash with the communities they work in over issues of morality. LGBT (lesbian, gay, bisexual, and transgender) teachers exemplify the tension between K-12 educators and the communities where they work because they take historically volatile issues, gender diversity and sexuality, and embody those issues in American schools. The extreme political diversity that existed between school districts because of the uniquely American system of local political control over K-12 education made navigating these tensions between 1970 and 1985 even more complicated. Teachers faced community expectations about their sexuality and openness as LGBT people that varied from school district to school district.

Teachers are easy to overlook; they are as ubiquitous in American communities as the schools where they work. The public often takes both schools and teachers for granted until there seems to be a problem with them. The teachers in this study had been forced to be unseen but refused to be invisible any longer. They left the anonymity of their desks and classrooms hoping that they would be able to return to them and teach without fear. By examining multiple LGB teachers' groups in their local and organizational contexts, this study highlights the diversity of LGB teachers' groups. It interrogates the conditions that were conducive to the initial LGB teachers' groups being able to form and pursue their goals. By utilizing oral histories gathered from individual LGB teacher activists and their allies, this study explores the narratives of LGB teachers' groups in greater detail than has been possible before. Finally, by viewing LGB teachers' groups through the lenses of LGBT history, labor history, and the history of education, this study locates LGB teachers' groups in these broader histories and shows how the narratives of LGB teachers' groups add significantly to our understanding of these three areas of history.

The Relevance of This Study

This book exists where the history of education, LGBT history, and labor history overlap. The history of education argues for the significance of education and institutions of education as sites for examining society as a whole. This study uses schools and the lives of teachers to explore the tremendous changes in societal acceptance of sexuality that occurred between 1970 and 1985 and illustrates that these changes were not limited to riots and Pride parades but were instead present in the seemingly most mundane of places, the K-12 classroom. LGBT history serves as an examination and critique of heteronormative social structures that typically conflate the statistical commonness of heterosexuality with inherent, and often exclusive, morality. This study presents how LGB teachers' groups argued and eventually convinced educational stakeholders that LGB teachers were as moral and as deserving of job security and a place in America's schools as their "straight" colleagues. Labor history examines the impact of organized labor on the lives of workers and the broad course of history by illustrating the effects of organized labor and the workplace with the rest of the human experience. This study definitively shows the negotiations between LGB teachers' groups and teachers' unions, the benefits that LGB teachers derived from organized labor, and how national teachers' unions gradually accepted the needs of their LGB members and LGB students as valid.

This book is relevant to the history of education because the organizing of LGB K-12 teachers and their inclusion into union policies and school-district-level nondiscrimination clauses represent an expansion of who was permitted to teach. In the same way that African American educators were a new "type" of teacher in desegregated schools in the 1960s, or Jewish teachers represented a new "type" of teacher in many urban schools throughout the early twentieth century, openly LGBT teachers were a new "type" of teacher in the 1970s and 1980s. Unlike most other "new types" of educators throughout the twentieth century, which were gradually and often controversially introduced to communities, LGBT educators were already present in classrooms across the United States but forced to remain hidden. Their reputations as educators were public knowledge even though their sexualities were not. School boards, administrators, and communities were faced with the reality that LGBT educators *were already in their schools* and doing their jobs for years. The sudden appearance of LGBT educators in *their* classrooms forced schools and communities to respond.

Within the history of education, this study fits into a broader trajectory of historical inquiry that examines educators and systems of education negotiating changes in society. These changes encompass the appearance and acceptance of "new types" of educators, teachers exercising political agency, and teachers claiming agency as a class of educational stakeholders. Including the historical narratives of LGB educators in this larger history of the American teaching profession makes it possible to examine this diversification at different levels. As LGB teachers came out, formed groups, and contested the discrimination they faced, they responded to local conditions while participating in a national trend of increasing acceptance that continues to this day.

Jackie Blount's *Fit to Teach: Same-Sex Desire, Gender, and School Work in the Twentieth Century* is the historical work this study is most indebted to. Blount's *Fit to Teach* remains the first and only comprehensive historical treatment of LGBT school workers in America covering the entirety of the twentieth century. Her work provides an overarching view of the broad shapes and trends that are apparent in that history and is in essence the foundational historical text regarding LGBT school workers in the United States. Blount includes accounts of LGB teachers' groups in her chapters, "Sometimes You Just Have to Take a Stand" and "How Sweet It Is," and details the formations of LGB teachers' groups and their activities.[2] Blount argues that the formation of organizations by LGBT school workers "gave significant momentum to the cause of employment rights for LGBT school workers," and places the development of these groups in the 1970s within the immediate context of the previous two decades.[3] Within this context, the formation of LGB teachers' groups and the efforts of individual LGBT teachers are the "Stand" taken against the oppression of the past. By focusing on the local/institutional contexts and diversity of challenges faced by specific LGB teachers' groups, this study will add to and complicate the overarching national narrative that Blount uncovered in her groundbreaking study of LGBT school workers.

Blount's research fits in a broader arc of writing about LGBT teachers and their history, which identifies the challenges faced by LGBT educators and explains the evolving roles of sexual orientation and gender diversity within the history of American education. Karen Graves's body of research on LGBT teachers, most notably her work *And They Were Wonderful Teachers: Florida's Purge of Gay and Lesbian Teachers*, establishes a detailed account of the perils facing gay and lesbian teachers in the context of Cold War witch hunts. Graves's work also establishes a case for the relevance of LGBT teachers to the broader history of education, positing that schools serve as "prime sites for cultural reproduction, contested terrain for those who wish to preserve or challenge the status quo."[4] LGBT teachers' position in these "prime sites" reflected and magnified the expectations for the sexuality of all teachers and continues doing so today.

Schools magnify the values and goals of a community. Teachers' experiences and the challenges they face indicate changes to those goals and values over time. This study demonstrates how LGB teachers skillfully negotiated the "contested terrain" of education between 1970 and 1985. LGB teachers' groups shifted that terrain from being de facto hostile to possessing the possibility of equity and also impacted the process of cultural reproduction inside American cities and teachers' unions to make protections based on sexual orientation a reality. These protections stand in stark contrast to the discrimination faced by LGB teachers in the 1950s and 1960s.

Craig Loftin utilizes the history of LGB teachers to illuminate the beliefs and realities of the Cold War in his work *Masked Voices: Gay Men and Lesbians in Cold War America*. His chapter on teachers, "Classroom Anxieties, Educators and Homosexuality," details the correspondence of gay male teachers to *ONE* magazine, the oldest gay male periodical in the United States, evidencing their awareness of both the persecution they personally faced as gay teachers and the widespread nature of that persecution in the 1950s and 1960s. This awareness occurred decades before LGB teachers organized professionally. Loftin's research confirms that gay male teachers nationwide discussed that they were constantly under pressure to avoid detection if they wanted to remain employed. His research also confirms that, by the late 1950s, gay male teachers were aware of persecutions in other parts of the country. Caught in the context of the Cold War, these teachers often felt helpless as individuals to combat their oppression as sexual minorities.[5]

The historical research of Karen Graves, Jackie Blount, and Craig Loftin builds on the first generation of histories written about LGBT teachers in the 1990s, which were pioneering in their efforts to establish LGBT teachers as a field of historical inquiry.[6] Research by Eric Rofes, Rita Kissen, James Sears, and Karen Harbeck about the experiences of LGBT teachers, often based on oral histories of those teachers, established an understanding of how the sexual orientation and gender diversity impacted LGBT teachers and the schools where they taught.[7] This understanding of the challenges faced by LGBT teachers at different points during the twentieth century serves as a basis for examining how LGBT teachers met those challenges and expressed political agency.

This study shows how LGB teachers and their allies came together in groups between 1970 and 1985 and utilized political agency to mitigate and overcome the challenges they shared with previous generations of LGBT educators. Coupled with more recent research by Loftin, Blount, and Graves, the earlier works by Harbeck, Kissen, and Rofes provide historiographical context for the agency of LGB teachers' groups and their impact on education. The addition of this study to queer educational historiography offers a deeper understanding of the diversity of challenges facing LGB teachers' groups at national, state, and local levels and how LGB K-12 educators and their allies addressed those challenges through organizing.

Historians have expanded the history of the LGBT community in the past twenty years by focusing their research on sites of activism and community that are less obvious. They have accomplished this by building on previous historical works that established a larger framework of queer history in the United States centered on major coastal cities and activist groups. Historians are now able to provide details for that larger framework by writing regional histories, histories concentrating on specific cities, and histories that examine the relationships between the LGBT rights movement and other social movements in the United States. It is clear from these studies that the development of the LGBT community in the United States and the struggle for LGBT rights occurred in numerous and diverse contexts. Historians have not adequately examined many of these contexts.[8]

Within the field of LGBT history, this study is most similar to works that examine political activity in settings outside traditional advocacy and activist groups. Jim Downs's *Stand By Me: The Forgotten History of Gay Liberation* exemplifies this type of history and serves as a model for organizing this study.[9] Downs focuses on, "a history that has often been overshadowed by the narrative that attempted to rationalize the spread of HIV." He argues that LGBT histories that did not support a rationale that gay men were hypersexualized beings, histories that included lesbian and transgender people as integral players, were not explored and have been neglected. To illustrate this neglect, he focuses each of his chapters on a different organizational site of gay liberation: a bar in New Orleans that was fire-bombed when a gay church met in there, a much loved gay bookstore in New York City, the work of the predominately LGBT Metropolitan Community Church, gay men who were incarcerated but engaged with the broader community, the act of writing gay history for the first time, and the publication of gay newspapers.[10]

In this way, Downs broadens what gay liberation meant and looked like for different people in the 1970s. This study will also examine what gay liberation and political organizing looked like for six teachers' groups. Downs's omission of LGB teachers' groups from his history of 1970s LGBT culture and organizing misses an opportunity to show that the alternative forms of organizing and political activity also occur in the context of professional groups. This book will illustrate how LGB teachers' groups were at the forefront of the broader movement toward LGBT equality and what the pursuit of that equality meant to LGB teachers.

There is a conspicuous absence of LGBT teachers in LGBT histories. There are several possible explanations for this absence. The simplest of which is that organization in the workplace by LGBT people has not received nearly as much attention as traditional political organizing by more militant groups. Another possibility is that the goals of LGBT teachers and LGB teachers' groups in this period are not revolutionary enough to draw the collective gaze of historians.[11] K-12 schools are so profoundly present in American communities they get passed over even in histories, like Downs's work, that focus on LGBT activism in less traditional settings. In researching this book, I found very few mentions of LGB teachers in the secondary literature aside from commentary on court cases and occasional first-person accounts.[12] When broader social histories of the LGBT community do not include LGBT teachers, what results is a form of erasure from these larger narratives. The research by Graves and Blount mentioned earlier in this introduction and the research detailed in this book show that this erasure is not justifiable.

This study contributes to labor history by establishing distinct ties between LGB activism and teachers' unions at local, state, and national levels. Specifically, this study details how LGB teachers in different settings viewed, negotiated with, participated in, and utilized teachers' unions to pursue their political goals. It presents a detailed historical account of these interactions between LGB teachers and teachers' unions, including local, state, and national activism and organization. This history of interaction is substantial, but because teachers were at the forefront of building alliances between the LGB community and organized labor they are even more critical to understand. The activities of LGB teachers' groups are among the earliest formal interactions between the LGB community and organized labor in the United States.[13] These interactions were spurred and sustained by the activism of LGB teachers and their allies who argued that lesbian, gay, and bisexual teachers were entitled to the same protection and representation as any other member of the union.

A small number of historians have examined the presence and impact of LGBT workers in American unions. Recent volumes that engage the roles sexuality and gender diversity played in the lives of American workers include Miriam Frank's *Out in the Union: A Labor History of Queer America* and Philip Tiemeyer's *Plane Queer: Labor, Sexuality, and AIDS in the History of Male Flight Attendants*. Frank's book presents an overview of the entire LGBT community and its relationship with organized labor, while Tiemeyer's research focuses on the airline industry. The connection between both works is the emphasis they place on LGBT people seeking out workplace protections in the context of organized labor. Neither makes the argument that being employed within the context of a union negated discrimination, but both present compelling evidence that the presence of a strong union gave LGBT workers the ability to contest discrimination consistently and successfully.[14]

This book will make a similar claim regarding the value of unions to LGB teachers; that belonging to a teachers' union positively impacted the ability of LGB teachers' groups to create change. Each of the cities in which early LGB teachers' groups developed had a strong teachers' union. Moreover, each of the city-based LGB teachers' groups discussed in this study actively sought out working relationships with their teachers' union as one of their initial actions. Frank's discussion of teachers' unions details resolutions passed by national and local levels of the unions and briefly outlines the progress of LGBT teachers. Frank also details a number of the interactions between LGB teachers' groups in San Francisco and New York City with local and national levels of their respective unions and characterizes the efforts of groups in these two cities as being "stymied" in their early efforts to engage their labor unions.[15] The city-based LGB teachers' groups, discussed in chapter 3 and chapter 4, are distinct within Frank's broader narrative. While they worked with unions, these groups intentionally maintained independence and autonomy, viewing themselves as allies of their cities' teachers' unions. Indeed, as we will see in the following chapters, the leaders of LGB teachers' groups in New York City, Los Angeles, and San Francisco went to significant lengths to work with their unions without being subsumed by larger organizations.

Teachers' unions have been the subject of significant historical research as organizations and educational stakeholders. This research covers overarching accounts of major national unions, biographies of union leaders, and histories of teachers' unions in specific states engaging in local politics.[16] The historical works that are most relevant to this study focus on the organizational structure and political activism of teachers' unions. Histories with this focus allow for an understanding of how teachers' unions engaged with politically active subgroups of educators, such as racial minorities or female teachers, and eventually incorporated some of the goals of those groups into the broader agenda of teachers' unions. Within this category, Marjorie Murphy's *Blackboard Unions* is the most comprehensive history of the two national teachers' unions, covering most of the twentieth century up to the late 1980s.

Murphy details the development of both the American Federation of Teachers (AFT) and the National Education Association (NEA) and pays particular attention to the differences between the two unions and their relationship as they developed over the first seventy years of the twentieth century.[17] While the NEA began as a professional organization with genteel aspirations and an "apolitical" educational agenda, the AFT had its origins as a "gadfly union" that utilized labor tactics, such as strikes and contract negotiation, from its inception.[18] Murphy posits that the primary concern of both teachers' unions in the 1950s and 1960s was the civil rights movement, with both the NEA and AFT vying to win a "contest of leadership" to see which union would win the support of diversifying and often politically liberal urban teachers. The AFT initially had the upper hand in this contest for urban teachers. Ultimately several bruising race-centered debates in the late 1960s, most notably the Ocean Hill controversy in New York City, left the NEA in a better position to "translate community demands into professional concerns."[19]

Wayne Urban's *Gender, Race, and the National Education Association: Professionalism and Its Limitations* supports Murphy's assertion that the NEA eclipsed the AFT in the arena of civil rights. Urban includes a significant discussion of the AFT because the AFT remained the NEA's only national competition during the 1970s and 1980s. He details how the NEA attempted to resolve the needs of female and African American teachers and how this compared to efforts by the AFT.[20] He concludes that the NEA was far more successful and equitable in its attempts to address the needs of female teachers early in the twentieth century than it was during the 1970s and 1980s for African American teachers. Urban also posits that the AFT made itself unattractive to politically moderate female teachers and minority teachers during the 1970s and 1980s because of the AFT's willingness to champion stereotypically white male causes through direct confrontation.[21]

This study deepens the analysis of Murphy and Urban by illustrating how teachers' unions at national and local levels engaged with LGB teachers between 1970 and 1985. It also details how LGB educators engaged the AFT and the NEA in a decades-long process to secure recognition and union support for LGB educators across the United States. The negotiations between LGB teachers' groups and national unions resulted in many political successes for LGB teachers' groups. The limitations of those political successes, and the path that individual LGB teachers' groups and their allies took to achieve them, add to our broader historical understanding of how teachers' unions responded to the demands and needs of minority teachers. By focusing on national-level debates within the NEA and AFT, this study highlights the distinctions between the two national unions and how their leadership and rank-and-file memberships perceived LGB teachers and students. Dialogues between teachers' unions and LGB teachers' groups also occurred in American cities locally. Teachers' unions played a pivotal role in local LGB teachers' groups achieving political victories.

The pattern that the NEA and AFT established during their engagement with the needs/goals of women and African American teachers also applies, to a significant degree, to LGB teachers' groups. As we will see in the following chapters, the NEA took longer to acknowledge the needs and goals of LGB teachers than the AFT but was far more willing to incorporate those needs and goals into the broader agenda of the association. In contrast, the AFT was very early in acknowledging LGB teachers but slow to extend formal recognition. The dynamic between the two national unions and LGB teachers between 1970 and 1985, while unique, is recognizable as a continuation of the NEA and AFT's previous engagement with other marginalized groups of educators.

The Scope of This Study

LGB teachers were among the first LGB people to organize professional groups. They were also among the first LGB people to secure commitments against discrimination from national-level labor unions. Working first to protect their employment rights and later to ensure the educational rights of LGBT students, LGB teachers' groups were at the forefront of shifting American schools toward greater inclusivity. I argue that the relevance of these LGB teachers' groups extends far beyond the individual experiences of their members. Expectations that Americans held, and continue to hold, for their schools and teachers are clearly present in the histories of these groups. LGB teachers' groups illustrate and exemplify the challenges faced by K-12 educators as they advocate for their interests and negotiate with other educational stakeholders over the future of American schools. LGB teachers' groups also provide a tremendous case study to examine the potential and limitations of K-12 teachers as agents of social change.

LGB teachers founded two types of groups between 1970 and 1985. The first variety centered on specific cities and focused on local conditions LGB teachers faced in those cities. The second variety worked within national teachers' unions and focused on the policies of those unions. The city-based LGB teachers' groups were more numerous. There is evidence of LGB teachers' groups being active in eight American cities between 1970 and 1985. Of these nine city-based groups, the groups in Chicago, Boston, Baltimore, Denver, and Portland, Oregon, left a minimal body of archival materials to examine.[22] Because of this archival limitation, I have focused on local LGB teachers' groups found in Los Angeles, New York City, and San Francisco.

LGB teachers' groups organized around national teachers' unions were less common simply because only two national teachers' unions were active between 1970 and 1985: the AFT and the NEA.[23] LGB teachers and their allies were active in both the NEA and the AFT. This activity manifested formally in the eventual formation of formal groups but also in informal groups, as evidenced by a continuous effort to change the policies of the AFT and the NEA regarding LGB teachers and students. The accomplishments of LGB teachers within the NEA and the AFT had the potential to impact teachers across the country because of the national reach of these two unions. Their large memberships, which numbered in the hundreds of thousands and included most teachers in the United States, were present in schools nationwide.[24]

Aside from the focus on LGB teachers acting in groups, rather than as individuals, another major boundary of this study is its time frame. I begin this study in 1970 because the earliest evidence of collective LGB teacher activism found in my research comes from that year. The end point for this study, 1985, was selected for two reasons. First, a fifteen-year time frame allows for an in-depth focus on a specific period of organizational history. Each of these groups operated under overarching beliefs and saw themselves as part of an effort to change education in America and the LGBT movement. This project is concerned with the beginnings of LGB teachers' groups and their development as they pursued their goals. Fifteen years is sufficient to broadly analyze the initial development of the six LGB teachers' groups selected for this project and understand their successes and shortfalls. The LGB teachers' groups discussed in this project all began and made significant strides in accomplishing their goals within this period.

Second, 1985 has significance for the broader history of the LGBT movement. In short, the advent of the AIDS crisis, which began earlier in the 1980s, fundamentally shifted the character of LGBT activism in the United States toward an epidemic claiming the lives of thousands of Americans. This fundamental shift in focus would last at least until the late 1990s, when drug treatments and the collective activism of the previous decade substantially mitigated the lethality of the epidemic among LGBT people in the United States. The AIDS crisis was a watershed moment in LGBT history. The issues, politics, and dangers faced by LGBT people in this period were categorically different than those that had come before.

So, while many of the political structures and legal protections developed in prior periods shaped the strategies and political dynamics of the AIDS crisis, it is a history that needs to be explored on its own and is beyond the scope of this study. This project will discuss how gay teachers' groups utilized the resources they had developed to grapple with the emergence of the AIDS crisis. Aside from these initial interactions, however, the long history of AIDS, the epidemic, and its impact on education, educators, and the LGBT community is outside this book's scope and will need to be addressed in further studies.[25]

Transgender teachers and students are largely absent from this study. This absence is not an omission or oversight. Transgender teachers and transgender students appear in the research done for this study a bare handful of times. This absence may be due to the time frame of the study. This absence may also be due to the particularly ferocious degree of oppression faced by transgender people during the fifteen years that this study is primarily concerned with. This heightened oppression would have made public participation in teacher activism extraordinarily challenging. I am not claiming that there were no transgender teachers in this period; there were.[26] There certainly were transgender students who suffered from a lack of advocacy on their behalf. But I have not found evidence of self-identified transgender teachers taking part in the activism of the teachers' groups discussed in this study. In the interest of accuracy and to avoid paving over the specific challenges that transgender teachers as a class of educators faced, and still face, or making this history more inclusive than it is, I use the acronym LGB (lesbian, gay, bisexual) when referring to the LGB teachers' groups researched in this book and LGBT (lesbian, gay, bisexual, and transgender) when referring to the LGBT community as a whole.

This study is an examination of beginnings and as such revolves around exceptions and exceptional circumstances. Historical beginnings are often exceptions; presenting something new offers the possibility of a more significant and widespread change in society. The exception examined in this study is the appearance of something breathtakingly new in 1970 and still startlingly uncommon fifteen years later in 1985; politically organized gay, lesbian, and bisexual K-12 teachers working together in groups.

I engage in three conversations throughout this book. First, I aim to show how LGB teachers created spaces for themselves as openly gay teachers and used those spaces to advocate for broader acceptance of LGBT educators and students. Second, I propose that the history of LGB teachers is a neglected portion of LGBT history and can be used to examine the evolving relationships between the queer community and K-12 education in the United States. Third, I highlight the unique identities that openly LGB teachers forged as professionals and the efficacy of their tactics which they derived from their experience with teachers' unions and LGBT activism.

The Plan of This Study

I have divided this book into four chapters. The National Education Association, the American Federation of Teachers, New York City, and the state of California, which includes activism in Los Angeles and San Francisco, are each the subject of a chapter. Each chapter proceeds chronologically, beginning with the first traceable instance of LGB teacher activism and ending in the 1980s. Readers can revisit important events and developments during this period from different angles and perspectives in subsequent chapters. For example, the impact of the 1978 Briggs Initiative, a ballot initiative that would have amended the California State Constitution, is discussed in multiple chapters.

The focus of discussion throughout this study will move between national, state, and local levels of organizing and activism. The first chapter details organizing in the NEA, and the second chapter discusses national LGB activism in the AFT. The third chapter shifts to the local-level activism in New York City. The fourth and final chapter discusses three local-level LGB teachers' groups participating in state and local activism in California. By shifting between different levels of activism and organization, we can examine the broad range of activities and goals LGB teachers' groups pursued between 1970 and 1985. Shifting focus between local-, state-, and national-level LGB teacher activism also illustrates the interplay and connections between different levels.

The first chapter, "The National Education Association: Teacher Sexuality and Professionalism," begins with the efforts of one gay teacher to change the policies of one of America's largest labor unions and to found an LGB teachers' caucus in 1972. The chapter contextualizes John Gish's efforts by examining the political climate of the NEA and the organizational and demographic changes that took place in the association in the years leading up to the early 1970s. The initial protections and commitments secured by LGB teachers and their allies arose from this context. The chapter then turns to the impact of geography on the formation of an LGB teachers' caucus. Organizing efforts at national meetings of the NEA and informal social gatherings throughout the 1970s and into the mid-1980s preceded the formation of an official caucus. Efforts by the LGB caucus led to the passage of numerous resolutions and an expansion of LGB teacher activism to include the needs of LGB students. The new LGB caucus's response to the AIDS crisis in the late 1980s showcased the group's development and efficacy in impacting NEA policy. The chapter concludes by discussing the benefits and limits of sanctioning teacher behavior through the construct of professionalism, paying particular attention to the lengthy timeline that professionalism as an ideal seems to impose on the process of change.

This chapter introduces the themes of professionalism and the right to maintain a distinction between personal and public life as a teacher. These two themes are apparent throughout the entirety of this study. Together they create the complicated dynamic of LGB teachers advocating for two distinct changes. First, administrators should not consider the sexuality of teachers when determining hiring and terminations. Second, LGB teachers whose sexuality was public had a right to job protections. LGB teachers' groups simultaneously argued for a right to privacy in some circumstances and a right to be out in others. They argued for both changes from the perspective of teacher professionalism.

While this might seem a contradiction, LGB teachers' groups viewed the juxtaposition of privacy and public life as something their heterosexual colleagues already possessed. Straight teachers had a right to privacy. Likewise, no one argued that heterosexual teachers had to hide their heterosexual relationships to maintain their employment; they could publicly acknowledge their husbands, wives, and partners and remain employed as K-12 teachers. Straight teachers had a right to be publicly heterosexual and still be considered professional. LGB teachers' groups believed they had the same rights and pursued those rights in contexts of labor unions and various political arenas.

The second chapter, "The American Federation of Teachers: Negotiating National Union Policy," analyzes the AFT's development of national-level union policy regarding LGB teachers. It begins with a discussion of the complicated relationship between the New York City's United Federation of Teachers (UFT), the AFT, and Albert Shanker, the man who would serve as leader of both unions for decades. After setting this internal context, the chapter discusses six resolutions and amendments about LGB teachers debated between 1970 and 1979 at the highest levels of the AFT. The language of these resolutions and their success, or failure, outlines the development of an understanding of LGB teachers in the AFT during the 1970s. This understanding underpinned a commitment to LGB teachers who were members of the union. Both the AFT's understanding and commitment had limitations, and these limitations were rooted in the institutional boundaries that existed for the AFT as a national organization. The AFT selectively interpreted and implemented resolutions passed at national conventions. The AFT's response to the Helm's Law, an anti-LGB-teacher statute in Oklahoma, illustrates this process of interpretation and implementation. The chapter closes by discussing the reach of national-level resolutions and their value for LGB teachers in different political and geographic contexts.

The second chapter points to the complicated negotiations that LGB teachers and their allies engaged in to accomplish their goals. This theme of negotiation is present throughout the narratives of each of the LGB teachers' groups examined in this study. LGB teachers were not only initially marginalized politically; they were deviants. Their deviant status fundamentally impacted how LGB teachers and their allies engaged in negotiation. First, they had to convince a significant portion of a group, like the AFT Delegate Assembly or AFT Executive Committee, that they were a legitimate group to negotiate with. Each LGB teachers' group had to achieve its right to negotiation early in its history because having any discussion was contingent on securing a seat at the negotiating table. The national-level union negotiations in chapters 1 and 2 provided firm rhetorical ground for local LGB teachers' groups. When met by a reluctant local-level union, or a state politician bent on passing discriminatory laws, local LGB teachers' groups could point to the commitments made by the AFT and NEA to LGB teachers and claim legitimacy. As we will see throughout this study, LGB teacher activists evidenced considerable skill in navigating the political environments in which they pursued their goals.

The third chapter, "The Gay Teachers Association of New York: Community and Relationships," details the efforts of LGB teachers in New York City and centers on the activities of the Gay Teachers Association (GTA). The chapter opens with a discussion of two local contexts that made New York City conducive to the organizing of LGB teachers. First, the city had a growing and politically vocal gay and lesbian community. Second, New York City had a long labor history that included what was arguably the country's most influential teachers' union, the UFT. The chapter then turns to the initial actions of the GTA to secure antidiscrimination commitments from both the UFT and the city's Board of Education. The GTA devoted considerable organizational energy to creating a community of LGB teachers that would be welcoming to both activists and LGB teachers who chose to remain closeted at work. While "closet rights" were respected, the ultimate goal of the GTA was to ensure schools did not discriminate against LGB teachers and students. To achieve this goal, the GTA was organized into numerous committees, which engaged the media, organized a speakers' bureau, interacted with politicians and other educational stakeholders, and engaged in student outreach.

Central to this chapter is the theme of community. Developing a community was essential to developing LGB teacher responsibility and LGB teachers actively working toward political goals. The GTA's newsletter conveyed this sense of responsibility through numerous articles and initiatives. LGB teachers in New York saw themselves as being responsible for two groups of people: other LGB teachers, who might still be in the closet by choice or be living in places where activism and remaining employed were mutually exclusive propositions, and LGB students, who as minors were in most respects at the mercy of their families and an educational bureaucracy that saw heterosexuality as normal and deviations from heterosexuality in students as problematic.

The GTA saw itself as a voice for both LGB teachers and LGB students. This theme of LGB teacher responsibility appears throughout this study. LGB teacher responsibility was an outgrowth of a broader history of American K-12 educators addressing social inequity through their unions, political engagement, and teaching. Indeed, some of the most vocal voices for LGB teachers and LGB students throughout this study came from heterosexual teachers who had seen their LGB colleagues and students treated unfairly and became allies of LGB teachers' groups. LGB teachers' groups were always a minority making moral arguments to a majority. Because of this demographic reality, straight allies were crucial in attaining local-, state-, and national-level gains for LGB teachers.

The fourth and final chapter, "California and the Image of LGB Teachers," examines the activities of the LGB teachers' groups in that state and discusses the portrayal of LGB teachers as a theme. This discussion encompasses how LGB teachers thought of themselves, how their political opponents portrayed them, and how popular media represented their struggles. The chapter begins with a discussion of California's political and demographic complexity and, from this position, moves on to discuss the foundation and efforts of the Gay Teachers of Los Angeles. The narrative then moves north and examines the activism of the Gay Teachers and School Workers Association of San Francisco and the Lesbian School Workers, who were each based in the Bay Area.

The activism of these three groups was made all the more urgent by the advent of Proposition 6 (a.k.a. the Briggs Initiative), a state ballot initiative that called for the firing of LGB teachers and a ban on the hiring of LGB people as teachers. The activism of these three LGB teachers' groups and how they portrayed themselves positively is juxtaposed against the negative portrayal of LGB teachers by the California Defend Our Children Campaign and State Senator John Briggs. This comparison provides an opportunity to discuss how the pro-Proposition 6 campaign attempted to motivate conservative voters. Finally, chapter 4 analyzes a series of political comics that ran in centrist and liberal newspapers during the Proposition 6 campaign. These comics critiqued the aims, arguments, and methods of State Senator John Briggs. They illustrate many of the reasons that activists defeated the Briggs Initiative and the changing role that sexuality played in American politics.

1

The National Education Association

Teacher Sexuality and
Professionalism

> One is tempted to conclude that it
> would have been better for John to have
> stayed in his closet. While he and his
> friends were hiding we weren't solving
> the problem, but we were avoiding it.
> Now they're out in the open and it's
> trouble for everybody.
> —*Washington Post* on the first LGB
> teachers' group

This chapter discusses the activism of LGBT teachers and their allies within the NEA between 1972 and 1988. It will detail the groups they formed, the agendas they pursued, the challenges they faced, and the goals they accomplished. LGBT teachers' activism within the NEA differs from similar activism found in U.S. cities in a key way: until 1987 it took place outside of an "official" group recognized by the association. In other settings, LGB educators formed groups in the 1970s that went on to serve different functions for their members and pursue a myriad of goals specific to the particular needs of a geographic or organizational space. Within the NEA, the accomplishments of LGB teachers and their allies appear to be disconnected because of the pacing of their activism. Activists came together at annual conventions and worked toward specific goals but did not maintain an official caucus until the late 1980s.[1] These disjointed periods of activity are misleading. A detailed analysis of primary and oral sources reveals an archipelago of motions, proposals, and activists breaking the waterline of silence only intermittently but connected nevertheless through social networks and the overarching arguments of gay liberation and civil rights.

Running through the history detailed in this chapter is the concept of professionalism—a vaguely understood, unclearly defined, yet nevertheless potent idea of how a teacher should fulfill their job responsibilities to their students and the community that employs them. Professionalism throughout this chapter will be most commonly described as "how a teacher should act." The question that follows from this definition is "Who determines how a teacher should act?" because the legitimacy of LGB teachers was based not only on how they acted but also on *who* judged those activities.

The NEA framed much of its advocacy around the concept of teacher professionalism but with the caveat that the collective professionalism and expertise of educators were best maintained and advanced not by outside authorities but by NEA members themselves. Educators could ensure the education of America's children through professionalism and garner the respect of the populace through their service. The history of LGB teachers' groups and activism within the NEA can be understood as a series of debates about that professionalism. Who qualified as a "good" teacher?[2] Who could the association publicly defend? Which teachers were unprofessional? For LGB teachers, the task then was in convincing their straight colleagues that they were entitled to the support of the NEA like any other teacher, not because they were oppressed, but because they were as competent as any other teacher. LGB teachers in the NEA would argue that for the NEA to be true to its institutional values, it had to defend and support LGB teachers and students.

The task of convincing their colleagues that they were professional and worth defending in courts of law and the court of public opinion hinged on debunking generations' worth of negative stereotypes around gay men and women. For gay male teachers, the myth that they actively preyed on young men, the so-called recruitment myth, had to be overcome. For lesbians, the major obstacle lay not only in the purportedly deviant nature of their sexuality but in the overarching "desexualization" of female teachers throughout American history.[3] This chapter details the long work of gaining the support of one of the nation's largest labor unions and then applying that support to the challenges faced by LGB teachers and students.[4]

John Gish and His Activism

LGBT activism in the NEA began with one man. John Gish decided that he was going to be a gay activist and a high school teacher. In 1971, and in Paramus, New Jersey, that was a remarkable decision. He had taught English at Paramus High School for six years without incident. Then in the summer of 1971 he and his partner, John Hannah, went to Riis Beach. There they met members of the Gay Activist Alliance (GAA) of New York, who were videotaping outtakes for a film to present to the mayor about what the gay community wanted from his administration.[5] Gish gave a statement and, being curious, asked where he could see the finished film. They told him to go to the "Firehouse in the Village." He was amazed and inspired by the vibrant activist community he found there and continued going to GAA events throughout the summer.[6]

When the other members of the GAA learned that Gish was from New Jersey they put him in touch with activists who also lived there and were interested in starting a GAA across the Hudson. Gish quickly became a founding member of GAA of New Jersey. Five months into the existence of this new group, the founding president resigned, leaving a hole in the New Jersey GAA's leadership. Gish saw that the alliance needed a committed leader and was interested in the role but thought "it would be pretty ridiculous to be the president of a gay group and not be out."[7] Gish understood that being a teacher and an out gay man were mutually exclusive propositions. Gish knew this directly, as the public relations representative of his local teachers' union, and viscerally, having grown up in 1940s and 1950s America. When he pointed this out, his partner responded, "Well do you really live and breathe teaching?" or in other words, "Are you willing to risk your job? How much is it worth to you?" To which Gish recalls responding, "it's getting a little stale." With that acknowledgment, he made the decision to come out publicly.

So, with the support of his partner and the full understanding that he would be likely be fired as a result, Gish told his colleagues in the Paramus School District that he was the president of the Gay Activist Alliance of New Jersey and would be lobbying for gay and lesbian rights at the upcoming NEA convention. His involvement in his school's teachers' union and the New Jersey Education Association made it a natural step for Gish to go to the NEA national convention in June to advocate for homosexual teachers. This was a form of activism that utilized his connections to a national organization to further the cause of gay liberation.

Gish had three goals in attending the national conference. First, he wanted the NEA to publicly acknowledge that there were gay and lesbian teachers in the association. Second, he wanted sexuality included in the NEA's nondiscrimination policy. Third, he hoped to find more members for the gay teachers caucus. Gish was nothing if not canny. He understood that, as a gay teacher, he would be instantly fired if he worked alone. He also understood that his local union, and likely the ACLU (American Civil Liberties Union), would support him against the local school district, provided that he was careful in how he presented himself. To secure the support of his local union, he took several steps, starting with framing his cause as a matter of free speech.

Before heading to NEA's annual meeting in Atlantic City, he contacted his local union and told them that he had accepted the presidency of the GAA of New Jersey. Gish also told the local union that he would be going to the national convention of the NEA to advocate for gay rights. Word of this spread faster than wildfire through Paramus, and the local superintendent swiftly called Gish to ask whether he intended to publicly advocate for gay rights. Gish responded that this was exactly what he planned. This statement prompted the superintendent to ask Gish directly if he was a homosexual. Gish responded, "What does my sexuality have to do with anything? I belong to the NAACP and I'm not black." Gish hoped to center the discussion on his right to politically advocate for a deeply unpopular group. Citing his membership in the NAACP (National Association for the Advancement of Colored People) connected the struggle for racial equality to the struggle for gay rights. [8]

Gish understood that if he admitted to being homosexual, he would be "out of the game, instantly," and because of that he classified not disclosing his sexuality as a tactical decision. The omission was a means to an end. [9] Casting himself as a political advocate and the Paramus School District as attempting to quash an employee's protected political speech gave Gish a more secure position from which to advocate. As a gay teacher, he could be instantly terminated, but as a teacher advocating gay rights, he could call on the institutional clout of the ACLU and the NEA.[10] There was a measure of safety in ambiguity. Gish had enough political awareness to understand that he had to play the system. This strategy followed a course of action that would prove successful for other LGBT activists; drawing their employers into a First Amendment legal battle because there were no legal protections safeguarding their employment.[11] The superintendent, likely having a similar political awareness, was unable to respond officially to these statements and ended the conversation.

Gish's political awareness and experience with the GAA of New Jersey also led him to an understanding of the utility of being viewed as part of a group of activists as opposed to working alone. His efforts at the convention could be more effective if he represented a caucus of teachers within the union rather than his individual goals. Alone, he was one teacher and could be isolated and ignored; as the leader of a group, that would be more difficult. The problem with founding a caucus lay in the scarcity of members. Openly LGBT teachers in 1972 were in short supply, presenting Gish with few options for collaborators. Fortunately, the *New York Times* had recently run an article on two gay teachers currently engaged in court battles: Joseph Acanfora and James Gaylord.[12] Gish had no way of contacting either of these men, but noticed that Acanfora was also from New Jersey and had a last name that seemed unique. Gish cold-called all the "Acanfora" numbers in the phone book and eventually contacted Acanfora's very supportive parents who put him in touch with their son. With that phone call, Gish founded the NEA Gay and Lesbian Caucus and as cochair prepared to go to Atlantic City to change the policy of one of the nation's largest unions. He was supported by a caucus of two teachers: himself and Joseph Acanfora.

Understanding what John Gish was trying to do and the challenges he faced requires examining the scope, organization, and history of the NEA. The NEA was, and remains, a megalithic organization. In 1970, the NEA had 943,000 members spread across all fifty states.[13] In addition to being among the largest labor organizations in America, the NEA was also profoundly decentralized. Each state had its own association acting in a mostly independent fashion that reflected and responded to the tremendous political diversity among states. Consider, for example, the similarities and differences in state educational politics and debates faced by the Massachusetts Education Association, where organized labor had wielded considerable power for generations, versus the Mississippi Education Association, which was a notably anti-labor state.[14] Each state association was itself comprised innumerable local associations representing school districts and these district-wide associations, in turn, comprised school-level associations. In this way, the NEA was national in scope, advising presidents and governors, while maintaining an intimate reach down to the level of individual classrooms.[15]

Every year, the Representative Assembly of the NEA met in a different city for a week and forged national policy through one of the largest democratic assemblies in the country. Thousands of representatives selected by their state and local associations make up the state-level caucuses, which in turn combine to form the national Representative Assembly.[16] Educators came from across the country to propose, debate, and vote on pressing educational and political issues.

Any representative could propose a business item for discussion on the floor of the assembly, provided they mustered the support of fifty fellow representatives. Likewise, any representative could speak to the entire assembly on any motion. Many representatives were elected to return to the convention year after year, allowing them to hone their prowess in this elaborate process over time. Hotels for miles around filled up with educators putting the finishing touches on the previous year's efforts and preparing to vote on this year's items of business. The floor of the convention became a cacophonous example of democracy in action. The back halls and meeting rooms of the convention floor were replete with all the deal-making and ideological clashes that are inherent in large groups of people with similar, but not identical, interests making decisions via a democratic process.

Balanced against the political mass of the Representative Assembly were the professional unionists of the national and state associations: the women and men whose livelihood was the maintenance and growth of the NEA. While most of the representatives went back to their schools, the national- and state-level staffers of the NEA worked year-round to push the agenda of the Association in Washington, D.C., and their respective state capitols. John Gish arrived in Atlantic City with his agenda of introducing LGBT activism in 1972 at a time of tremendous change in the organization of the NEA. The association was in the middle of shifting from a rather cautious professional association run by a small group of staffers and dominated by educational administrators to a functioning union dominated by members who were K-12 teachers.

The NEA did not begin its history as a union; it started as a professional organization concerned with professionalism in the field of education. This stands in contrast to its counterpart and rival, the AFT, which was unabashedly founded as a labor union.[17] It was not until 1973, after years of debate and pressure from its rank-and-file membership, that the NEA became a teachers' union both in practice and organization.[18] Before that shift, the NEA was principally an organization run by a professional staff based out of Washington, D.C., and dominated by the portions of the association that comprised administrators and school superintendents.[19]

K-12 teachers in the United States have endured a distinct lack of prestige for at least a century.[20] This lack of prestige has physically manifested as meager wages, little input into their workplaces, and few job protections beyond the patronage of their principals. Teachers' lack of prestige is especially apparent in comparison to other professions requiring postsecondary education. In the first half of the twentieth century, teachers were roused to action; they generally capitalized on their role as nurturers and caretakers, appealing to moral arguments and their own role as educational experts, to lobby mayors, school boards, and governors into action.[21] Teachers were faced with the dilemma of how to better the situation of their profession and the state of education in the United States. The teachers of the NEA wanted not only to secure for themselves better material conditions but also to increase the prestige of being a teacher. Being associated with unions and hourly workers from the lower classes might add material benefits to the lives of teachers but would it add anything to the prestige of the profession?

The willingness of rank-and-file teachers to be led by administrators should be analyzed within the frameworks of professionalism and precedent; specifically, the reality that most teachers were women. The teachers of the NEA in the first half of the twentieth century conceived of teaching as a career that would provide security to the individual and guide education in the nation.[22] These two goals were intertwined and could not be achieved if the public saw teachers as the equivalent of plumbers or dockworkers. In contrast to the blue-collar possibility of unions, a genteel professional association headed by educational leaders working respectfully to alter the course of education seemed more effective, or at the very least more prestigious.

Civil servants organizing unions and engaging in collective bargaining was illegal in most jurisdictions until the 1960s. Public servants in the federal government did not gain the legal right to organize until President Kennedy signed Executive Order 10988 in 1962. This action in turn set off a series of legislative initiatives in state and local jurisdictions mirroring Executive Order 10988.[23] Teachers in the NEA before this unionization of the public sector attempted to gain prestige by association with the educational professionals that society held in higher esteem: principals, superintendents, and educational researchers.

John Gish's founding of the NEA Gay and Lesbian Caucus and, more broadly, the spread of "gay liberation" as the dominant political narrative of the LGBT community, coincided with the NEA teachers' increasing suspicion that relying on their school districts to respect the "professionalism" of teachers had failed to improve the lives of American educators. Becoming a functional union had distinct political costs for the NEA. Much of the NEA's prestige and ability to work in states that had a history of hostility toward organized labor was predicated on being perceived as nonpartisan, apolitical, and limiting its lobbying to the arena of education policy. Before 1973, many of the departments inside the NEA were under the direct supervision of a board-appointed executive officer. This executive officer was paid four times more than the membership-elected president and proposed much of the organization's national agenda.[24]

Informally, after the Executive Office itself, the Research Division of the NEA represented the most influential group of employees in the association. The Research Division in the postwar period derived its power from two factors. First, the division represented a collection of skills and expertise in education research that was on par with, if not superior to, any major research university's education department in the 1960s. Second, the Research Division housed the collected data of decades of surveys and studies. This arguably gave the NEA the most comprehensive understanding of education in America.[25] That expertise was widely acknowledged in Washington, D.C., and was the source of considerable prestige and political clout for the NEA. The combination of expertise and political neutrality allowed the NEA to participate in many joint projects with federal and state departments of education. This prestige from participation with government provided small comfort to the mass of educators who made the vast majority of NEA membership and had the unenviable challenge of making ends meet on a teacher's salary. It is not surprising that, by the beginning of the 1970s, the NEA leadership's promises of respect and prosperity through apolitical professionalism were wearing thin.[26]

The political shift that occurred within the NEA during the late 1960s and early 1970s can be described as a change from an organization that utilized members who were teachers to promote an educational agenda, to an organization centered on the needs of teachers. Before the 1960s, the NEA as an organization utilized the political clout that came with numbering hundreds of thousands of K-12 educators among its members. Those teachers in turn benefited from being a member of the association, but benefiting those hundreds of thousands of teachers directly was not the goal of the NEA. While teachers certainly had input into the decisions and policies of the NEA, their input was secondary to the voices of educational administrators. Hypothetically, if John Gish had wanted to lobby the NEA in 1965 to change its policies regarding homosexual teachers, he would have been wise to seek the support of principals, superintendents, and the paid staff of the NEA.[27] But by the late 1960s, the K-12 teachers of the NEA were successfully moving the association in a direction that made it resemble a labor union as state and local associations engaged in collective bargaining and lobbied for teachers' employment rights. Because of this shift in power within the NEA, and the reality that while he was connected to the New Jersey Education Association Gish did not have access to the power brokers of the NEA, Gish targeted his efforts at the teachers attending the annual convention.

Gish arrived at the NEA convention in Atlantic City to find the annual meeting in full swing. Armed with a bag full of flyers, he stood in the middle of the main entrance to the convention handing out his flyers and chanting, "Stop the war against gay America!" These flyers implored gay teachers to unite and "Break the chains of oppression!" and featured images of a naked man and woman with broken manacles uniting to "Free Ourselves" and "Smash Sexism" (see figure 1.1). They also contained directions to the hotel at which he was staying and news of the District of Columbia passing a nondiscrimination clause for homosexual teachers.[28] Gish was quickly noticed by convention organizers who ushered him into the back corridors of the hall where he was shown to rooms full of copiers to make more flyers, given the schedule of events that he might want to attend, and told what business items were being considered. Additionally, despite the impromptu appearance of Gish, a meeting of the gay caucus was announced from the main stage of the convention alongside announcements for other interest groups within the NEA.[29] The individuals who provided these services never identified themselves. On reflection, Gish concluded that they were

GAY TEACHERS UNITE!
You've nothing to lose but oppression.

What Will the NEA Gay Teachers' Caucus Do?

1. Educators concerned with Gay Teachers' issues come to the National Education Association (NEA) in order to "Promote and Protect Human Civil Rights," one of the major objectives of the proposed Constitution (see Preamble).

2. We come to the NEA because its proposed Constitution (Article I; Section 2) states: "Nothing in the Constitution or Bylaws shall be construed to prevent the Association from adopting additional objectives consistent with the Association's basic goals." We would like to indicate certain objectives for the Constitution.

3. We come to propose that Article II, Section 1:b be amended to include the phrase "Sexual Orientation" between "Creed" and "Or national origin."

4. We come to propose that the term "Ethnic-Minority" (Article III; Section 2:b) be clearly defined so as to include gay members; and that the section should read: "Bylaws shall provide for ethnic and/or counterculture minority representation in the Representative Assembly." See Item 7.

5. We come to be assured that no gay person may be censured, pressured, suspended or expelled from the United Teaching Profession because of his/her sexual orientation (see Article VII; Section 1:b).

6. We come to support in its entirety Section I; "Names & Goals," of the proposed bylaws.

7. We come to propose amendment to Bylaw 3-3 Ethnic Minority Representation whereby "Identified Ethnic-Minority Populations" be clarified to include contemporary sociological statistics (see Kinsey Report).

For further Convention Information:
John N. Gish, Jr., Chairman pro tem.
NEA Gay Teachers' Caucus
32 Bridge Street
Hackensack, N.J. 07601
Telephone: 201 343-6402

FIGURE 1.1 John Gish, flyer: "Gay Teachers Unite!," 1972. (Author's collection.)

sympathetic NEA staffers that could not officially support him but were personally in favor of his advocacy. Throughout the rest of the convention, Gish recalled being met mostly with support from the attendees. He left Atlantic City at the end of the week and considered the trip a success.[30]

There are at least two ways to interpret the assistance that Gish received at the NEA convention in Atlantic City. The first is what Gish himself believed: that there were a few NEA staff members or member volunteers working at the convention who were sympathetic to his cause and decided to help Gish navigate the labyrinth of bureaucracy. The second interpretation of Gish's experiences at the convention is that the help he received from the NEA was a form of damage control. NEA conventions were widely covered by local and national media. Gish's nascent gay teachers caucus was just one of the dozens of caucuses that often held views that were more politically radical than the official positions of the NEA. The staffers of the NEA were likely experienced with minimizing disruptions to the convention.

In the case of John Gish, they had to decide whether to leave a teacher to loudly chant in the lobby with the possibility of talking to any random reporter, or to manage the situation. Gish was a credentialed member of the NEA and had every right to be present, so getting rid of him was not a viable option.[31] Alternatively, they could choose to help Gish and gently direct him as part of that help. While this interpretation may seem calculating, there is no reason that it would not be compatible with Gish's understanding of what occurred; the unofficial assistance he received from NEA staffers could have been meant both to help his advocacy and to direct that advocacy in a way that was less disruptive to the workings of the convention.

Throughout the week, Gish met dozens of teachers at a variety of functions, spoke to the leaders of delegations, gave interviews to the media, and served as a symbol of liberation for gay and lesbian educators who remained closeted.[32] From the floor of the convention, he proposed that a study be undertaken by the NEA to "provide a program of public information in regards to human rights of gay teachers.[33] Such studies were often a precursor to the NEA taking a specific political stance on an issue or amending internal policies. Gish also proposed that the membership of the association be surveyed with regards to their stance on sexuality. Protocol dictated that any proposal that would incur a significant expense for the NEA be referred to the treasurer who in this case estimated the cost of Gish's survey to be $10,000. It was voted down and so the numbers and needs of LGBT teachers in the NEA remained a mystery.[34]

Gish returned from the convention and was met with the loss of his teaching job. He then embarked on a series of legal battles that would extend for more than a decade.[35] Two of Gish's goals, recognition of gay and lesbian teachers in the NEA and their inclusion in the association's nondiscrimination clause, would be achieved within two years. The final goal of founding a viable gay and lesbian caucus within the national association was not realized until fifteen years later. Gish himself spent the years of his legal battle doing curriculum work for the Paramus School District, illustrating the complexities of LGBT rights and teaching. The school board was willing to employ a person they suspected of being gay and even one who advocated for gay rights, but not as a teacher.[36] Gish continued to be active with the New Jersey GAA and worked toward the passage of laws benefiting LGBT in his home state. With Gish's departure from the teaching profession, the initial incarnation of the NEA Gay and Lesbian Caucus came to an end. Activism aimed at securing protections for LGBT teachers and students would continue to move forward despite the lack of an official organization. Crucial to understanding that forward momentum is an understanding of changes that took place within the NEA during the 1960s and 1970s that were conducive to the success of LGBT activism and would pave the way for a permanent caucus.

Changes within the NEA

Why were teacher unions the first labor unions to endorse and pursue protections for gay and lesbian workers? John Gish found a ready audience among the teachers in 1972 at the NEA convention, a mere three years after the 1969 Stonewall riots accelerated LGBT activism across the United States. What conditions were in place in teachers' unions that made them fertile ground for gay and lesbian activism? I propose two distinct but related changes that occurred within the NEA during the 1960s and 1970s that collectively created conditions that were supportive of gay and lesbian worker's rights and broad equality for LGBT Americans. First, the NEA merged with the historically African American teachers' association, the American Teachers Association (ATA) in 1966, increasing racial diversity in the NEA. Second, the role of women in the workplace shifted profoundly, impacting both the profession of teaching, which was majority female, and the NEA, which comprised mostly teachers. While many of the NEA's circumstances are particular to the association and K-12 teachers, the increasing presence of African Americans and women in American schools were part of a trend that saw both groups included to a greater degree in the general workforce. Political activism by women and African Americans to ensure this inclusion precipitated similar shifts for LGBT people in the American workforce.[37]

When the NEA met for the 1973 annual convention in Portland, Oregon, two topics dominated the convention floor: the recent adoption of a new association constitution and a possible merger with the AFT.[38] The new constitution greatly increased the authority of officials elected by the Representative Assembly and reflected what many commentators saw as the "increased politicization" of the NEA, mandating, among many other things, a quota system for nominees to elected positions, ensuring ethnic minorities were present on the candidate slate, and mandating 20 percent of the Executive Committee being from ethnic minorities.[39] The proposed merger with the AFT had been actively pursued by leadership in both the NEA and AFT and would have created the largest union in the country with over two million members. This merger was ultimately voted down. The NEA wished to maintain its independence from outside influences and the AFT as a member of the AFL-CIO (American Federation of Labor and Congress of Industrial Organizations) had no desire to leave that labor coalition.[40] A merger of the two teachers' unions never occurred but, in the early 1970s, unionists held out hope that it would eventually happen. Their hopes were bolstered by precedent; in 1966 the NEA merged with the historically African American teachers' association, the ATA.

The merger with the ATA was the product of more than a decade of negotiation between the NEA and the ATA. Merging with the ATA significantly increased the racial diversity of the NEA membership, particularly in southern states. In addition to simply increasing the number of African Americans in the NEA, the merger also imported the experienced professional and activist core of the national ATA into the NEA and provided African American educators who were already members of the NEA with a larger platform to get elected to national-level positions within the NEA. This occurred almost immediately; in 1968 Elizabeth Duncan Koontz was elected as the first African American NEA president. Koontz had previously served as president of the Department of Classroom Teachers, from 1964 to 1965.[41] Additional impacts of the ATA merger could be felt at the state level as state affiliates integrated, resisted desegregation, and in some cases formed all-white teachers' associations in competition with the newly integrated state-level associations.[42]

The NEA had been engaged in a process of desegregating its state associations in the South since 1964. This integration was formally mandated in the initial national-level merger agreement between the NEA with the ATA. All state-level associations were given two years to integrate.[43] The process of desegregation was complicated by the structure of the NEA and its relationship to state associations. The state associations of the

NEA were organizationally independent of the national organization and, until 1973, it was possible to be a member of a state-level association but not be part of the NEA.[44] While the NEA's rival, the AFT, was centered in urban areas and tied to the distinctly urban racial unrest taking place throughout the country's largest cities, the NEA primarily functioned in rural areas, suburbs, and small- to mid-sized cities. It was in these areas in the American South that the NEA as a national organization negotiated the complexities of integrating African American and white teachers' associations that had existed as separate entities for decades.

The autonomy of state associations allowed them to act swiftly and with intimate knowledge of their locales, but it also provided the opportunity to balk at mandates to integrate with state-level ATAs. The process of integrating the state associations lasted until 1976 and was only resolved after the last two holdout states, Alabama and Mississippi, had been each separately expelled and readmitted to the NEA after finally agreeing to integrate.[45] With these final agreements, and the mandate that members of state associations were automatically enrolled as members of the NEA, the African American membership of the NEA grew considerably. This growth impacted the political stance of the NEA as a whole.

Women's majority in NEA membership mirrored the demographic dominance of women in K-12 teaching. For at least a hundred years, most K-12 educators have been women. Between 60 and 70 percent of teachers were women in the 1970s and 1980s. In elementary schools, 82 to 88 percent of teachers were women and in high schools 46 to 56 percent of teachers were women.[46] Throughout the twentieth century, the proportion of female K-12 teachers wavered up and down but never fell below 60 percent.[47] By virtue of these demographics, American students have been primarily educated by women for generations.[48] Less obvious are the impacts that a female-dominated teaching force has had on American expectations regarding the behavior, morals, and compensation of educators. In short, what was "proper behavior" for women became the model of proper behavior for teachers, education became firmly attached to a "maternal" virtue, and the salary of teachers never grew to the same level of male-dominated professions.[49]

Women who taught faced obstacles their male colleagues did not. These obstacles ranged from female-specific morality clauses in their contracts to not being able to remain in the profession if they became pregnant. Within K-12 education, men were clearly favored in many ways; for example, ascending into school administration was considerably more difficult for women with principal and superintendent positions being disproportionately held by men throughout the twentieth century.[50] That being said, it is reasonable to argue that male K-12 teachers throughout the twentieth century had their salaries, work norms, and profession as a whole significantly impacted by the reality that most American educators were female. Male teachers were less affected by their profession being viewed as "women's work" than their female colleagues but the indirect impacts of sexism on K-12 teaching, even for men, were unmistakable.

The reality of teaching as "women's work" was significantly complicated in the second half of the twentieth century by the headway women made in other workplaces across the country. In the first half of the twentieth century, secretarial work, teaching, and nursing were among the few professions that women could aspire to and also attain professional status. Throughout the mid-century, women's options for employment widened as the number of women in the workforce steadily increased.[51] Women as a portion of the workforce steadily rose from 29 percent in 1950, to 35 percent in 1965, and, by 1975, 40 percent of the workforce was female. A total of 70 percent of working women in 1970 were employed full time, but in 1950 only 50 percent of wage-earning women were working full-time jobs.[52] The women entering the workforce in the millions did not acquiesce to traditional gender roles that often saw women relegated to de facto subservience. Instead, the workplace and issues of workplace equity became a political platform for women to organize around and an arena for the broader struggle for gender equality. The glaringly unfair treatment of women at work, the inequality of pay, and the grim reality of sexual harassment each became rallying cries for second and third wave feminism.[53] Women and their allies advocated both for legal protections and for change within the workplace by attaining managerial positions and through union activism.[54]

The growth of teachers' unions in the 1960s and 1970s can be described as part of the efforts of American women to benefit from the security that unions offered. In a similar vein, it can also be viewed as an expansion of the labor movement into the "industry" of education similar to the attempted expansion of unions into other female dominated industries in the 1970s and 1980s. Anna Lane-Windham describes these attempts in her book *Knocking on Labor's Door: Union Organizing and the Origins of the New Economic Divide (1968–1985)*, which chronicles the efforts of women and people of color to achieve the prosperity enjoyed by white male union members. Windham illustrates how these efforts were complicated and often thwarted by the combination of institutionalized sexism/racism and corporate America becoming adept at halting the spread of unions into the Sunbelt and nonunionized industries.[55]

K-12 teachers avoided the reach of private industry, lobbyists, and militantly anti-labor managers in the 1970s and 1980s because they were employed in the public sector. The public sector experienced a tremendous degree of labor organizing in the 1970s and, because of this timeline, became political targets later than private-sector unions.[56] K-12 educators were distinctly susceptible to the local political trends, as most teachers were and remain employees of local-level governments, and so the areas of the country that had little tradition of private-sector unionism often also had little or no growth in teachers' unions because of fierce local opposition.

An action by teachers' unions in the 1970s and 1980s meant to secure better conditions for either educators or their students was, by default, an action engaged in with or by women.[57] These actions might not have been explicitly feminist in their goals, yet this point could be extensively debated in either direction. Regardless of the feminist bona fides of these actions, opponents of teachers' unions often interpreted them as women illegitimately attempting to wield power. Jon Shelton, in *Teacher Strike! Public Education and the Making of a New American Political Order*, examines how teacher strikes were perceived as gendered actions by the public and how those actions came to represent the labor movement in America as a whole. As the labor movement as a whole went into stagnation and decline, the public activities of teachers' unions became the dominant narrative of organized labor for many Americans.

Shelton meticulously chronicles the role gender played in teachers' strikes in Detroit, Pittsburgh, Newark, New York City, Philadelphia, and Saint Louis, establishing a recurring theme that pitted feminine power of teachers' unions against the "public good"/dominant order that was by default male.[58] Teachers, who were expected to embody "feminine virtues" like patience and caring, transgressed the gendered societal expectations of their profession by advocating for themselves and entering into public conflicts with elected officials. This gendered conflict of power was exasperated by the fact that almost all teacher strikes were illegal. Laws preventing state employees from striking made such actions by teachers' unions appear to be disrespectful; suddenly the average American child was being taught third grade math by a teacher who broke the law. Elected school boards, who were often predominantly male, could prosecute teachers for breaking anti-strike laws, but that prosecution was a public relations nightmare that entailed sending scores of middle-class college-educated women to prison.[59]

All teachers had to grapple with long hours, few job protections, and a low salary based on decades of discrimination, which was founded in large part on gender discrimination against the women who had for generations comprised the majority of K-12 teachers.[60] Low pay coupled with the inflation of the late 1960s and 1970s made many teachers in America eager to unionize.[61] Membership in the NEA grew significantly as it took on the collective bargaining and other tasks associated with labor unions. From a purely transactional perspective, this growth could be viewed as the NEA providing services that potential members were willing to pay dues for. In 1960, the NEA boasted 714,000 members. Between 1960 and 1970, the NEA gained a significant 32 percent in membership, rising to 943,000 members. By 1986, 77 percent of teachers surveyed by the NEA in their national surveys reported membership in the NEA.[62]

Both the explicit inclusion of African Americans and substantial participation of women in the NEA were indicative of a movement toward greater inclusion of formerly marginalized groups within the power structures of the NEA. For African American educators, this inclusion was in the context of being historically segregated entirely and the NEA mandating the integration of state-level associations. For women, this inclusion was in the context of having been the majority of the NEA for generations but being sequestered from positions of leadership. In each of these examples, a group that had been excluded negotiated a position within the NEA that was, if not equitable, significantly better for members of these groups than had previously been the case. LGBT educators in the NEA benefited from these developments in two distinct ways. First, they could model their activism on the efforts of African Americans and women within the NEA. Second, they could potentially find allies within the NEA who themselves had experienced exclusion and discrimination.

Efforts to secure LGBT protections and found a gay caucus in the NEA were part of a broader movement by gay and lesbian activists to engage liberal heterosexual Americans. Historians have long noted that the gay rights movement benefited from the labor movement, women's rights movement, and civil rights movement, not only because it achieved prominence after these movements and appeared in their midst but also because the gay rights movement derived many of its early victories by convincing other groups in the American Left that LGBT rights were a valid cause.[63] One of the most significant and successful tactics of LGBT activists has been arguing for the inclusion of LGBT rights in the broad struggle for equality. These arguments were received with varying degrees of acceptance from other minority groups and social activists.

It is difficult to establish a causal connection between a specific group having experienced discrimination and their being more likely to support other groups that are also experiencing discrimination. It is possible, however, to argue that there is a distinct correlation between having experienced discrimination and being willing to support other groups that are also experiencing discrimination. This reading of history is perhaps optimistic considering the countless examples of oppressed groups attaining a measure of security only to later deny that security to others. But it is important to acknowledge that early LGB teacher activists like John Gish were notably optimistic. There were many educators inside the NEA that had systemically had their actions as teachers and their participation in the association questioned and contested by virtue of being a member of a marginalized group. LGB activists like John Gish understood that alliances with other groups within the NEA were necessary to achieve any real change within the association from the purely pragmatic perspective that LGB people would never have a majority. While Gish and later LGBT activists understood that there were many women and teachers of color in the NEA who would not support them, they also understood that the likelihood of finding support could be greater among women and teachers of color. Changes that had occurred in the previous decade placed women, younger teachers, and people of color in positions of power within the association. Many of these changes had occurred through the activism of the same groups that benefited from them. LGB teachers in the NEA would come to rely on these straight allies to help accomplish their goals and provide models for activism.

Initial Protections

The initial protection resolution for gay and lesbian NEA members in 1974 has been something of a mystery for historians of education. Karen Harbeck, in her groundbreaking *Gay and Lesbian Educators: Personal Freedoms, Public Constraints*, describes the proposal as being put together by an ad hoc group of delegates. Harbeck notes that the victories that occurred in the 1970s for LGBT educators followed a "domino pattern." This pattern consisted of adding sexual orientation to the list of other categories that had already been acknowledged as warranting protection from discrimination.[64] Like dominoes falling in a sequence, each subsequent victory added momentum to future civil rights actions, making them easier to achieve insofar as they could be modeled on previous victories. In the case of the 1974 resolution, the words "sexual orientation" were added to the end of an already existing civil rights provision that included numerous racial groups and women.

Part of this mystery is resolved through a close reading of the word-for-word minutes kept from each annual convention. These minutes provide an outline that reveals the activism of straight allies like Jane Stern, who as a teacher and delegate attended NEA conventions for many years and supported a number of liberal causes.[65] Stern recalled receiving a button from John Gish in 1972 and his activism more generally. While Gish's proposal to provide information to the public about the rights of gay teachers in 1972 was voted down without debate, a proposal to amend the NEA nondiscrimination policy to include sexual orientation was briefly debated on the floor of the convention and eventually passed.

According to Stern, delegates at the NEA convention were atypical compared to members of the NEA in general in both their level of involvement with the association and in their political leanings. Particularly in the early 1970s, the politics of the association skewed significantly to the Left. She recalled the politics and delegates of the time saying, "you have to understand that the people who came to the convention in those days were pretty liberal."[66] This political leaning colored many of the proposals for new business items that came before the Representative Assembly. Achieving a winning majority of votes, more than half for most business items and more than two-thirds to amend a governing policy, was difficult. Comparatively, proposing a new business item was simple and could be done by any delegate who had another delegate to second the motion. While many of the more radical new business items were simply voted down, the sheer variety of new business items considered by the Representative Assembly frames the breadth of discussions that were occurring at NEA conventions.

In 1974, the Representative Assembly voted on 109 new business items in addition to numerous rules and policy changes, including adding sexual orientation to the NEA's nondiscrimination policy. Alongside the general business of the association, including debates over insurance, delegate badges, and budget expenditures, were political statements and initiatives.

40 • Not Alone

Delegates voted on whether to support the impeachment of President Nixon, working to elect a veto-proof Congress, and to clarify NEA legislative activities regarding the Indochina War. Also included in the 109 new business items for 1974 were a number aimed at adding to diversity and equity in the NEA. Among these were establishing a Minority Affairs Division in the NEA, providing funds for aid in West Africa, and removing sexist language from NEA documents.[67] In the context of this assemblage of proposals and business items, the inclusion of sexual orientation protections for teachers was bold but not out of place.

When the provision to add sexual orientation as a protected group, C-30, came to the floor of the convention, it was not written off as beyond the scope of the NEA or too politically charged to engage. The debate began with an outright attempt at removing the words "sexual orientation" altogether through amending the proposal to replace those words and instead add "family relationships." Implicit in this amendment was the reality that homosexual relationships were not legally "family relationships" and so would not be included as a protected group. Richard Harper, a delegate from Utah, justified his amendment by creating a dichotomy between "new" and "old" morality saying, "I am opposed to the addition of sexual orientation to the Resolution. Sexual orientation implies homosexual orientation. It could include some aspects of the new morality. Some teachers recognize the new morality as just being the old immorality."

Harper attempted to appeal to the middle ground of the debate. He was not claiming that homosexuals were viewed as immoral by everyone or even that the NEA should not defend them. Instead, he claimed that a sizable portion of the delegates might think homosexuals were immoral and so the NEA should not commit to the "new morality." To prevent fellow delegates from thinking that he was willing to trample the rights of fellow teachers, Harper went on to say:

> But what about human rights you might ask? What a teacher does in private should be no concern to others, should it? While not wanting to violate anyone's human rights, it should be pointed out that there is such a thing as personal responsibility. It would seem that part of that responsibility is keeping private that which is private. It might also be the responsibility for those who practice the new morality to teach and live in communities whose standards are compatible with their own. Rest assured the NEA should and does fight for due process in the hiring and firing of teachers. But let's not ask

the NEA to defend the right to practice the new morality without specifying some responsibilities which go along with such rights. I urge you to vote for this amendment.[68]

This argument, along with the statement of support that followed it, reveals a considerable amount about the opposition to the amendment and LGB issues in the NEA.

Harper correctly asserted that the NEA already defended the rights of LGBT teachers to due process in hiring and firing. At the local and state level, they had provided legal and fiscal support to a number of teachers in the early 1970s who had been fired based on their sexuality, including John Gish.[69] His issue was not that the NEA was providing support for those teachers. Rather he was concerned that the NEA as an organization was breaching the boundary between private and public. This boundary crossing threw into question the responsibilities of the individual and more particularly the rights of local communities to decide who should teach in their schools. Harper was not claiming that homosexuals should not teach but instead that they should only teach in the places that wanted them. In his view, the NEA would be foolish to declare that every American community should view LGB teachers as morally neutral. Some American communities would continue to follow the "old" morality and the NEA was risking alienating that conservative portion of the country by taking unnecessary stands.

The argument made by Harper was elaborated on by Bob Bower, who seconded the motion to amend. Bower, also from the Utah delegation, framed the amendment in moral terms and asked the Representative Assembly to proceed with caution saying: "I would like to point out to the body that whether we like it or not I think the term 'sexual orientation' at least connotatively speaks of that which is moral and that which is immoral. And morality or immorality is certainly an area of closed and individual concern. We concede that. But I think it ill behooves this body to pass a national mandate that would force large segments of the educational community and families across this land to violate their own moral standards."[70]

Bower, in "conceding" that there might be LGB teachers and that there might be people who do not find those teachers to be immoral, did not concede any ground in his argument. Instead, he attempted to shift the offensive action, infringing on other people's rights, onto the people proposing C-30, LGB people more broadly, and potentially the NEA as a whole. The question at the heart of Bower and Harper's amendment to C-30 was whether the NEA should force educators to take sides in a hotly charged political debate over what more conservative members of the Representative Assembly considered private morality.

Of course, as mentioned earlier in this section, the NEA often declared its support for one side of politically charged issues. It seems, however, that, at least in the minds of those speaking against C-30, supporting homosexual teachers was a bridge too far. Bower continued his indictment of adding sexual orientation to the nondiscrimination policy saying, "we as a professional body would be caught in the posture of having to defend that which is considered by a given community as perhaps illicit or promiscuous in its nature. I think we as educators can ill afford to portray this image."

This warning encapsulated both the concerns of the opposition and how those concerns were specific to teaching as a profession. Bower invoked the ill-defined but constant specter of professionalism to remind his fellow delegates that they are expected to act according to the expectations of the broader community. He reminded them, as Harper did previously, that there was variability in what communities considered moral and immoral. In this context, recommending the removal of sexual orientation was again a recommendation for political moderation. Why should teachers risk the anger of large segments of the population for the sake of homosexuals? The benefits of taking an unpopular political position were minimal and the cost was potentially great—a cost that Bower reminded his fellow delegates they could "ill afford."[71] In this way the Utah delegation was attempting to appeal both to a moral argument, respecting individual consciences, and a realpolitik that was ultimately pragmatic.

It seems that the majority of delegates were unimpressed with this attempt to negate the original intention of C-30. Harper and Bower were correct in asserting that the point of adding sexual orientation to the nondiscrimination policy was the inclusion of homosexuals as a protected class. They were also correct in asserting that this could potentially lead the NEA into conflict with many conservative communities. The association as a national organization would have to support due process for firing its homosexual members, or at least it could be called on for that support. The NEA was already providing that support on an individual basis and C-30 could be considered more of a public declaration than a policy change. With a swift show of hands, the Representative Assembly voted Harper's Amendment down and returned to the main proposal.

Marshall Ellstein, a delegate from Illinois, spoke in favor of the bill, rebutting the opposition, and saying that the resolution was about teachers' rights. To underscore this point, he quoted Senator McGovern, the failed Democratic presidential candidate in the 1972 election, regarding equality: "I hope for the day when we do not need to specify that liberty and justice for all includes, Chicanos, American Indians, women, homosexuals or any other group—'all' means all." Ellstein further clarified his position by categorically denying that the resolution promoted homosexuality in any way. The resolution especially was not, "advocating homosexuality or lesbianism between teacher and student any more than coeducation advocates heterosexual relations." According to Ellstein, a vote for C-30 was simply a vote for human rights and so should be passed.[72]

C-30 passed by majority vote a moment after Ellstein stopped speaking. With its passage, LGB teachers in the NEA suddenly had the explicitly defined right to call on the association to defend them from workplace discrimination based on their sexual orientation. The passage of this resolution was a historic moment for LGBT teachers but the limitations of this resolution and the nondiscrimination policy of the NEA are readily apparent. Read broadly, the resolution obligated the NEA to be proactive in the defense of its LGB members but such a broad reading is likely overly optimistic. Instead, LGBT teachers had to initiate the protections outlined in the nondiscrimination policy either as a reaction to a specific act of discrimination or in reaction to a general climate of discrimination. The burden of proof remained on LGBT teachers to come forward and claim protection. As we will discuss in the next section, many teachers were unwilling or unable to come forward and trade the known, if tenuous, security of anonymity for the new and uncertain commitments of their fellow teachers.

Geography, the Closet, and the Ichabod Crane Debating Society

Richard Rubino thought that hiding his sexuality was unnecessary. At the same time, he thought that discussing his sexuality at work was also unnecessary. He counted himself lucky to be employed in Prince George's County, Maryland, as a science teacher, specializing in science instruction for elementary school students. As a gay man he never denied anything but didn't offer any information about his sexuality to colleagues. He had been involved with both his Prince George's County local and the state-level Maryland Education Association for years. In that time, he actively sought protections for LGBT people in his local union without ever explicitly declaring his sexuality. His sexuality was, however, an open secret to other teachers involved in the union. Whenever the convention for the NEA was held close to Baltimore, he attended, and while at these conventions he met other gay and lesbian teachers through the social events that occurred after the daily debates and meetings were over.

Just before the 1985 NEA convention held in Washington, D.C., Rubino arrived home to find a letter in his mailbox. It was in a plain envelope, had no return address, and contained an invitation from the Ichabod Crane Debating Society to a party during the convention. The letter had a list of fourteen other names but no indication of what the party was being held for. Rubino did not know any of the other names on the list, or how his name had ended up on it, or even what the party was for. The message was tremendously vague but the location of the event, the Lost and Found in Washington, D.C., let him know what sort of party he had been invited to.[73] Located far from any public transportation in a strip of businesses close to the Potomac River between an asphalt plant and a bus garage, the Lost and Found was one of the District's best-known gay dance clubs.

When Richard got to the Lost and Found a few weeks later, he found there "were many more than fourteen men" dancing.[74] He also learned that these parties had been going on for years and that invites were usually by word of mouth. He never learned who had invited him or how they got his name and address. The exact beginnings of the Ichabod Crane Debating Society are currently unknown. Official NEA timelines of LGBT activism within the association are unclear, placing the start of the "off-site social get-togethers" in the early 1970s.[75] The parties lasted at least a decade and were an annual occurrence at NEA conventions. It is unclear whether they predated the initial activism of John Gish in 1972 detailed earlier in this chapter.

What is clear is that there was a recurring meeting of LGB teachers during annual NEA conventions. This begs the question, "Why didn't these teachers form a caucus in the NEA?" They were attending the convention and this was 1985; a solid thirteen years after John Gish initiated LGBT activism in the NEA. Officially, the NEA had supported nondiscrimination against teachers based on sexuality for more than a decade. Surely there had been enough time for teachers to be "out"; if not in their home school districts then at least at the convention. Vast numbers of LGB teacher delegates were not needed to form a caucus. Even if only 5 percent of the nine thousand delegates at the NEA convention were LGBT, there were 450 potential LGBT caucus members. If even a quarter of those delegates were willing to form a caucus, they would have numbered more than a hundred.

The benefits of having an official caucus were obvious. Caucuses received space at the convention, were mentioned in official publications, and, perhaps most importantly, could propose agenda items as an entity on the convention floor. Thousands of delegates listening to the motions of the floor would hear, "Speaking on behalf of the Gay and Lesbian Caucus I propose that" announcing the presence and actions of gay and lesbian educators within the NEA to the entire association and any media covering the convention. So why in 1985 were there unmarked envelopes containing invitations being sent out for clandestine parties and why was there still no official NEA gay and lesbian caucus? A possible answer lies in the intersection of the closet with the organizational structure and geography of the NEA.

Historians of gay and lesbian history have often observed the creation of queer space in which the constraints placed on sexual minorities and gender nonconforming people are loosened. Histories of the gay bar, same-sex relationships at women's colleges, Southern queer culture, and homosexuality in the World War II military each point to the value, necessity, and continuous existence of separate space. These spaces arose either opportunistically within societal conditions that mandated gender segregation; for example, the military during World War II or all women colleges, or were created by LGBT people for the specific purpose of safety and socializing.[76]

LGBT bars in particular offered both shelter and anonymity where people could meet regardless of whether or not they were in the closet, have a drink, and dance; they were, and remain, integral to LGBT culture.[77] Many of the most seminal moments of queer history in the United States, both positive and negative, have occurred in these social spaces. The Stonewall riots, which are popularly credited with accelerating the gay rights movement, were sparked when police, who had routinely been raiding gay bars for decades, invaded one such space.[78] The two largest massacres of gay and lesbian Americans both occurred inside gay bars; in 1973 at the UpStairs Lounge in New Orleans bar where thirty-two people were killed by arson and in 2016 when forty-nine people were killed in a mass shooting at the Pulse Nightclub in Orlando.[79]

The Ichabod Crane Debating Society fits into this broader history of explicitly LGBT spaces. Annual dance parties fulfilled very real needs for gay and lesbian teachers; space to socialize away from their heterosexual colleagues and space to see other gay and lesbian teachers.[80] Fulfilling these basic needs is a recurring theme in the histories of different LGBT teachers' groups and will be discussed in different contexts throughout this study. Bringing educators from across rural, suburban, and urban areas throughout the United States to one place for a week at a time to engage in the business of the association offered gay and lesbian educators an opportunity to temporarily create spaces that were specifically for them. The wide range of places that teachers came from also explains the enduring appeal of these dance parties.

Richard Rubino could have been dancing at the Ichabod Crane Debating Society party next to a teacher from San Francisco and on his other side might have been a teacher from Tulsa. While the progress of gay and lesbian Americans as a whole from 1970 to 1985 was remarkable and unquestionable, the progress of gay and lesbian Americans in particular places, for example in Tulsa, during those fifteen years is debatable. Secrecy remained useful and necessary for many of the gay and lesbian delegates coming to the NEA convention. Despite being hundreds or thousands of miles from their home school district, the cost of being out and identifiable as a gay or lesbian remained far too high for many LGBT delegates to the NEA annual meeting well into the 1980s.

The public nature of being a delegate to the NEA annual meeting complicated the possibility of having an LGB caucus. Delegates were chosen by their state- and local-level education associations. The convention itself was an open space with visitors and press in attendance. While it is difficult to ascertain the actual level of risk a delegate might face, insofar as being uncovered as a homosexual by their employer because of their actions at a teachers' union convention, the actual level of risk is not what concerned LGB teachers. Instead, it was the possibility that LGBT teachers were concerned with. For LBGT Americans in general, the threat of losing their livelihoods and community standing hung as a threat in the background, ever present and always possible.

The balancing of activism with the need for some, if not most, teachers to remain closeted to keep their jobs recurs throughout the histories of different LGB teachers' groups. In the case of the NEA, it becomes clear that the balance was tilted in favor of secrecy. Secrecy was an option available to gay and lesbian teachers even as most other minority teachers could not take advantage of it.[81] Sexual minorities were invisible until they revealed themselves or were forcibly revealed.[82] There were varying degrees of secrecy, dimensions to the closet, and the creation of space for something as simple as a gay dance party for teachers in the 1970s in the context of a national professional convention was itself a form of activism.[83] While an official caucus would fulfill the social needs of teachers who were willing to be publicly out, the Ichabod Crane Debating Society provided a space for teachers who were out and actively working in the NEA *and* those who were not willing, or able to leave the closet.

A Gay and Lesbian Caucus

For the thirteen years between 1972 and 1985, progress on LGBT issues within the NEA occurred, but it was driven primarily by the agendas of small groups of activists coming together for a specific initiative and then disbanding. Despite this, progress throughout the 1970s and early 1980s was steady and evidenced by the NEA's sequence of commitments to LGB teachers. That steady progress may have even dissuaded many LGB teachers from forming an official caucus. Why take unnecessary risks when progress was already being made? By the time Jeff Horton became deeply involved with the NEA in 1986, the limitations of hidden parties and secrecy had become apparent. Horton lived in Los Angeles and had taught for almost a decade in schools throughout the city. As a member of the LA Unified Teachers Union, he belonged to both the NEA and the AFT.[84] Living in Los Angeles, which had a long history of LGBT activism and politically powerful LGB communities, Horton believed that an open and active caucus would accomplish more for LGB teachers and students than was possible working behind the scenes. He was aware of the Ichabod Crane Debating Society but thought that it was time for there to be an official caucus. There was an open LGB teachers' group in Los Angeles and he saw no reason for there to not be a similar group nationally.[85] Horton's desire to have an official and visible organization for LGB teachers and the consignment of earlier forms of semi-closeted activist to the past was in keeping with broader political developments within the LGBT community during the AIDS crisis.

Horton thought unions were prime sites for gay and lesbian activism and that gay rights were in keeping with the goals of teachers' unions and the labor movement in general.[86] The unease that Horton felt at the secretive nature of the Ichabod Crane Debating Society was not only because of the constraints and limits that secrecy placed on activism but also from an underlying sense that being forced to work from the shadows was undignified. Horton came to LGBT activism through both the civil rights movement and the labor movement; after teaching for a few years he became involved in a group of "leftist" teachers who were actively working toward racial integration in Los Angeles public schools.[87] These teachers were actively lobbying the teachers' union and, through this activity, Horton became involved with the union at a citywide level. During the early 1980s, he joined a gay teachers' group in Los Angeles, which he described as being a continuation of activism around the Briggs Initiative in 1978: the Gay Teachers of Los Angeles, which will be discussed in the final chapter of this book.[88]

Dr. Mary Futrell, who was president of the NEA in 1987 when the NEA Gay and Lesbian Caucus was founded, recalled that even then a lot of people were reticent to speak out on LGB issues for fear of being ostracized.[89] Horton himself embodied many of the complexities of being an openly gay teacher in the 1980s; although he was president of the NEA Gay and Lesbian Caucus, he was not completely out of the closet at his high school back in Los Angeles. He would not reveal himself as a gay man publicly until 1991 when he ran for a position on the Los Angeles school board.[90] This foray into local politics saw him leave teaching for almost a decade and so he was unable to remain involved with the NEA caucus for long.[91] Fortunately, Horton realized early on the need for gender diversity from the beginning of the new caucus and included provisions for a male and female cochair of the caucus in the founding bylaws of the organization. This foresight would provide the caucus with steady leadership in the person of Carol Watchler, who became the first female cochair.

Watchler found out about the caucus by walking around the floor of the convention exhibition hall and seeing a table for the newly formed Gay and Lesbian Caucus. She was told the caucus would be meeting later in the week. Remembering the event in an interview for this project, she recalled a "sigh of relief when she entered the meeting" from the participants because, of the thirty-odd people in the room, only two or three were women and the gay men in the group wanted a balance between genders.[92] Much later, Watchler concluded that a thriving and well-established women's caucus was likely attracting many of the politically active lesbian delegates at the convention. Watchler, who came from a feminist and anti-war activist background, decided that the new caucus would be a worthwhile effort and so agreed to be a cochair the following year in 1988.[93] She would go on to lead the caucus for more than a decade and was intimately involved in the negotiation and crafting of the multiple resolutions that the Gay and Lesbian Caucus would propose during that time.[94]

The initial two Representative Assemblies that the Gay and Lesbian Caucus participated in presented several opportunities for the new organization to actively pursue equity for LGB teachers and students. Entering the 1980s, the LGBT community had enjoyed a solid decade of advances and steady progress; discrimination certainly was pervasive, but it was not as pervasive as it had been. The advent of the HIV epidemic challenged that progressive and positivist view. As the full magnitude of the epidemic became known to the LGBT community and the broader public it also came to dominate much of the discourse within the LGBT community and about the LGBT community. In his book *Making Gay History*, Eric Marcus titles the chapter covering the 1980s to the early 1990s "In the Shadow of AIDS" and details the ways that the epidemic impacted daily life and the political development of the LGBT community.[95]

While in the past LGBT people in the United States were actively persecuted, government oppression during the HIV epidemic often took the form of neglect, with official responses to the new disease proving utterly insufficient to the magnitude of the epidemic.[96] The LGBT community in many ways came of age as a politically vocal minority inside the context of responding to the threat of the AIDS crisis.[97] In response to what activists perceived as the willful ignorance of the political establishment, the LGBT community organized to a greater degree, forming both professional lobbying initiatives and direct-action organizations such as ACT UP to demand action from the government.[98]

The HIV epidemic and the NEA's commitment to LGB rights are entwined rhetorically in a number of the resolutions and business items considered by the Representative Assembly in 1987 and 1988. As the epidemic widened in its impact from primarily queer men to all segments of society, large national organizations like the NEA began to pay attention. New Business Item 18, approved in 1987 reads, "That in accordance with NEA Resolution H-13 supporting civil rights for all regardless of sexual orientation, the NEA supports the March on Washington for Lesbian and Gay Rights scheduled for October 11, 1987."[99] The delegate who proposed the amendment, Ed Foglia, spoke in support of his business item saying:

New Business Item 18 gives us the opportunity to reaffirm our commitment at a time when the rights of a particular group, gay and lesbian persons, are under vicious attack. Gains we have made during recent years are in jeopardy. The tragic timing of the AIDs epidemic has given those who always oppose any group besides their own the opportunity to promote mandatory testing, invasion of privacy, and outright harassment of individuals and educators. We must let the nation know where we stand in this moral and legal crisis . . . I am not gay, but I think they should have the right to express themselves in a free area.[100]

This paragraph is a masterful piece of argument. Foglia calls on the assembly to reaffirm its support; to keep its promises. He then in no uncertain terms identifies the opponents of LGBT rights as "those who always oppose any group besides their own" and as people who would take advantage of an epidemic. By definitively stating that he was not gay, Foglia broadened the issue from the purview of a special interest group to a matter that warrants the attention of everyone in the assembly. Finally, by invoking the freedoms of speech and assembly, Foglia questions the opposition's commitment to constitutional freedoms enjoyed by all Americans.

In response to Foglia's statement, a delegate speaking in opposition to the business item questioned whether this was an appropriate business for the NEA to be considering. Jeff Horton, who had seconded Foglia's initial motion and would be identified later as the chair of the newly formed Gay and Lesbian Caucus, responded: "A commonly accepted figure for the percentage of gays and lesbians in the population is ten percent. That means that there are over 180,000 members of this organization who are gay or lesbian educators. And if that doesn't make this our business I don't know what does. They are in particular at this point under attack. There are calls for mandatory testing for dismissal . . . it is an issue for this organization, and it is appropriate that we take it up now. Because our members, members of this organization are at risk here. Thank you."[101] Horton played on the twin themes of unionism and professionalism that formed the basis of the NEA's stated mission in his response. It was untenable for the union to abandon 10 percent of its members and remain credible in the eyes of the other 90 percent.

Horton's reference to "mandatory testing" concerned a new assault on the rights of teachers: proposals for mandatory HIV testing. Schools were seen as an integral part of national, state, and local responses to the epidemic.[102] In addition to providing teachers with training on HIV and educational materials to teach their students, a number of school boards and even state level boards of education considered mandating HIV testing for teachers as a condition of employment. [103] As far as Horton was concerned, being unwilling to support the LGB community while such attacks on the rights of LGB teachers, and by proxy the privacy of teachers as a whole, was unthinkable.

While no delegate at the Representative Assembly was willing to voice support for the mandatory screening of teachers for HIV as a precondition for employment, there was opposition to supporting AIDS education and the March on Washington. NEA President Mary Futrell deflated the most carefully framed opposition statement to New Business Item 18, voiced by Bill McCormick, a delegate from Kentucky. Utilizing the point of information parliamentary procedure, McCormick requested three questions from the president. First, he asked the president to read an earlier business item that had passed the Representative Assembly. President Futrell obliged reading the business item, which stated that the NEA "urged a comprehensive AIDS/sexually transmitted disease prevention program in schools ... including abstinence and medically accepted devices."

> MR. MCCORMICK: Are we not by supporting the—I guess you might say "supporting"—the march in Washington of the gay and lesbian group, supporting and advocating the practice of what is absolutely the opposite of abstinence?

> PRESIDENT FUTRELL: I don't believe that is correct, since there has been no indication that we are being asked, if this should pass, to encourage anyone to engage in any kind of sexual activity. [Applause]

> Your third and final point, please.

> MR. MCCORMICK: Considering the response of the body in regard to your response to my question, I feel that it would be—I guess the word would be "a hopeless cause" to ask my third. I thank you.

This wry response from the NEA president and the amusement of the assembled delegates ensured that New Business Item 18 was referred to committee and summarily adopted. Aside from hinting at where she stood on this particular issue, Futrell's response and the ensuing laughter reveal that, in the minds of many of the delegates, homosexual rights and homosexual sex were not the same. The applause from thousands of delegates to Futrell's rebuttal informed Bill McCormick that his objections were "a hopeless cause" and indicate the considerable level of support that LGB issues received at the NEA conventions by 1987.

This dedication to teacher privacy and the NEA's commitment to it runs through the discourse on LGB educators. Even before the HIV epidemic, when considering whether they should oppose the Briggs Initiative in 1978, the NEA clearly classified sexual orientation as private.[104] When asked what sexual orientation "meant to the NEA," Mr. Bob Chanin, the NEA legal counsel, responded: " in the broadest sense, a person's private life. Whether you or dealing with sexual preference or any other aspect of private life is not in and of itself a relevant criteria to discipline or dismiss that person. That person's job and job security should be based on what he or she does in the classroom. Unless it can be shown that sexual preference or sexual activity in some way impinges on the effectiveness of the person or teacher, he or she should not be disciplined or discharged."[105]

By maintaining a distinction between teacher effectiveness and a teacher's behavior outside the school setting, the NEA established a clear basis for defending its members who faced discrimination based on their sexuality. As far as the NEA was concerned, school districts and the public writ large had no business judging the morality of teachers who taught in their communities, unless they could prove that morality impacted the professional abilities of a teacher. Homosexual teachers were added into the larger group of protected teachers by classifying their homosexuality as a private matter, which, alongside other private matters, was only relevant if it directly impacted a teacher's measurable performance. A personal distaste of homosexual sex, or their disapproval of extramarital sex in general, was not a justification for denying homosexual educators the support of the union.

Moving homosexuality from a classification of "abhorrent" to one of "distasteful but private" allowed the NEA to defend its members from being fired for being gay. Jackie Blount frames this discussion around whether or not an individual or group was "fit to teach."[106] There were certainly behaviors that de facto excluded groups of people from the classroom. For LGBT teachers' groups, the initial goal was to convince a substantial majority of their colleagues that being gay, lesbian, bisexual, or transgender did not automatically disqualify a person from teaching. After that goal was accomplished, then LGBT teachers and their allies could work to move school districts and the greater public to actively support LGBT teachers and eventually LGBT students. Within the NEA, this shift from intolerable to

Students, Sexuality, and the AIDS Crisis

The welfare of LGBT students became a topic of debate at NEA conventions by the middle of the 1980s. Alongside the discussion of LGB students was the grim realization that the AIDS crisis impacted children and adolescents as well as adults. Defending the rights of students was integral to NEA members' conceptions of themselves as teachers, regardless of who the students were. Many teachers had personally seen the difficulties that LGBT students had faced and some of those educators eventually rose to a leadership position in the association. In an interview for this book, NEA president Mary Futrell recalled that her first interaction with a gay person occurred years before she became union NEA president and had involved one of her students while she was still a teacher in Virginia. Futrell was rounding a corner in the halls of her school when she encountered two male students beating up another young man in a stairwell. After breaking up the fight, she listened to the student who explained through his tears that he was being attacked because the other students knew he was homosexual. She told him, "you respect yourself and respect who you are."[107] Futrell remembered this incident during an interview conducted for this study; specifically, in the context of a student's right to an education.

For Futrell, who had been elected as the first African American president of the Virginia Education Association in 1978, one of the major goals of the NEA lay in ensuring that all students would receive the education necessary to succeed in life and that the right to that education was integral to the functioning of the United States.[108] Teachers' unions ensured the protection of those rights by actively advocating for students and creating positive working conditions for their teachers, by implementing policies voted on by the Representative Assembly and lobbying politicians to support those policies. The defense of minority students, whether they were part of a racial minority or a sexual minority, was integral to the NEA fulfilling its mission. All students had a right to a good and factually accurate education and threats to that right needed to be contested. Teachers' unions were in the best position to ensure these rights.[109]

In 1988, Futrell and the NEA demonstrated their commitment to the educational rights of all students by inviting Ryan White to give the opening address in New Orleans. Ryan White was a high school student who suffered from hemophilia. He had contracted HIV via his medication, which was made from human blood. His diagnosis had made him and his family pariahs in their hometown of Kokomo, Indiana, and a poster child for the AIDS crisis. White represented the cause of people living with HIV, particularly students, exceptionally well. Being a child and having contracted HIV in a way that could be viewed as both innocent and utterly tragic, White could effectively advocate to Americans across a broad political spectrum. Futrell recalled that police officers in New Orleans were unwilling to escort White to the convention. Even members of the NEA asked her if touching him was "a good idea." Futrell walked across the stage and in full view of thousands of delegates hugged Ryan White welcoming him on behalf of America's teachers.[110]

White gave a stirring speech to the Representative Assembly. He recounted how people in Kokomo had reacted fearfully when knowledge of his diagnosis became public, and how he was "given six months to live." He spoke of how some parents had founded their own school and removed their students from contact with Ryan. At school, people put folders in his locker marked "fag" and he was the subject of "Ryan White" jokes about AIDS. He spoke of how he "had been labeled a trouble maker and my mom an unfit mother, and I was not welcome anywhere." He looked forward to graduating from high school in 1991. His family eventually moved to a new community where the teachers were supportive. He asked the teachers of the NEA "to help me fight this disease."[111] Many of the teachers in the audience were moved to tears.

Two days after Ryan White's speech, the Gay and Lesbian Caucus proposed Resolution C-11 to lobby for counseling in all schools for gay and lesbian students. C-11 reads: "The National Education Association believes that all persons regardless of sexual orientation should be afforded equal opportunity within the public education system. The Association further believes that every school district should provide counseling by trained personnel for students who are struggling with their sexual/gender orientation." The final two words of this proposal are the first examples of the NEA, or any national labor union, explicitly supporting nonbinary gender diversity and transgender rights. This proposal was groundbreaking because, while there were earlier instances of transgender rights being included in union-negotiated contracts, those contracts were between adults.[112] With this proposal, the NEA acknowledged the existence of LGBT students and declared those students had specific needs that adults could, and should, address. In 1988, at the height of the AIDS crisis and during the second Reagan administration, his proposal was nothing short of remarkable.

Roxanne Bradshaw, the secretary treasurer of the NEA, opened debate on the proposal, recounting how her first time speaking on the floor of the Representative Assembly was in 1974 on behalf of the original inclusion of LGB people in the NEA nondiscrimination policy. Bradshaw had been moved to action after helping a student in 1972 recover from a coma that had been a result of attempted suicide due to depression about her sexuality. After watching her student "in a state of convulsion for over 70 hours sitting by her bedside, I vowed I would never again be silent on this issue." Bradshaw concluded by asking delegates for your "enlightened and your educated support," which was needed "Particularly in this time of ignorance surrounding the issue of AIDS."[113]

Another delegate spoke of a student he had counseled years before who had attempted to hang himself because a school administrator had told him "he would die in the streets as a result of drugs, prostitution, and AIDS if he continued to believe he was gay," but that, because of counseling, the student had become a productive member of society.[114] The major opposition to C-11 took the form of an amendment to the resolution removing the words "gay and lesbian" and making the resolution a generic commitment to counseling for all students. The rationale behind this change was not that there was no need for gay and lesbian students to receive counseling but that having a specific resolution for gay and lesbian students might make getting counseling to those students more difficult for NEA members in conservative places. This proposal was rebutted by Clyde McQueen, a delegate from Michigan, who explained to the assembly that gay and lesbian students were "hurting in a very special and hard way" and reprimanded the proponents of the amendment saying "I hope we can say the words 'gay' and 'lesbian' and not cringe."[115] The proposal proceeded to a vote without the amendment and the NEA resolved to lobby for counseling in all schools for gay and lesbian students.[116]

Following on the heels of the LGBT student counseling proposal and Ryan White's speech, the Representative Assembly approved three new business items regarding students and HIV/AIDS: to support AIDS education and the development of curricula for that purpose, to oppose the mandatory testing of students for HIV/AIDS, and to guarantee a least restrictive educational environment for students diagnosed with HIV/AIDS.[117] Of these three proposals, the one involving the most nuanced debate involved the mandatory testing of students for HIV.

This proposal came as a response to a number of initiatives and plans from politicians across the country for various segments of the population to be routinely and mandatorily tested. Political leaders at the national level, including Secretary of Education William J. Bennet and President Reagan, saw such testing as a precautionary measure against exposing the general populace to AIDS and lent their clout to the debate over mandatory HIV testing.[118] The NEA opposed these blanket proposals and was concerned that there would be a significant stigma attached to the act of being tested. There was also concern that specific populations, including gay students, would be targeted by any policies that mandated testing. At the same time, some delegates were unwilling to go on the record condemning all mandatory testing of students. Instead, they argued over which circumstances justified requiring a student to be tested for HIV without implying criminal activity or inciting discrimination.[119] Eventually, the proposed new business item passed as a blanket condemnation of mandatory/involuntary testing but not before a significant debate over what conditions might justify a school district requiring a student or employee be tested for HIV.

The Measured Pace of Professionalism

LGBT teacher activism within the NEA grew in a way that was determined in large part by the national character of the NEA and the public nature of the Representative Assembly. LGBT teachers from communities across the political spectrum came together at the NEA Annual Meeting, making it a prime spot for LGBT activism. Activists made significant, and indeed historic, strides in their pursuit of equality for LGBT educators inside the NEA. The amount of time it took to achieve those accomplishments was extended significantly by the structure of NEA governance through the NEA Annual Meeting. Coming to a democratic consensus about an issue as contentious as homosexuality and LGB teachers took many years. The accomplishments of LGBT activists and their allies within the NEA were also significantly limited by the need to satisfy the condition of professionalism for the majority of delegates before the association would broadly support a motion.

LGBT teachers in the NEA did not successfully form a caucus until 1987 and because of this their activism at the national level remained centered on the annual meeting for a solid fifteen years.[120] LGB teachers organizing outside the annual meeting before the founding of an official caucus in 1987 is certainly a possibility, and even likely, but it is not evidenced in the archival record. Being centered on pushing business through the labyrinth of the Representative Assembly meant that progress on issues affecting LGBT teachers and students was slow and appears almost sporadic.

John Gish understood the importance of having an official caucus in 1972 and so made it one of his initial goals. This importance had not decreased when Jeff Horton founded a caucus in 1987, which is still active in its pursuit of LGBT equality in education today.[121] With the foundation of an official caucus in 1987, LGBT teachers in the NEA could exert consistent influence on the national association and sympathetic state-level education associations. Perhaps more importantly, they could conduct this lobbying year round. Developing relationships with other interest groups, delegations, and caucuses within the NEA rested on having a person, in this case the leadership of the Gay and Lesbian Caucus, to speak with and form coalitions with. Before 1987, LGBT teachers in the NEA lacked this structure and so had to rely on semisecret organizations and social groups like the Ichabod Crane Debating Society to maintain relationships with each other.

John Gish, Jeff Horton, Carol Watchler, and all the other LGBT teachers actively pursuing equity within the NEA were arguing for an expansion of the conditions of professionalism that would include lesbian, gay, bisexual, and eventually transgender teachers. They were joined in this argument by heterosexual allies who felt that the values of the NEA as an organization and/or their professional politics necessitated taking a political stance for equity. Working within this framework of professionalism and in the context of a national organization presented challenges—crafting proposals that could gain the support of thousands of delegates—and opportunities—the ability to alter the policies and political stances of one of the largest labor organizations in the United States.

The emergence of LGBT educators in large numbers posed distinct challenges for K-12 education as a profession. While the professional boundaries of proper behavior for heterosexual teachers had been a source of constant debate in American education, that debate was based on precedent. LGBT teachers were a new category of variability within the profession, sexuality/gender conformity, and were creating a new precedent. The difference between the new openly gay teachers of the 1970s/1980s and the hidden/closeted teachers of previous decades lay in which actors were ascribing value and defining terms of inclusion and exclusion.[122] Prior to the 1970s, LGBT teachers had very little input into the discussion of what way, either positive or negative, their sexuality and gender diversity impacted their value as teachers because they were categorically excluded from the conversation.

With the advent of LGBT teachers' activism and organizations in the 1970s, gay and lesbian educators personally entered into the conversation about whether or not they should be employed as K-12 teachers. Where before they were told "No" and summarily fired, now there was discussion and debate. This debate was in keeping with the core values of the NEA, which saw teachers as educational stakeholders who were not obligated to blindly follow the orders of administrators. The NEA saw K-12 teachers as political actors who had the professional responsibility to exercise their agency at local, state, and national levels. In the public eye, a good "teacher" embodied virtues of humility and self-sacrificing service while placing the needs of students before their own needs. This trapped K-12 educators in a situation of being expected to work for the welfare of students but as apolitical martyrs: to implement curriculum but seldom instigate change. The exercise of agency by teachers has rarely, if ever, occurred without significant opposition precisely because teacher agency can so easily be construed as unprofessional. Teachers routinely expressing and acting on political interests, particularly self-interests, opposes the archetype of self-sacrifice that has been constructed around their profession.

Other stakeholders had input into what was considered "professional" for a K-12 educator because education was, and remains, a community endeavor that is publicly funded. Stakeholders who were not teachers decided who was symbolically acceptable in America's classrooms and whether their presence would have any practical impact on the process of education. In short, the scale by which teachers were judged and the lowest acceptable quality measured on that scale, in the case of this study adherence to gender/sexuality norms, were both largely beyond the control of teachers.

LGBT K-12 educators exemplified and magnified the dilemma faced by all teachers regarding professionalism precisely because coming out of the closet as a teacher was an explicit political act that forced other stakeholders to realign their expectations of what a teacher should be. In 1970, the majority of Americans viewed LGBT people as unsuitable to teach their children and the weight of that belief was uncontested. Moreover, there were no communities in which LGBT people made up a majority that would have innately secured them a "safe" place where the populace implicitly did not question their professionalism as teachers. With the rise of LGBT teacher activism in the NEA, and as we will see in the following chapters, throughout the country, LGBT teachers created spaces where they could engage in activism without being removed from their classrooms. LGBT teachers called on other educators to respect their dignity, honor their integrity as professionals, and help them advocate for equality. By winning the support of the NEA, LGBT K-12 educators added a powerful and respected organization to the growing chorus of voices advocating for equitable working conditions for LGBT adults and equitable educational opportunities for LGBT children and adolescents.

2

The American Federation of Teachers

Negotiating National Union Policy

> Now, we are faced with another issue, that of another human rights issue, that of discrimination against gay people. Now this is not a particularly "fashionable" thing to do at this time but I think the public is becoming more accepting of this sort of thing.
> —Robert Holden, president of local 1934, at the 1979 AFT convention

This chapter examines the organization, activities, and goals of LGB teachers and their allies within the AFT. It traces the evolution of LGB advocacy in the AFT and focuses specifically on the language used in resolutions regarding LGB teachers and the debates surrounding those resolutions. Teachers' unions at the national level were an arena in which teachers with diverse politics and differing understandings of the role of unions could meet, negotiate, and reach compromises. This process of compromise and crafting official political positions and policies could last years.

The positions reached represented a middle ground that balanced the desires of activists, the prevailing political tolerances of an assembly of union delegates selected from locals across the country, and the tacit approval of union leadership. By analyzing these resolutions, I will illustrate how the AFT, at the highest levels and through democratic processes at national conventions, attempted to reconcile its historic commitment to civil rights with the pragmatism required to maintain a national labor union. The appearance of LGB teachers in the 1970s and 1980s presented teachers' unions at all levels with an opportunity to reaffirm their commitment to defending the rights of minority teachers and students. This chapter discusses how a commitment to the workers' rights of LGB teachers was developed, justified, and pursued.

The timeline of progress for LGBT rights within the AFT is notably long, both because it began early and stretched out well past the period this study is concerned with. In 1970, the AFT was the first American union to call for privacy protections for homosexual teachers, but it would not be until 1988 that an LGB caucus specific to the AFT would be founded.[1] Including sexual orientation in the AFT's constitution as part of a nondiscrimination policy, a feat accomplished by the NEA in 1974, did not occur until the early 1990s, despite the AFT being the first national American labor union to explicitly support job protections based on sexuality. There is little previous scholarship analyzing the progression of national AFT policy regarding LGBT teachers. This chapter addresses that gap in the research.[2]

While researching this study, it became readily apparent that the records of LGB teacher activism and organizations in the AFT between 1970 and 1985 are noticeably less abundant than the primary sources available for the other sites of LGBT teacher activism discussed in this study. The causes for this are unclear. There clearly was activity, as evidenced by the resolutions discussed in this chapter. Possible explanations may lie in the record-keeping culture of the AFT, the late founding of an official LGB AFT caucus, an unfortunate loss of records over time, or some combination of these factors. This relative dearth of primary sources, coupled with few secondary sources and oral histories, makes presenting a compelling analysis of the history of LGBT teachers, their organizations, and activism inside the AFT difficult. So why write a chapter on the AFT if all this is true? There are two reasons.

First, the sources that are available present us with each step the AFT took as an organization to protect LGB teachers mapping out an organizational timeline that warrants close examination. Second, the progression of LGB causes within the AFT presents a compelling illustration of the organizational barriers confronted by LGBT teachers and their allies as those barriers shifted over time.

Discussing the particulars of a thread of activism and how that activism was reacted to is challenging, particularly when the names, numbers, and motivations of many of the activists are unknown. Fortunately, there is a series of resolutions and amendments at national conventions and reactions by AFT leadership to LGB issues that can be traced through the 1970s and into the 1980s. Using this sequence as a starting point, it is possible to construct a history of the progress of LGB teachers in the AFT.

To examine this history, the chapter will proceed chronologically through five AFT resolutions that passed during the 1970s and are explicitly concerned with LGBT teachers. This analysis will highlight the connections between these resolutions and the commitments they entailed and how they were based on preceding resolutions. It is possible to illustrate how the understanding of LGB teachers evolved throughout the decade by constructing a progression of concepts as they appear in these proposals. These proposals were vetted through a democratic process and established support for LGB teachers but applied that support on a case-by-case basis. Moving into the 1980s, the chapter will examine the limitations of AFT commitment to LGB teachers and their causes, as illustrated by an attempt to enlist the AFT to repeal an Oklahoma antigay teacher law in 1981.

Before engaging in this analysis though, it is necessary to understand the shifting political context in which these resolutions occurred. The AFT had 59,000 members in 1960 and increased that number to 205,000 in 1970. Between 1970 and 1980, AFT membership would increase by another 346,359 members, for a total of 551,359 members nationally.[3] The AFT grew a staggering 934 percent between 1960 and 1980. The union comprised a diverse group of dozens of small locals, powerful state federations, and a handful of large urban local unions that determined many of the AFT's goals and political stances. The relationship of the AFT to one of those urban locals, the UFT of New York City, provides the background needed for understanding the progress of LGB activism in the union. The importance of this relationship rests on the fact that, unlike the NEA, which had term limits on executives, the AFT would be led by one president for three decades. Because of this, the LGB teacher activism in the NEA and AFT occurred in very different environments.

The AFT, the UFT, and an LGB Caucus

The AFT had a complicated relationship with many of the locals that made up its membership. Cities and states could have a large influence on national AFT policy by obtaining leadership positions for members of their local unions and ensuring a literal seat at the table. The largest and most powerful of these locals in the 1970s and 1980s was the UFT of New York City. While in the NEA no one local or even state delegation was large enough as a portion of the total membership of the national union to attain dominance, in the AFT this was not the case. The activity surrounding LGB teachers and the resolutions passed in favor of them needs to be examined in this organizational context.

The importance of the New York City local, the UFT, to the AFT as a whole is difficult to overstate. The addition of UFT members nearly doubled the size of the national organization and UFT members became the single largest voting bloc in the AFT after joining the union in 1960. So, while the AFT experienced tremendous growth in the 1960s, much of that growth was a result of the New York teachers affiliating with the AFT.[4] The UFT remained the largest local in the national union and maintained tremendous voting power by virtue of its size. UFT leadership was in a position to set and approve the national agenda of the AFT by using those votes to their fullest potential. If UFT delegates voted in unison on key issues, it was difficult for any other voting bloc in the AFT to determine the outcome of a debate.

The possibility of controlling the AFT's national agenda was not capitalized on until the UFT brought all the delegates to which it was entitled to the national convention and utterly dominated the proceedings. Before the 1970s, sending a full contingent of delegates to the national convention was an expense that most AFT locals avoided. Instead, they sent a portion of their delegates, and the agendas at the conventions were often heavily influenced by geography.[5] AFT locals closer to the site of the convention sent the most delegates, while locals from across the country sent fewer delegates.[6] In the early 1970s, under UFT president Al Shanker, the UFT began paying for each delegate to which they were entitled according to the AFT constitution to attend the national convention. As the largest local, this gave the UFT a critical edge in floor battles over resolutions and in electing the leaders of the AFT.

The parliamentary weight of the UFT at national conventions was amplified by the fact that the UFT was also the largest AFT local, by almost an order of magnitude, in New York State. The UFT was in a position to greatly influence the actions of both the AFT state-level affiliate, the New York State Teachers' Union, and the Empire State's caucus at the national convention because of its sheer size. By giving or withholding support at the convention, or at the state Capitol, the UFT could command significant loyalty both inside the AFT and in the halls of power in Albany.[7] Even without allies from other AFT locals, this gave the UFT a distinct edge in any parliamentary procedures. After shifting political tactics to take full advantage of their numbers, UFT support became crucial for anyone seeking national office in the AFT.[8] Outvoting the UFT under these circumstances required coalitions of other large locals acting in conjunction. The complexity of such coalitions and their political cost likely explains their rarity, particularly after Al Shanker became AFT president in 1974.[9]

Louis Weiner, a long-time union activist and teacher who would eventually become a professor critically researching teachers' unions, recalled the early 1970s as a window of opportunity for dissenting views within the AFT. During the late 1960s and into the beginning of the 1970s it was possible to express dissent and to move contentious political causes forward inside the AFT. According to Weiner, this window was closed by the Progressive Caucus of the AFT, which was led by Shanker. Debates around provocative issues seemed to decrease as the Progressive Caucus increased its dominance on the floor of the national convention and through leadership roles. Whereas in the late 1960s independent caucuses of delegates organized around political issues—for example, a strong women's caucus supported many progressive causes, including LGBT workers' rights—in the 1970s these independent caucuses were subsumed by committees and working groups officially sanctioned by AFT leadership.[10]

The causes behind the UFT leadership's historical ascendance to national prominence as leaders of the AFT and the impact of that ascendance on the democratic traditions of the AFT are debatable. These debates are beyond the scope of this study and so will not be engaged here. What is not debatable is the fact that UFT members and UFT leadership had their concerns and experiences raised onto a national platform. What happened in New York echoed within the AFT and could be amplified onto a national stage.

Shanker's impact is difficult to overstate. From the early 1970s until 1994, when he resigned as president, politically contentious national policy had to get past either Shanker or his allies. This does not mean Shanker personally had to approve every particular proposal. The Progressive Caucus could exercise a de facto veto by signaling their lack of support during a floor vote. From the perspective of moving a contentious proposal forward, securing the approval of the Progressive Caucus added an extra step to the process. While it might be argued that this would be necessary for any parliamentary procedure, that there is always a dominant group or coalition that needs to be convinced to support or at the very least to not oppose a given measure, the strength of Shanker and his allies in the AFT was tremendous and had a notable impact on AFT policy.

The UFT leadership's considerable control over the AFT also had a positive impact on LGBT teachers in the AFT. LGBT political activists and LGBT teachers in New York City could have a greater national impact because the UFT leaders they engaged for many years would go on to lead the AFT. In this way, the dominance of the UFT within the AFT was inadvertently beneficial to LGBT teachers across the United States. So, while UFT dominance may have slowed the progress of LGBT issues, as we will discuss in the rest of this chapter, that progress was constant throughout the 1970s and 1980s. This progress was driven by activists within the AFT nationally and by activism in large urban AFT locals like New York City, San Francisco, and Los Angeles. These cities had their own active LGB teachers' groups by the mid-1970s, which will be discussed in detail later in this book.

The First Resolution

At the December meeting of the executive council of the AFT in 1970, two locals brought forward a resolution that would initiate the process of committing the AFT to defend the rights of homosexual teachers. This initial resolution did not have its origins in a K-12 teachers' union but instead was proposed by locals based at San Jose State University and the student workers' local at San Francisco State University. Colleges in the Bay area had been roiled by student and professor strikes throughout the end of the 1960s.

These strikes centered on the creation and implementation of racially equitable conditions and curriculum.[11] The participation of AFT locals for these actions ranged from support of students to full-blown strikes and placed these university AFT locals in the most liberal vanguard of the national union.[12] Both the AFT and the NEA had postsecondary education locals, but the academy had proven to be rocky soil for teachers' unions. Higher education locals had full rights within the AFT to send delegates to the biennial convention and to make proposals to both the assembled convention and the Executive Council of the AFT and so their political stances could have an impact on the AFT as a whole.

Before examining the text of the resolution and what it reveals about how AFT members thought of LGB teachers, two underlying questions need to be asked. First, "Why was the Executive Council of the AFT willing to take such an unpopular political stance so early?" Second, "Why after taking such an early stand did it twenty years for the AFT to add sexuality to their nondiscrimination policy?" The answers to these questions may lie with the political climate of the AFT at the end of the 1960s. Louis Weiner describes a brief window for significantly progressive actions by the AFT in an interview for this study. Inside this window of time, the AFT was large enough to have national influence and had a membership that was politically progressive but had not yet come under the political control of the Progressive Caucus headed by Al Shanker.[13] It is impossible given available sources of information to determine exactly the motivations of members of the Executive Council in 1970. We do not know how individual members reacted to pressure from within the union. However, the timeline of proposals and actions that I will detail throughout this chapter seems to indicate that as the Progressive Caucus of the AFT gained greater control, the likelihood of outlier proposals gaining traction and passing a vote in the Delegate Assembly or Executive Council decreased.

The initial resolution is bold due to its timing but also measured because of the limited scope of its obligation. The 1970 resolution reads:

> WHEREAS professional people insist that they be judged on the basis of professional and not personal criteria; and
>
> WHEREAS it the responsibility of labor unions to provide job protection from all forms of discrimination that is not based on performance such as race, color, sex, religion, age, or ethnic origin, be it

> RESOLVED, that the American Federation of Teachers protests any personnel actions taken against any teacher merely because he or she practices homosexual behavior in private life.[14]

The boldness of this resolution lay in the fact that it was the first such statement by any labor union in the United States at a national level and, to date, is the earliest known statement regarding equitable treatment for homosexuals at any level by a national labor union in the United States. It would take another four years before other unions, two American Federation of State, County, and Municipal Employees locals and the NEA, would make similar moves including sexual orientation in negotiated contracts and nondiscrimination policies.[15] By any standard, this resolution was groundbreaking; it placed the AFT and teachers' unions at the forefront of advancing LGBT rights in the workplace.

The measured nature of the 1970 resolution lies in the ambiguity of the word "protests." What does "protests any actions taken against any teacher merely because he or she practices homosexual behavior in private life" actually entail? The AFT was declaring that it was inappropriate and unprofessional to hold the sexuality of a teacher against them as far as personnel actions were concerned. The resolution set the default official position of the national union against politicians, school boards, and administrators investigating the private sexual lives of teachers. It did not commit the AFT to act in favor of LGB teachers but instead argued that the category of sexuality was an invalid way to judge educators and should not be used to make personnel decisions.

The activists behind the 1970 resolution, like their counterparts in the NEA, understood that one route to LGBT rights lay in being included in already existing categories of protection. In the case of the AFT, this protection included categories "such as race, color, sex, religion, age, or ethnic origin." Including sexuality in this list of designations that according to the AFT had no bearing on teacher performance appealed to the professional character of teachers' unionism. Appealing to professionalism was complicated by all the political factors surrounding the construction of teacher identity discussed in chapter 1. Read narrowly, this resolution only commits the AFT to voice disapproval over personnel actions but does not entail taking any actions beyond voicing disapproval. The 1970 resolution still limits that support to teachers practicing homosexual behavior in their private lives. Even if we read the mandate to protest using sexuality as a criterion for personnel decisions as broadly as possible, the qualifier of "private" excludes "public" homosexuals and again draws our attention to the murky boundary between the private and public lives of LGBT teachers.

Who qualified as a teacher who "practices homosexual behavior" in their private life? This is decidedly unclear. Arguably any homosexual teacher who was professionally known to be homosexual was no longer a teacher who "practices homosexuality in their private lives," or at the very least, not exclusively in their private lives. The act of identifying or being identified as a homosexual placed the teacher's sexuality into the public sphere. The act of defending oneself against the accusation of homosexuality was also in the public sphere.[16] Centering the conversation around the homosexual act remaining unseen made the 1970 resolution a matter of interpretation. It did not commit the AFT to do anything but protest, which, while groundbreaking, was of little practical use to an LGBT teacher hypothetically faced with termination because of "public" homosexuality. LGBT teachers attempting to use this resolution to enlist the AFT to help them would have to argue that their activities as homosexuals were private without a clear definition of what qualified as private.

The 1970 resolution signaled to activists within the AFT that they could gain traction with union leadership and pass resolutions that dealt with the concerns of LGB teachers. Likewise, this resolution signaled to more progressive locals within the AFT that the national union would not oppose, and might even tentatively support, LGB activism under the aegis of teacher unionism. The resolution, though it was limited, set the groundwork for future resolutions that would commit the AFT to actually defending the rights of LGBT teachers. The 1970 resolution also laid out the framework in which AFT leadership would be willing to defend those rights: as part of a broader commitment to minority rights that had been historically made by labor unions.[17] Activists writing subsequent proposals would return to this understanding of the AFT's historic commitments in their efforts to secure job recognition and protections for LGBT teachers. Reaching that goal would require many small victories, each of which involved overcoming significant obstacles, and, from the benefit of historical hindsight, a constant negotiation between the progressive activists of the AFT and the cautious leadership of the union.

1973 and the Absence of "Homosexual"

The next proposal having to do with LGBT teachers came when the AFT met for their biennial convention in Saint Paul. Unlike the 1970 resolution, which was passed through the Executive Council, the 1973 resolution was passed by a majority vote of the Delegate Assembly, a body numbering in the hundreds and drawn from AFT locals across the country. The size of the Delegate Assembly and their geographic distribution gives us an indication that protecting the rights of homosexual teachers had considerable support in AFT beyond just the highest circles of the union.

The 1973 resolution appears in AFT records as "Resolution #9: Teachers' Right to Privacy" and begins by invoking what would become a seminal court case in California: WHEREAS on November 20th, 1969, the California Supreme Court in the case *Morrison v. the State Board of Education* held that a teacher's life credential could not be revoked unless it could be proven that acts committed in his private life which are grounds for credential revocation can be shown to affect his fitness to teach; and WHEREAS the American Federation of Teachers has always opposed interference of school officials with the lives of private teachers; therefore be it.[18] *Morrison v. the State Board of Education* was a sweeping ruling by the California Supreme Court regarding the moral turpitude law of California that allowed administrators to terminate a teacher's employment. Most states had similar laws on the books but as Stuart Biegel notes in his study of LGBT teachers and the law, *The Right to Be Out*, it was not until the *Morrison* case in 1969 that the vague words "immoral or unprofessional conduct," found in the state law governing teacher dismissal, were interpreted by a major court. Without judicial interpretation, the limits of these clauses, specifically the circumstances in which an administrator or school board was justified legally to terminate a teacher's employment, remained undefined and unchecked by any authority but the moral judgment of the individuals doing the firing.[19]

Morrison was by all accounts a competent teacher who had a brief physical relationship, a single week that both parties described as "noncriminal," with another male teacher. When the other teacher made this week-long transgression of social mores public a few years later, Morrison was pressured to resign from his teaching job and the State Board of Education revoked his teaching credential. Morrison took the state to court and won. Morrison never claimed to be homosexual. Morrison's lawyers instead argued that his activities had no impact on his professional capacities as a teacher and as such could not be cause for termination. The Board of Education had overstepped its authority by revoking his teaching license because of an "offense" that had nothing to do with teaching.[20]

The California Supreme Court agreed with Morrison's argument, finding no evidence that Morrison's actions impacted his teaching and, more importantly, determining that such evidence was necessary to justify revoking a teacher's credential. Citing Robert Harris Jr.'s work *Private Consensual Adult Behavior: The Requirement of Harm to Others in the Enforcement of Morality*, Justice Tobriner pointed out that "there may be a plurality of moralities. Whose morals shall be enforced? There is a tendency to say that public morals should be enforced. But that just begs the question. Whose morals are the public morals?" Indeed, as the court noted, even within a single community there could be multiple interpretations of what constituted morality and that "in the opinion of many people laziness, gluttony, vanity, selfishness, avarice and cowardice constitute immoral conduct." Given this reality, how could the State Board of Education revoke Morrison's teaching credential but allow cowards and gluttons to remain in California's classroom? The State Board of Education was interpreting what was moral and immoral. Their interpretation was relative and, as Justice Tobriner noted, "the Legislature surely did not mean to endow the employing agency with the power to terminate any employee whose personal, private conduct incurred its disapproval."[21]

By citing *Morrison v. the State Board of Education*, the authors of the 1973 resolution were not only invoking judicial authority to bolster their cause but were also attempting to align the long-standing AFT position on teacher privacy with the California Supreme Court's understanding of the gravity of depriving a person of their employment.[22] The second stanza of the resolution is an escalation of commitment compared to the 1970 resolution and represents significant progress for LGBT teachers and their allies. While both resolutions appeal to the AFT's history of commitment to teacher privacy, the 1973 resolution claims that the AFT had *always opposed interference* by school officials. This frames the resolution rhetorically as a continuation of a long-standing policy commitment. Rather than being a move into unexplored territory for the AFT, this resolution reiterates a commitment to teachers' privacy and includes supporting gay and lesbian teachers in that history of opposing school officials. The resolution was potentially more palatable to a larger number of delegates because of this positioning. The lack of explicitly mentioning homosexual teachers as the beneficiaries of the proposal does call into question whether delegates necessarily understood that they were voting for or against the privacy of homosexual teachers; however, in all likelihood they understood the resolution was about LGB teachers, particularly in light of the forceful language used in the second half of the resolution.

The resolution goes on in its third and fourth stanzas to strengthen the AFT's commitment to teacher privacy by not only taking a stance of active opposition but also encouraging its state and local affiliates to do the same through repealing punitive laws: RESOLVED that the American Federation of Teachers opposes any punitive action taken against teachers for acts committed in their private lives unless such act can be shown to effect fitness to teach, and be it finally RESOLVED that American Federation of Teachers urges its state federations and locals to work for the repeal of state laws and local school district regulations which attempt to punish acts committed by teachers in the course of their private lives unless such act can be shown to effect fitness to teach.[23] The 1973 resolution achieves many of the goals attempted in the 1970 resolution. In addition to shifting the official language of the AFT regarding teacher privacy from "protests" to "opposes," the 1973 resolution also called on the federation of the AFT to exercise their considerable political might on behalf of teachers' privacy. It also showed activists within the AFT that it was possible to achieve a majority vote in the Delegate Assembly that helped the cause of LGBT teachers provided that the language of the proposal was carefully crafted.

The absence of an explicit reference to homosexual teachers in the 1973 resolution can be interpreted in several ways. First, it is possible that the omission was an effort to avoid naming a contentious group of educators as the primary beneficiaries of this resolution to gain more votes within the Delegate Assembly. Or, second, it is possible the word homosexual was omitted to avoid drawing outside attention, for example from the national media, to the vote. Of these two options, the second seems more likely for a simple reason. If the resolution's authors intended to obfuscate the aim of their resolution, strengthening the AFT's commitment to teachers' privacy and repealing discriminatory and punitive laws, they could have avoided referencing *Morrison v. the State Board of Education*.

While it is reasonable to assert that many of the delegates might not know this particular court case, or its impact, surely some delegates did and could have easily spread that knowledge to the rest of the delegation via either debate or the meetings held by state delegations to explain and discuss proposed resolutions. The sleight of hand present in the 1973 resolution was possibly directed at observing outsiders ready to offer praise or castigation, or more likely both, given the polarized view of the AFT in the press.[24] Because popular opinion was firmly against LGB teachers, the vague language utilized in the resolution offered the AFT, and perhaps locals facing more conservative politics at home, the benefit of plausible deniability. Not deniability in the sense that the resolution did not apply to homosexual teachers but rather the ability to deny that these protections *only* applied to homosexual teachers. In this way, the AFT was insulated from accusations of giving "special rights" to a minority by the absence of the word "homosexuality."

Like the 1970 resolution, the practical value of the 1973 resolution to LGB teachers in the AFT's state and local federation was limited by including the caveat "in their private lives." The AFT was already committed to defending the private lives of its members from educational administrators and community members inclined to use moral judgments as a pretext for firing K-12 teachers. Even with these limitations, it would be a mistake to downplay the importance of both the 1970 and 1973 resolutions and the progress they represented. Despite the 1970 resolution explicitly naming homosexual teachers, it was the 1973 resolution that would be cited in future resolutions as justification for the AFT's continued support of LGBT causes. While both types of resolution, either voted on by delegates or Executive Council, accomplished the same policy outcome, the democratic stamp of approval granted by a resolution that had passed the Delegate Assembly seems to have given the 1973 resolution greater significance in the AFT's evolving position on LGBT teachers during this period.

After the convention in 1973, the AFT was committed, albeit in an obfuscated way, to defending the employment of LGBT teachers and to working to oppose "punitive laws." The 1973 resolution called for direct action by the AFT and its affiliates rather than calling for symbolic action of protest. This call for action by a national union was itself groundbreaking coming a year before the NEA added sexual orientation to its nondiscrimination clause and four years before any other national labor union made such a commitment to the rights of LGBT people in the American workplace.[25]

1977 and Sexual Preference

The lack of clarity surrounding which private lives the second largest organization of teachers in the United States had committed to defending lasted four years. Then, in 1977, the AFT passed a resolution defending the personal and political choices of all teachers that explicitly referred to sexual preference:

> WHEREAS a person's lifestyle, sexual preference, and political association, are an individual's choice, with freedom of choice being an integral part of the democratic process, and
> WHEREAS the activities which educational workers and others carry on in their private lives do not relate to their abilities to perform in a professional capacity;
> RESOLVED that the 1977 AFT Convention go on record supporting legislation and other reforms which prohibit discrimination and abrogation of individual liberties based on an individual's personal and political preferences.[26]

It is unclear exactly what prompted the passage of this resolution. A distinct possibility was the threat of conservative activists politicizing teacher sexuality to push their agendas. The AFT had had ample opportunity to assess the damage that could be done by conservatives bent on making gay teachers into political scapegoats.

Teachers across the country watched the political drama unfold in Dade County, Florida, as Anita Bryant and her Save Our Children campaign squared off against a loose coalition of progressive groups to repeal a local ordinance that included homosexuals in the county's nondiscrimination law. The teachers' union in Dade County was an AFT local that represented fifteen thousand teachers. AFT local 1974 strongly opposed Bryant's efforts, going on the record numerous times against the repeal. The local produced materials arguing against Bryant's campaign based on contractual and constitutional rights.[27] The majority of rank-and-file union members were not opposed to the Dade County union's political stance to keep the protection ordinance; however, five hundred members did quit to protest their local's actions.[28] Little if any help came from the rest of organized labor in Florida, which, as Frank notes, was a "right to work state" where unions had minimal influence on public policy. There was, however, a large retired community in Florida, many of whom had been union workers, which could have been mobilized. National unions appeared even more silent than their Florida affiliates; neither the NEA nor the AFT issued statements condemning the Save Our Children campaign. The job protections ordinance in Dade County was repealed on June 7, 1977 with almost 70 percent of the vote.[29]

It is possible that the AFT was not silent on the Save Our Children campaign but was muted in its criticism, preferring to speak circumspectly about the issue after the repeal had taken place. Bryant's campaign and the 1977 AFT convention occurred during the same summer. The AFT convention convened in Boston a month after the landslide vote to repeal the nondiscrimination ordinance took place in early July.[30] The motivations of the writers of the 1977 resolution and the intent of the hundreds of delegates who voted to pass the resolution are difficult to determine without verbatim transcripts of the debate surrounding this resolution. Whether the delegates were responding specifically to Anita Bryant or more broadly to a national political climate that was becoming more aware of and explicitly hostile toward LGB teachers in American schools is unclear. What is clear is that the passage of this resolution set the stage for the AFT to actively oppose "legislation and reforms" that were detrimental to LGB teachers. Speaking out against Bryant's campaign after the fact did not help gay and lesbian activists during their fight against the repeal of the Dade County ordinance, but the AFT would have another opportunity to confront antigay activism at the 1978 convention, this time before voters in California went to the polls.

1978 and the Briggs Initiative

Flush with victory in Florida, Bryant's ideas spread across the country. Groups inspired by her success won repeals of local ordinances that protected workers' sexual privacy in Eugene, Saint Paul, and Wichita. It also inspired other conservatives to not only attempt to repeal already existing employment protection ordinances but to pass state laws banning homosexual teachers from classrooms altogether. These efforts failed in Seattle but were easily passed in Oklahoma.[31]

Historian Jackie Blount concisely details the motivations and actions of Anita Bryant and her campaign, which was then copied in other states, pointing out the particular effectiveness of appealing to voters through the "recruitment myth." Television ads showed footage of a San Francisco Gay Pride parade and claimed the parade included "Men hugging men. Cavorting with little boys" while newspaper ads asked, "and who qualifies as a likely recruit: a 35-year-old father or mother of two . . . or a teenage boy or girl who is surging with sexual awareness?"[32] Despite the spread of Bryant's rhetoric throughout the country, it was not until State Senator John Briggs, who had worked with Bryant in Florida, introduced a ballot initiative to bar LGB teachers and their supporters from schools in California that the AFT and NEA voiced their opposition as national organizations.[33] The state and local affiliates of the AFT in California pulled out all the stops in their efforts to defeat Proposition 6 while at the national level the AFT forcefully denounced the Briggs Initiative during their 1978 national convention.[34]

The Briggs Initiative (Proposition 6) was startling in its scope and sparked a national conversation about gay and lesbian teachers even beyond what Anita Bryant had inspired.[35] Across the country pundits, scholars, and politicians weighed in on the merits and flaws of Briggs's efforts, the likeliness that the initiative would pass, and the greater significance of even having a political discussion about gay and lesbian teachers.[36] The AFT based opposition to the Briggs Initiative squarely on the 1973 resolution. While five years earlier including "homosexual" in a resolution had been a bridge too far, in the face of the Briggs Initiative the Delegate Assembly of the AFT swiftly and decisively condemned the ballot initiative in California. The 1978 resolution cites the 1973 resolution twice and also cites the opposition of the California Federation of Teachers and the California Labor Federation.[37]

The major shift in language that occurs between the "Opposition to Briggs Initiative" proposal and previous LGB-centered resolutions centers on the fact that this is the first time the AFT classified a threat to LGB teachers as a threat to the AFT and all teachers. The details of the Briggs Initiative—invasion of privacy by subjecting teachers to the moral judgment local boards tasked with ferreting out homosexuals—were so threatening to LGB teachers, so broad, and so devastating to the rights of teachers as a whole that the AFT not only felt a need to voice opposition, but they specifically named the law outright. The possibility that the Briggs Initiative might spark similar laws in other states only added to the need for a forceful statement of opposition. Including the California Federation of Labor in the text of the resolution served to reiterate the point that the Briggs Initiative was beyond the pale.

Proposition 6 did not just involve LGB teachers; instead, the Briggs Initiative threatened the rights of *all workers* in California. The rationale behind this was simple: if homosexuals could be denied employment as teachers, barred by direct democracy from an entire profession, what would prevent barring homosexuals from other professions? And, if a class of people, even a class of people that were historically disapproved of by much of the population, could be barred by the political process from one profession why not other classes of people and other professions? The Briggs Initiative presented labor leaders with a slippery slope scenario that required a swift response because it broadly threatened political expression in the workplace.[38]

1979 and the AFT Constitution

The next appearance of LGBT issues at a national level within the AFT occurred the following year when activists within the AFT attempted to amend the union's nondiscrimination policy to include sexuality. This had to have been a key moment for LGB teachers and their allies in the AFT; during the previous two conventions, the Delegate Assembly had passed resolutions that opposed discriminatory laws against LGB teachers. Despite this positive track record, LGB teachers and their allies faced a significant challenge. Amending the AFT constitution was significantly more difficult than passing a resolution: an amendment could not be voted on by the Executive Council, it had to go through the Delegate Assembly. A constitutional amendment needed to receive a one-third vote of confidence from the delegates to even be brought to the floor for debate. More pressingly, any amendment to the constitution had to receive a two-thirds majority vote, or 66 percent of all delegates in attendance at the convention, rather than a simple 50 percent majority vote.[39] A proof of the verbatim transcript for this resolution exists and provides valuable insight into the debates surrounding LGB teachers within the AFT at the end of the 1970s.

Because of the verbatim transcript, we have a name to associate with this resolution. Robert Holden was the president of local 1934 at Grossmont Community College and had served as secretary for the Women in Education Committee of the California Federation of Teachers; he was notably the only male teacher on the committee.[40] Holden was remembered for proposing resolutions and amendments at national conventions and so his sponsorship of an amendment championing LGB rights was in keeping with a history of personal activism. The 1979 resolution attempted to amend the AFT's existing nondiscrimination clause by adding the words "sexual preference."[41] Holden opened the debate with a speech that directly tied the discrimination faced by gay and lesbian teachers to the forms of discrimination that the AFT had successfully opposed and reminded delegates that:

> The AFT was for human rights before it was fashionable. In 1956 the AFT led the fight against race discrimination in education. We expelled locals which were segregating on the basis of race.
>
> We have also led the fight against sexism in education. We have passed a number of resolutions, and we have also amended our constitution to make sex discrimination illegal.
>
> Now, we are faced with another issue, that of another human rights issue, that of discrimination against gay people. Now this is not a particularly "fashionable" thing to do at this time but I think the public is becoming more accepting of this sort of thing.[42]

This introductory speech hammered home two points. First, it connected the constitutional amendment on the table to the AFT's long-standing history of supporting human rights causes, citing the civil rights movement of the 1950s and the women's rights movement of the 1960s and 1970s. The delegates listening were reminded of not too distant days when a stance of supporting the rights of African Americans or women in the workplace was an outlier. Second, the term "fashionable" heaps a fair amount of scorn on delegates who might oppose the amendment. In 1979, the majority of delegates at the assembly had living memory of both Jim Crow laws and an America where women were barred from the vast majority of professions. It was fashionable in much of the country, and within the lifetimes of the majority of those delegates, to think that women and racial minorities should have fewer rights. In the same way, it was fashionable in much of America in 1979 to think that sexual minorities should not have rights at all.

This opening statement was an appeal to the collective conscience of the delegates listening. By recounting that the AFT had been on the "right side of history," the opening statement also reminded delegates that they did not want to be on the wrong side of history. This line of reasoning indicates that by 1979 the activists working for LGBT rights within the AFT perceived that there were a significant number of other delegates who would agree with, or be swayed by, the idea that "gay people" were entitled to human rights on a similar footing with other minorities. This argument was a far cry from the language of just six years before, which made the support of the AFT contingent on homosexuality remaining in the "private lives" of teachers.[43] By 1979, the struggle to end discrimination toward "gay people" was being discussed as being similar to discrimination toward African Americans and women. Not only had the public "become more accepting of this sort of thing," but so had the delegates of the AFT.

Holden went on to remind the assembly that the AFT had passed resolutions in 1973 supporting gay teachers and that they had opposed the Briggs Initiative the year before. He cites the defeat of the Briggs Initiative—58 percent of voters in California rejected it—as evidence that the public had indeed become more accepting and was "ready to come out against discrimination against gay people."[44] The year 1979 was a moment where the AFT could again show leadership in a human rights struggle and take a stance that, while not fashionable, was at least becoming more acceptable to the public. The vote to entertain the motion easily got the one-third vote needed for real debate to begin.[45]

Having jumped over the first hurdle, Holden moved on making a second speech to address concerns delegates might have. Attempting to get ahead of the opposition, he pointed out that "The only reason I can see for voting these things down is political expediency. I think the correct position is to pass them and get them into our constitution. Before you vote I ask you to examine your conscience now. Are you in favor of bigotry against gay people or not?" A major concern was that some of the delegates would vote against the resolution out of fear that it would "hurt the union." Holden reminded delegates that "all delegates are free to vote the way they wish. You're uninstructed unless you were specifically instructed by your local in this matter."[46]

Opposition to the amendment was wide ranging. One delegate stridently said, "I rise to speak against the amendment against discrimination against gays, against discrimination against vegetarians; against non-swimmers, and others who are not mentioned in this particular amendment." The amendment was in his view "unnecessary" and represented a sort of frivolous attempt to legislate away problems that "preclude discrimination that may have cropped up in this organization in the past. I do not feel that this organization is guilty of such discrimination." Another delegate presented the same idea in a more nuanced way and pointed out that the "AFT is already on record within its bylaws and within its constitution of affirming the rights of every teacher to secure his or her job or his or her civil liberty."[47] According to this view, an amendment specifically mentioning sexual preference was not needed because the AFT had already made a commitment to gay and lesbian teachers as part of its already existing commitments to teachers as a whole. Why clutter the constitution with a panoply of specific amendments for particular categories when those groups were already covered in the general clauses that the AFT had supported since its inception?

In response to this contention, a delegate in favor of the amendment pointed out that "At one point we thought that the constitution of the United States was written for everyone. We later found out that there were some omissions. And we sought to include those people within that constitution by amending it." Another delegate wryly noted that "As far as I know there is no prejudice against vegetarians for being members of the union at this time. Within the real world there are problems. There are people that will discriminate against people on the basis of their sexual preference." He went on to ask: "If we were going to go up to a potential member and say, you are a member of this bargaining unit, will you be a member of this union?—by the way who do you sleep with?"[48] For proponents of the amendment, adding sexual preference cost little and was an affirmation of the AFT's commitments to human rights.

For opponents of the resolution, the issue was not whether gay and lesbian teachers deserved equality in the sight of the union; the opposition assumed that equality already existed and reiterating it was redundant. No delegate spoke in opposition of LGB teachers per se; instead, they spoke in opposition of making "a list" of discriminated against people. One delegate speaking in opposition said she would offer an amendment to the amendment adding handicapped people, saying, "So if you want one, you'll get two," and was met with applause loud enough to be noted in the transcript.[49]

The debate over this single amendment ranges over forty pages of the verbatim transcript, with delegates arguing passionately for and against. An amendment was proposed to change the words of the amendment from "sexual preference" to "lifestyle choice," which would "take care of all these people that are worried about the vegetarians and non-swimmers and other people that have been left out." That proposed change was met with incredulity by supporters of the amendment; delegates were reminded that Dade County and Anita Bryant had occurred just two years before and this was not an issue limited to "San Francisco and California." Against the contention that gay and lesbian teachers were already protected by general nondiscrimination clauses, supporters of the resolution pointed out that there was a difference between reality and what was written in policies. While a general nondiscrimination clause could be interpreted to include gay and lesbian teachers, that possibility was weighed against the reality that they had not been historically included and so needed a "positive action," or explicit inclusion, to counter the years of exclusion. In the context of historic exclusion, altering the resolution with the words "lifestyle choice" would only further obfuscate the issue. The motion to alter the resolution was defeated; after a lengthy debate over just what "lifestyle" meant, no satisfactory definition was agreed on, and the original debate continued.[50]

The amendment to the AFT constitution in 1979 failed by an extremely narrow margin. The vote was so close that Al Shanker, looking out at the show of hands, initially declared that it had passed. When the room was divided by vote and a headcount taken, a tally of 808 delegates voted in favor of the amendment to add sexual preference to the constitution and 423 voted against it. According to the bylaws, a two-thirds majority vote was needed, and the amendment had missed that by just 14 votes. The amendment was defeated by less than 1 percent of the 1,231 delegates on the convention floor. Going into the 1980s, LGBT members of the AFT would benefit from the numerous resolutions passed in the previous decade but it would take multiple attempts before the AFT included sexual preference or sexual orientation protections in its constitution.[51]

1979 and Job Discrimination

Even though efforts to add sexual preference as a category in the AFT constitution failed, gay and lesbian teachers left San Francisco in 1979 with a substantial, if smaller, victory.[52] In addition to the more ambitious effort of amending the constitution, activists had prepared a resolution addressing job discrimination against gay and lesbian Americans in general. This resolution was in many ways the culmination of efforts by LGBT teachers and their allies during the 1970s and directly builds on each of the decade's prior resolutions.

The resolution opens with the familiar pattern of citing the AFT's historic commitments to equality: WHEREAS The American Federation of Teachers has in the past strongly supported laws against job discrimination based on race, color, sex, or national origin, and. . . . It then goes on to draw a direct equivalency between those groups and homosexuals by citing the 1973 resolution. Unlike the 1973 resolution, which was concerned specifically with teachers, the 1979 resolution encompasses all Americans: this broadness of scope is based on the 1977 resolution, which tied individual choice to a well-functioning democratic process. To hammer home that point, the third stanza of the resolution cites the AFT and AFL-CIO opposition to the Briggs Initiative and even explains that the Briggs Initiative would "have if passed required homosexual teachers to be fired for engaging in homosexual activity in private."[53] For AFT members, the Briggs Initiative served as a powerful example of how the democratic process could be used to attack teachers.

Attacks on teachers from elected officials, through the legislative process or direct democracy in the form of ballot initiatives and referendums, presented a particular challenge to teachers' unions. Even in the best of circumstances, supporting a popular cause, a teachers' union could be easily portrayed as obstructionist, undemocratic, a "special interest," or "against the public good" as articulated by any number of other rhetorical devices.[54] When teachers' unions were confronted with unpopular or politically divisive causes, like the rights of LGB teachers, the task of maintaining positive public opinion became even more difficult. This difficulty was compounded by the fact that politicians, like California state senator John Briggs, saw schools and teachers as an opportunity to highlight the issues of the culture wars and garner greater support.

Combine the political vulnerabilities of teachers with the morally questionable LGB community in the 1970s and you have what in hindsight seems like the perfect group to inspire moral panic among conservative and even centrist citizens. Fred Fejes discusses the central role of moral panic in his book, *Gay Rights and Moral Panic: The Origins of America's Debate on Homosexuality*. Fejes offers a thorough examination of the campaigns of the late 1970s aimed at repealing pro-gay ordinances that had been passed during the previous decade and preemptive campaigns to prevent such ordinances from making it onto the law books. While Fejes's research exhaustively documents these campaigns and their participants, the activities of LGB teachers are notably absent from his analysis.[55] If the origin of America's debate on homosexuality was the moral panic caused by the prospect of homosexual teachers, a discussion of what those teachers did in response to this panic is needed. A lack of that discussion makes LGBT teachers and teachers in general, seem passive and lacking in agency. This impression is misleading because teachers' unions and local LGBT teachers' groups actively contested these discriminatory campaigns.

Overcoming the moral panic that Fejes describes and preventing that moral panic from arising in the future was one of the greatest challenges that LGB teacher activists and their allies faced. Within the AFT, they attempted to do this by adding sexual preference to the AFT constitution. Though the amendment to the constitution failed, activists were successful in passing a job discrimination resolution that was predicated on the idea that "No employee should be discriminated against because of their sexual preference." The 1979 job discrimination resolution built on the 1977 resolution not only "supporting legislation and other reforms" but specifically stating what needed to be reformed: RESOLVED that the American Federation of Teachers supports amendment of the federal laws relating to job discrimination to include discrimination because of sexual preference.[56] This focus on laws at the federal level was likely a response to the repeal of local laws in Florida, Kansas, Minnesota, and Oregon. A federal law would reinforce local gay positive ordinances, invalidate discriminatory local ordinances, and negate the ability of local politicians to assault the livelihoods of gay and lesbian teachers across the entire country.

A federal law would likewise blunt the impact of state-level actions against gay and lesbian teachers. In California, the Briggs Initiative had failed, but in deeply conservative Oklahoma the Helm's bill enshrined discrimination against LGB teachers in that state's law. There were attempts to introduce nondiscrimination legislation at the federal level in the 1970s, and in each successive decade, but none of these attempts was successful. To date, the passage of a federal law protecting Americans on the basis of sexuality and/or gender diversity has eluded LGBT rights advocates and remained one of the greatest goals for LGBT advocates.[57] While activists within the AFT could not muster a two-thirds majority to pass a constitutional amendment by the end of the 1970s, they had proven repeatedly that they could get a simple majority vote on LGB issues. These resolutions and the support of a majority of AFT delegates placed the AFT as a labor union at the forefront of efforts to secure LGB rights in the American workplace.

Limits of AFT Support for LGB Causes in the 1980s

Before delineating the boundaries of AFT support for LGB causes in the 1980s, it is important to discuss the options that teachers' unions had for supporting LGB causes. What were unions able to do on behalf of their LGB members and LGB Americans as a whole? These options can be divided into internal and external categories. Internally, unions could pass resolutions, amend their constitutions, and prevent discrimination within the union itself. Externally, unions had two major options. First, at a local level, they could include nondiscrimination clauses in their collective bargaining agreements and support individual teachers fired within the context of these negotiated agreements Second, they could lend political support to LGBT-friendly legislation/litigation and publicly oppose anti-LGBT legislation/litigation.

The *Gish* and *Acanfora* court cases of the early 1970s are examples of unions providing legal and material resources for members they believed to be wrongfully, or potentially wrongfully, terminated based on terms outlined in negotiated agreements.[58] However, in the early 1970s, LGB teachers had to rely on being classified as protected through the umbrella of overarching employee protections. Teachers' unions had the possibility of supporting pro-LGB legislation on their own but, by the late 1970s and early 1980s, another avenue had opened. The increasing political strength of the LGBT community presented teachers' unions at all levels with the opportunity to join LGBT advocacy groups in litigation aimed at establishing a precedent for LGBT rights.

Some of the first academic examinations of LGB teachers occurred in legal journals and were specifically concerned with job protections. Joshua Dressler's analysis of the situation of LGB teachers and their legal rights, or lack of legal rights, may be the first of these published legal articles. It is notable for two reasons: first, for the thoroughness with which it traces anti-sodomy laws and lists the challenges and stereotypes faced by homosexuals as a result of the aforementioned laws sanctioning those negative stereotypes. Second, Dressler's scholarship accurately predicts the legal arguments that would be utilized by LGBT advocacy groups in the following decades in seminal court cases, *Lawrence v. Texas* (2003) and *Obergefell v. Hodges* (2015), which would strike down anti-sodomy laws and establish nationwide marriage equality for LGBT Americans.

Dressler accurately predicted that such cases would be predicated on the right to privacy established in *Griswold v. Connecticut* (1965) and subsequently applied in other Supreme Court cases, including those involving marriage such as *Eisenstadt v. Baird* (1972).[59] While being interviewed for this study, Dressler stated that his motivations were based on an overarching sense of injustice being done to these teachers and that he had been contacted after the article's publication by LGB organizations and individuals expressing gratitude for his efforts.[60]

The lack of legal opinion about LGBT teachers likely had a significant impact on the actions of the AFT. Because legal scholarship on LGB teachers was scarce, teachers' unions had very little to base their actions on aside from professional opinion of the union's own legal counsel and the guiding political or moral principles of the union. In this context, the likelihood of winning a court case for LGB rights had to be measured against the political cost of being affiliated with explicitly gay and lesbian organizations that made supporting such litigation unappealing well into the 1980s. Defending the rights of an individual gay or lesbian union member whose rights had been infringed on through breach of contract was an integral part of the AFT's agreement with its members. Adding the AFT's resources to broader battles for LGBT rights, even when they directly involved LGB teachers, was a different matter altogether.

We have one example of the AFT declining to participate in such a battle, and, while this example does not overshadow the union's progressive record, it does illustrate the complexities and limitations of being a national union engaging the political spectrum of the United States. The GAA corresponded with the UFT in New York City beginning in the early 1970s and engaged in a number of actions aimed at moving the city's school board there to provide better working conditions for LGBT teachers and better schools for LGB students.[61] Similarly, the National Gay Task Force (NGTF) maintained a steady correspondence with the AFT throughout the mid- and late 1970s, informing the AFT of events occurring throughout the country that impacted gay and lesbian teachers and students.[62] On April 4, 1979, the NGTF sent a letter to Al Shanker, containing a copy of a proposed law in Oklahoma, to enlist the AFT against the bill.[63]

The Helm's bill was a success for the conservative movement in its decades-long battle against gay and lesbian Americans. State Senator Mary Helm of Oklahoma proposed the bill, which would bear her name, and proposed adding "public homosexual activity" to the list of reasons that a school district could fire a teacher. "Public homosexual activity" was narrowly defined in reference to acts that fell under Section 896 of Title 21 of the Oklahoma Statutes. Title 21 was an anti-sodomy law passed in 1910, which stated, "Every person who is guilty of the detestable and abominable crime against nature committed with mankind or with beast is punishable by imprisonment in the penitentiary not exceeding ten years."[64] The Helm's bill was met with very little opposition and passed both houses of the state legislature easily with only a handful of lawmakers voting against it.[65] The ease with which the bill passed was disheartening to the leadership of the NGTF, but the specific concern that they brought to AFT was the response of Oklahoma teachers' unions to the bill: a resounding silence.[66]

Neither the NEA nor the AFT state affiliates in Oklahoma took a stance on the Helm's bill before its passage, according to statements taken by the local newspaper in Tulsa. Oklahoma Federation of Teachers president Mike Barlow promised that, if it came up, the bill would be "discussed and analyzed by the membership." Doctor Richard Morgan, the Oklahoma State Education Association executive secretary, voiced no concerns about the content of the bill and pointed out that, "I think that every teacher knows that there are two statutory grounds for dismissal that appear to cover the subject—immorality and moral turpitude. The reason that we haven't paid any attention is that we thought it was already covered."[67] And so with no recorded opposition from local teachers' organizations and the support of Oklahoma's legislators, the Helm bill became law.

The NGTF immediately began planning legal challenges to the Helm law, and, in 1981, the ACLU brought a challenge against the law in court. The NGTF also asked the AFT to join them as co-plaintiffs in the initial case tried in Oklahoma, saying that the case would "substantiate the policy statement adopted in 1970 entitled: 'Discrimination Against Homosexuals Denounced' and aid our efforts significantly."[68] The AFT declined to join the case, which proceeded without the help of the teachers' union.

The appellate court decision in *Board of Education of Oklahoma City v. National Gay Task Force* had ruled that the Helm's law was unconstitutional on First Amendment grounds because it deterred political speech.[69] The Helm's law allowed for the firing of any teacher who "advocated" homosexuality in addition to firing teachers accused of homosexuality.[70] The school board then took the case before the Supreme Court where the ACLU aimed for an affirmation of the lower court decision.[71] As part of this legal effort, the ACLU and the NGTF began asking liberal organizations around the country, including the AFL-CIO, to file amicus curiae briefs in the upcoming case with the Supreme Court.[72] The ACLU approached the NEA and the AFT, considering the teachers' unions to be natural allies in the fight to repeal the Oklahoma statute.[73]

Considering that the AFT had been on record for fourteen years, since 1970, supporting the legal rights of gay and lesbian teachers and had resolutions passed by the delegate assembly that explicitly spoke in favor of the repeal of anti-gay and lesbian laws that were punitive, this was a reasonable request on the part of the ACLU. Both the AFT and the NEA had members in Oklahoma directly affected by the Helm's law. The AFT did not file an amicus brief while the NEA was willing to do so. The reasons for the AFT's lack of participation in the case are unclear.

A possible answer lies filed away next to the other correspondence that the AFT had with the National Gay and Lesbian Task Force (NGLTF) over two decades, in what appears to be a draft of an unsent letter to either the ACLU or the NGLTF. The letter is not addressed or signed. In it, an unknown author presents a list of reasons why the AFT would not file an amicus brief. While the anonymity of this source makes its ultimate relevance questionable, it does reveal another perspective ostensibly within the AFT, regarding LGB teachers, and should be examined. The author of this draft presents four reasons that the AFT would not participate in the NGTF's court case.[74]

The first issue raised is that supporting the case would imperil the AFT's overarching goal "to advance the public image of the teaching profession, to secure recognition of the importance of teachers to students and the community, and to defend public school system from attempts to privatize education." These efforts would be measured concretely by "more money for public education and teacher salaries." While it is not explicitly stated by the author, the implication is that joining the NEA in a court case to repeal the Helm's law before the Supreme Court would not aid in the pursuit of these three goals or the securing of larger sums of money for teachers or schools. *Board of Education of Oklahoma City v. National Gay Task Force* was deemed superfluous to the AFT's goals. The superfluous nature of the case was heightened by the second reason given: "Homosexuality is considered by many to be aberrant, illegal, antisocial, and offensive to the social values of the people."[75] In short, how could the AFT expect the public to support teachers and their unions if those unions advocated for aberrant, illegal, antisocial, and offensive individuals?

Third, according to this unsigned document, it would be irresponsible for the AFT to use "its limited resources to assert a right to advocate ideas whose expression does not necessarily implicate serious First Amendment concerns." This was particularly the case in light of the fourth reason presented: "Finally, the AFT continuously adheres to its policy of providing legal counsel to its members punished for private conduct. We have, in the past, provided this assistance on due process grounds to teachers accused of homosexuality and will continue to do so."[76] According to the writer of this draft, the AFT was already using its limited resources to defend gay and lesbian members as individuals and saw no need to take up an unpopular cause that could detract from the economic goals of the union.

It would be a simple matter to write off the sentiments expressed in this anonymous letter as outliers if they did not align with many of the sentiments expressed by AFT president Al Shanker. Historians Jackie Blount and Karen Harbeck each note the reticence with which Shanker approached gay and lesbian rights and the broader impact of his framing of those rights. Shanker was on record numerous times hedging around the issues facing gay and lesbian teachers and generally preferred issues that were less divisive and politically expensive.[77] From Shanker's perspective, the AFT needed to pursue causes and issues that would benefit teachers as a whole and he remained unconvinced throughout the 1970s and into the 1980s that supporting LGB teachers as a group, rather than as individual union members, benefited the AFT. While Shanker's articulation of these concerns was certainly more nuanced than the arguments found in the anonymous letter, they are effectively the same; both valued political expediencies more highly than appeals to moral arguments. A sizable portion of the AFT, and likely the NEA as well, would have agreed with this assessment. In the face of an increasingly hostile political climate for organized labor in the United States, teachers' unions had to be strategic with their resources.

The Supreme Court affirmed the ruling of the appellate court with a 4–4 vote that ruled part of the law unconstitutional.[78] In the deliberation over the law, Justice Rehnquist, questioning whether the court should be hearing the case at all, noted that the law had "never been applied to a living person." Attorney Lawrence Tribe responded that, regardless of the law's

88 • Not Alone

application, it represented a "chilling" and "Draconian" violation of speech that could and should be addressed by the court.[79] The Helm's law was not a threat because of what it did. It was a threat because it had the potential to initiate McCarthy-style witch hunts for LGB teachers elsewhere.

The Reach of Resolutions

There are significant reasons to be critical of resolutions passed by national teachers' unions like the NEA and the AFT. The most prominent of these reasons revolve around the reach of resolutions passed by national groups. How much impact did these resolutions have, what type of impact, and where did they have an impact? The reach of these resolutions is limited by two factors: geographic limitations and organizational limitations. These two categories are not entirely distinct; they often overlapped and, when this overlap occurred, it seems there was greater resistance to centralized initiatives. The AFT's responses to the Helm's bill and later *Board of Education of Oklahoma City v. National Gay Task Force* illustrate both the organizational and geographic limitations of national resolutions.

The organizational limits placed on resolutions passed by the national conventions of the AFT were political and pragmatic. Like the NEA, the AFT comprised a multitude of bargaining units that functioned as educational stakeholders at state and local levels. These affiliate teachers' unions in turn negotiated with other local-level educational stakeholders. The AFT had to balance the degree to which national-level leadership was willing to intervene in local politics to enforce national-level resolutions. Generally, local unions were left to pursue their own agendas as long as they did not run completely counter to highly publicized actions by the AFT Delegate Assembly or national leadership. The AFT expelling locals that refused to desegregate in the early 1960s despite resolutions passed at national conferences mandating racial integration remains the classic example of AFT forcing the state and local affiliates to act.[80] This stands in distinct contrast to how resolutions regarding the equality of gay and lesbian teachers and laws that punished gay and lesbian teachers were implemented.

Organizationally, it fell on the leadership of the AFT to enforce and implement resolutions passed by the Delegate Assembly. If the leadership was not convinced of the merit of a cause, or it was easy for them to withhold AFT support for a particular case, AFT leadership could choose to not weigh in on state or local issues even if the compiled resolutions and political record of the AFT would indicate otherwise. The political climate in Oklahoma in 1978 was profoundly conservative on the issue of LGB teachers; only 11 percent of voters polled approved of homosexuals being teachers. When the Helm's bill was announced, the local Ku Klux Klan chapter declared that on hundred teenage boys had joined the Klan to fight homosexuals, with some of the teenagers attacking patrons of a local gay bar with baseball bats.[81] Local teachers' unions needed to be willing to risk being portrayed as supporting homosexuals in an overwhelmingly conservative state. This was a risk they were unwilling to take, and a risk that their national union was unwilling to force on them.

A second dimension of the organizational limitation on the reach of resolutions can be seen in the reticence of the AFT to support the NGLTF in *Board of Education of Oklahoma City v. National Gay Task Force.* AFT leadership was not held accountable for its lack of support. Who was there to hold Al Shanker or other elected officials within the union personally accountable for not fulfilling resolutions passed by the Delegate Assembly? There was no organized group of LGB teachers within the AFT to be outraged at the lack of support until 1988, and within an organization with hundreds of thousands of members, the efficacy of individual activists was limited. As mentioned earlier in this chapter, special interest caucuses in the AFT were sanctioned by AFT leadership and were in essence official arms of the national union working in specific arenas. These caucuses could be viewed as a gauge for when the entrenched AFT leadership found a specific political cause palatable and extended their approval for that cause. In the case of gay and lesbian teachers, this was not until 1988. While the centralized power structure of the national AFT could work in favor of LGB teachers and their allies, it could also slow the formation of organized advocacy within the union. This meant that AFT leadership choosing not to act on a politically controversial matter would receive little organized opposition from within the union.

The geographic limitations on the reach of national-level resolutions within the AFT stem from the fact that the vast majority of AFT's membership came from urban areas. In the NEA, the issues faced by LGBT teachers and their allies involved negotiating progress with the hundreds of thousands of teachers, and the political realities faced by those teachers, from suburban and rural school districts. The LGBT teachers and their allies in the AFT had an advantage in passing union policy but a disadvantage in applying that policy nationally. The largest locals within the AFT were in New York City, Chicago, Los Angeles, San Francisco, and Philadelphia; all of which had sizable LGBT populations and relatively liberal political leanings. The rest of the United States, places like Oklahoma, were significantly more conservative than the urban centers that were bastions of the AFT and organized labor. Putting pro-gay policies into action in conservative spaces had a commensurately higher political cost because of this difference and it was a cost that AFT leadership was not willing to pay in Oklahoma.

Imagine Al Shanker demanding that the AFT state affiliate in Oklahoma came out in force against the Helm's law, or that they organize protests against it after the bill became law. In what way would that help the prestige, social standing, or pay rate of teachers in Tulsa? Would such demands attract more members to the Oklahoma Federation of Teachers? If the AFT had joined as coplaintiff with the NGTF in suing the Tulsa School Board, would any of these bread-and-butter labor issues have benefited? These were the questions faced by leaders in the AFT and the Oklahoma Federation of Teachers. Even if those leaders were personally committed to the advancement and equality of LGB teachers, they had an obligation to their membership to ascertain the best course of action for their unions.

Would the gains for the AFT justify the cost of publicly supporting LGB teachers? As far as Oklahoma was concerned in 1978, many in the AFT clearly thought "No"; in 1981 again they clearly thought "No"; and in 1984, as the NGTF was about to go before the Supreme Court, the leadership of the AFT still said "No." The lack of action by the AFT contradicted the string of resolutions passed by the AFT throughout the 1970s. The Helm's law punished teachers for actions committed in their private lives and hung over the heads of teachers in Oklahoma, threatening their reputations and livelihoods. It was exactly the sort of law that the AFT had committed to repeal in multiple resolutions. But without organized political pressure from within the national union, the mandate for a forceful response was measured against the pragmatism of inaction, and the AFT remained silent on the Helm's law.

Resolutions passed at a national convention were limited in how far they could reach organizationally within the union because of the hierarchy of the AFT. The impact made by resolutions were also limited geographically by local politics and the place of teachers' unions within those politics.

While the AFT was in de jure support of LGB teachers in this particular instance, the union was a de facto nonentity. The potency of resolutions passed by national level organizations was limited by local political factors, such as the presence of a strong local union. The perceived political cost of supporting LGB teachers in different geographic contexts substantially impacted the willingness of the AFT to implement resolutions. In short, the commitment of the AFT to LGB teachers was groundbreaking and well ahead of its time, but the implementation of that commitment was subject to the same political forces that impacted the rest of the union.

3

The Gay Teachers
Association of New York

Community and Relationships

> Wearing a mask to hide beauty is always
> a poignant and painful experience.
> —Marc Rubin, GTA co-founder
> in 1978

Marc Rubin was already an experienced educator when he decided to publicly come out as a gay teacher.[1] In 1974, he and another teacher, Miss Mil-
lay, who used a pseudonym to protect her job, gave an interview at the
headquarters of the NGLTF about being gay teachers. They were both board
members at the NGLTF and wanted to advocate for the rights of LGB
teachers in New York City. Their argument was simple: being homosexual
had no impact on their being teachers. Rubin's motivation to go public as a
gay teacher was equally simple; he thought that the public had been lied to
about LGB teachers.

The LGBT community had made significant gains in New York City. A
proposal, Intro 2, was before the city council and, if passed, would ban discrimination against homosexuals in employment, housing, and public

accommodation. The Catholic Archdiocese of New York took issue with the portion of the bill that would protect openly gay teachers in the city's schools. The archdiocese contended that the presence of such teachers "could harm persons in their formative years." Rubin felt the need to respond to this accusation and, in an interview, explained his reasons for going public, saying, "There's got to be a response to all those lies the archdiocese was spreading."[2] Rubin would go on to be a founding member of an LGB teachers' group in the city that would continuously respond to such accusations and defend the rights of LGB teachers and students.

This chapter examines the activism of the Gay Teachers Association of New York between its founding in 1974 and 1985.[3] (See figure 3.1.) During this time, the GTA expanded from a handful of activists to an organization that regularly hosted events, lobbied city hall and state politicians, participated in debates in the media and with community members, and produced a monthly newsletter that was distributed nationally. The GTA made significant gains in three distinct but overlapping activities: forging relationships between LGB teachers through community building, establishing working relationships with the UFT and the New York City Board of Education, and, finally, advocating for LGB students within the school system. Each of these goals was interlocking, building upon and strengthening the GTA's ability to pursue goals in the other two areas. In this chapter, I examine each of these three areas of activity individually, showing how the capacity of the GTA to engage in organizational activities in pursuit of equality for LGB New Yorkers in the city's schools shifted over the course of eleven years.

Why was New York the site of the first successful LGB teachers' group and what conditions were in place in early 1970s New York that were conducive to the establishment and success of an LGBT teachers' group? I argue that two major factors contributed significantly to the success of the GTA: the strength of the city's teachers' union and the surging politicization of the city's gay and lesbian community. The growth of the UFT was influenced by New York City itself; the city's long history of racial and ethnic diversity, the conflicts that occurred in its streets and were mirrored in its public schools, and the strength of its industrial labor unions all influenced the teachers' union. New York City's LGBT community was likewise uniquely a product of the myriad social factors coming together in America's largest city. The goals and activities of the GTA were aided by two factors: the urban context of New York's LGBT community and the labor

FIGURE 3.1 Artist unknown, "Logo of the Gay Teachers Association," 1978. (Lesbian and Gay Teachers Association of New York Collection, box 1, file 2, LGBT Community Center National Archives, New York.)

context of the UFT. Understanding these two contexts allows us to examine the GTA from a number of angles and to place the GTA within the broader labor movement and the LGBT rights movement within the city.

Organizers of the GTA championed being an out LGB teacher but did not denigrate remaining in the closet. This was accomplished in part by balancing out political activities with social events and maintaining a policy of welcome regardless of how out a teacher might be. This policy of openness, which maintained the size of the organization, gave the GTA a strong position to operate from. As time went on, the GTA expanded their legislative outreach to include state-level officials and, having secured protections for themselves, the rights of LGB students.

I argue that the GTA's advocacy for LGB students was rooted in their conception of teacher responsibility and the student–teacher relationship. I also argue that this concept of teacher responsibility developed over the first ten years of the GTA's existence but was apparent from the beginning of the group. To examine the GTA's advocacy for LGB students, I first analyze how the GTA constructed the concept of teacher responsibility and how teacher responsibility related to organizing the association. Second, I examine the portrayal of LGB students by the GTA in their newsletter focusing on the presentation of LGB students as being in great need but having great potential. Finally, I present the three main ways the GTA engaged in advocacy for LGB students focusing on the balance that LGB teachers maintained between that advocacy and the political restraint historically expected of K-12 educators. Closing the chapter, I discuss the GTA's multiple levels of impact on the personal lives of teachers and students, other LGBT teachers' groups, and the policies and politics of sexuality in New York's schools.

An Urban Context

Audacious may not be a strong enough word to describe the hopes of early LGBT teacher activists. These educators faced tremendous odds and potentially devastating personal consequences. These odds were not only determined by the general outlook toward homosexuality in the 1970s but were derived from a specific and more intense negative animus directed at LGB educators. Public opinion in the 1970s slowly but steadily increased in favor of LGB rights, but the prospect of LGB teachers in public schools remained a negative outlier late into the decade. A Gallup poll in 1977 found that 56 percent of Americans believed homosexuals should receive "equal employment opportunities" but that poll also found that the same people opposed gay teachers in K-12 schools—65 percent—with only 27 percent "in favor" of them. A Harris poll conducted in the same year with a national sample found a similar result with 55 percent of the public against homosexual teachers and only 35 percent in favor.[4] It is clear that the prospect of a gay or lesbian teacher in the classroom was significantly more offensive to a larger swathe of the American public than an LGB person owning a store or working for a local business.

LGB advocacy in public K-12 education from 1970 to 1985 is striking in this context of widespread and specific public disapproval.[5] While in other economic sectors the presence of perceived immorality was distasteful, in education immorality was presented as directly threatening the prerogatives of parents and local communities to determine the moral instruction of their children. LGB advocacy in K-12 public schools amounted to telling parents, at least half of whom did not want homosexual teachers in their community schools, that they did not know what was best for their own children.

There was a distinctly fiscal dimension to opposition to LGB teachers, which echoed the talking points of the New Right. The idea that not only would your child be taught by someone that you and your church perceived as immoral but that you as a taxpayer would have to pay for that immoral educator's salary added insult to injury. A disapproving individual had the opportunity to opt out of purchasing flowers, or insurance, or any other number of goods and services from businesses they found morally suspect; education was government funded and legally mandated. Certainly, there were private schools for the wealthy, or those middle-class parents willing to make substantial monetary sacrifices for their personal morality, but being forced to retreat from the public schools was itself an unprecedented admission of defeat.[6]

LGB teachers' groups inside teachers' associations and unions were in many ways insulated from the harshest political winds faced by other LGB teachers. In the previous chapter, I stressed the complications created by centering activism on an annual meeting with a changing location. This scenario does have certain advantages though when compared to activism in a static geographic space; for example, a large urban school district like New York City. Being activists at a distance from the place they were employed offered a measure of anonymity for LGB teachers in the NEA and the AFT.

This partial anonymity meant activists in national-level organizations were less likely to attract local opposition.

Imagine for a moment that you are a conservative parent or perhaps the religious leader of a local congregation which maintains a stance that homosexuality is inherently immoral in 1975.[7] Consider the difference between knowing that there are LGB teachers in some liberal union of educators compared to knowing that there is an LGB teacher in your child's classroom or working at the school down the road from your church. The distinction between events that are disapproved of occurring at a distance versus "in my backyard" can be a tremendously powerful one. The offense at a distance can be easily ignored but the closer the offending activity comes, the more likely it is to elicit a reaction.[8] Because they were not operating directly in anyone else's "back yard," LGB teachers and their allies in national teachers' unions initially only had other educators to contend with. The possible opposition LGB teachers' groups faced in teachers' unions came from other unionists. A lack of outside opposition did not guarantee that LGB activists in the NEA and the AFT would be successful in their efforts. But not having to expend energy combatting outside opposition was likely beneficial to LGB teachers' groups operating inside teachers' unions.

The earliest manifestations of LGB teacher activism occurred in professional teachers' associations and labor unions but were soon followed by LGB teachers' groups in American cities. By 1980, there were eight LGB teachers' groups centered on a specific geographic location in the United States and devoted to addressing the specific conditions facing LGB teachers locally.[9] The size and scope of the groups, and their longevity, varied enormously but a unifying factor in the foundation of all but one of these organizations was an urban setting.[10] The liberal political climate that allowed for, while still not actively supporting, the long-standing existence of the gay and lesbian community proved beneficial to LGB teachers.

Cities offered the benefit of relative anonymity to K-12 teachers. An individual could live and work in separate locations with miles and thousands of people separating their personal and professional life.[11] Juxtaposed against the narratives of LGBT people living in smaller cities or rural America, the degree of freedom that LGBT communities in large urban communities exercised, while of course mitigated by oppressive laws and an overarching societal stigma, was markedly greater. As detailed in previous chapters, being open about one's sexuality exists along a spectrum. If that spectrum is conceived of as having an utter lack of openness about one's sexuality and/or gender identity on one extreme and an utter openness on the opposite extreme, LGBT Americans living in urban centers in the 1970s and 1980s had greater possibilities for openness with less of a risk than other LGBT people in the United States. In short, while being an LGBT person during this period could not be described as "easy" in an American city for most LGBT people, it was "easier" than being anywhere else in the country.

It is unsurprising that following labor unions, American cities were the next setting in which LGBT teachers' groups appear. Urban Americans were in many ways inured to the reality of people "in their backyards" that they did not approve of. Put plainly, urban Americans often lived closer to people they considered undesirable and who were categorically "different from them." The trope of cities as warrens of vice and immorality predates America by millennia extending at least as far back, in this instance ironically, to Sodom and Gomorrah. The residents of small towns and rural areas potentially had greater degrees of moral, religious, and even racial homogeneity to bolster their sense of certainty and moral indignation. Cities have been places where differences were, if not celebrated, at least relatively tolerated out of sheer pragmatism. The majority in American cities were already in some way inured to the presence of "immorality," and as a result had a higher threshold for deviations from the norm.[12]

The first city-based LGB teachers' group was founded in Chicago in 1972. The Chicago Gay Teachers' Association is evidenced by a single flyer published during the winter of 1973, celebrating the first anniversary of the organization.[13] Beyond knowing that the organization existed and that it marched in the 1973 Chicago Gay Pride parade, there is scant evidence of the Chicago GTA's activities.[14] Based on the mission statement of the association, we know that the Chicago GTA was planning on having a woman's caucus, pursuing talks with city hall, organizing a "sex-ed task force," and a gay studies program for adults.[15] The realization of any of these goals never materialized and the group dissipated in 1974, leaving Chicago without an LGB teacher activist group until the early 1990s.[16] While urban areas provided beneficial conditions for LGB teacher activism, the example of Chicago underscores the difficulties of maintaining group cohesion even with the favorable conditions of a large city.[17]

The Chicago GTA's Statement of Purpose provides a succinct two-paragraph outline of the goals of the organization and illustrates the hopes and fears of many LGBT teachers. The organization was "composed of professional educators and other people in the education field who realize that our first commitment is to the children we serve." The organization would take on "the task of educating the public that homosexuality and lesbianism are viable, healthy alternative lifestyles which are in no way related to classroom competence."[18] Tellingly, however, these goals and the membership of the Chicago GTA were framed in the context of what historians of LGBT history have termed the "recruitment myth"; the idea that gay men and women "recruit" or lure young men and women into their deviant lifestyle.[19]

That the Chicago GTA felt the need to explicitly engage the recruitment myth in its short mission statement not once but twice is pertinent. They stress not only that "homosexuality and lesbianism are unrelated to child molestation" but also that "under no circumstances can we condone acts of sexual aggression directed towards children." The Chicago GTA wanted to make clear that "Gay women and Gay men are as responsible for the separation of their private and professional lives as are our heterosexual colleagues."[20] Compared to similar documents from later LGB teachers' groups, this statement is extremely cautious. Ultimately, the impact of this caution is unknown. The Chicago GTA disbanded before they could pursue any of their goals, and so to understand how LGBT teachers organized in American cities and were effective, we need to look to New York City.

Nowhere in the United States were the advantages of living in an urban space more apparent than in New York City. George Chauncey's seminal work on the city, *Gay New York*, references the draw of the city to gay men, noting that in the 1930s, "Many men arrived in the city with only a vague understanding of what they might find, but, fearful they would never fit in in their hometowns were drawn simply by the city's reputation as a center of 'Nonconformist' or 'bohemian behavior.'" These men were often guided by older gay men who showed them "that there were gay restaurants, that there were gay clubs, that there was a gay beach, that there was a gay world."[21] Lesbians were also drawn by the "bohemian" reputation of New York City throughout the twentieth century, establishing their own world of social circles, clubs, and institutions, and while these two homosexual worlds sometimes overlapped, they developed and maintained distinct social spheres.[22]

The size of the gay and lesbian communities in American cities grew as young men and women who had served in World War II moved to urban areas in the thousands. After World War II the political constraints of the Cold War were certainly felt by gay men and lesbians in New York City but arguably to a lesser degree than outside the sanctuary offered by America's largest metropolis.[23] Specific neighborhoods, most notably Greenwich Village, became associated with the gay male community and the number of gay bars, businesses, and groups grew throughout the 1950s and 1960s despite systemic harassment by law enforcement. The postwar period also saw an increase in efforts by lesbians and gay men to be politically active. By 1960, the Mattachine Society and the Daughters of Bilitis had both formed activist communities among the city's gay men and lesbians.[24] These groups argued for measured and steady attainment of equality through respectable civil actions and peaceful protest as part of the homophile movement.[25] The moment that upended this measured approach for LGBT people in New York City, and arguably the United States as a whole, came in 1969 at a dive bar in The Village called the Stonewall Inn.

That the Stonewall riots were a watershed moment for the LGBT community is readily apparent.[26] Before Stonewall, the majority of LGBT people hoped to be left alone, to avoid persecution and prosecution. After Stonewall, LGBT people formed visible communities devoted to pursuing political agendas that made demands rather than asked for recognition. The tenor of the conversation had changed dramatically to demanding political rights. It was in this context that LGBT political and professional groups, like the GTA, were founded. The members of the GTA had the advantage of living in New York City and they had the advantage of a vibrant LGBT activist community in New York City. As educators in New York City, GTA members had another advantage: they benefited from a vigorous teachers' union, which was itself a part of a powerful labor federation.

The Labor Context

While there were cities in the United States where union members comprised a greater portion of workers, there is arguably nowhere that unions had more political clout than in New York.[27] Compared to many other industries, K-12 education was slow to unionize and K-12 teachers were even slower to unify under the aegis of a single union in New York City. Instead, in the first half of the twentieth century, teachers formed professional organizations based on the school level or the subject matter that they taught, their political affiliation, or the borough they lived in.[28] This dispersal of political power meant that teachers in the city were also slow to garner the benefits of collective bargaining: salary schedules, grievance procedures, and due process. The process of unifying these disparate groups took the better part of the 1950s and when, in 1961, the teachers of New York finally voted to be represented by a single entity, they chose to be represented by a local of the AFT, the United Federation of Teachers.[29]

The single event that lifted the AFT from the status of a small "gadfly union" to a nationally important union was its selection by the UFT in New York City as the bargaining unit for the city's public schools in 1961. Representing teachers in the nation's largest school district swelled the ranks of the AFT, almost doubling national membership. This dramatic increase also drew the attention of local and national labor leaders.[30] The AFT as part of the AFL-CIO had access to expertise from generations of union organizers/activists across numerous industries. By joining the AFT the leadership of New York's teacher union benefited from the legal, organizational, and political counsel of the AFL-CIO and its constituent unions and ostensibly passed these benefits onto the rank-and-file members. The next year, in 1962, another set of teacher strikes vaulted the UFT into the national spotlight where it stayed for a solid decade of contentious union actions and negotiations.

In the spring of 1963, the UFT led teachers in a strike for the legal certainties provided by a contract. Before this contract, teachers were often promised salary increases but later told that the local boards' hands were tied by the state legislature or other budget constraints.[31] During the 1963 strike and other UFT strikes in the 1960s and 1970s, the city's labor unions offered their support and services as mediators between city hall and the teachers.[32] This set a precedent for the UFT of seeking boardroom deals between the leadership of the city's political elite and the UFT leadership rather than relying on a more democratic process of negotiation through union-wide resolutions. In effect, the UFT learned how to efficiently negotiate in the same way that private-sector unions had over the previous three decades. The leaders of the UFT were schooled in labor negotiations by the experienced leadership of New York City's labor movement.

The UFT's tactics and the personal leadership of Albert Shanker, who would go on to lead both the AFT and UFT for decades, were both put to the test in the late 1960s over the issue of local school control.[33] The UFT acknowledged pervasive and even systemic issues facing schools with large minority populations but did not acknowledge or critique "teachers' abilities or their attitudes" as a significant contributor to those issues. Instead, the UFT focused on reforms that they claimed impacted all students, like small class size, and on ensuring that teachers maintained authority over their own classrooms. Teachers and the UFT often justified the underperformance of minority students by relying on psychological explanations of children living in poverty as being unwilling or unable, by virtue of their circumstances and "home life," to learn with the same ease.[34] One African American parent summed up the concerns of the African American community faced with the prejudices of white teachers by saying, "I don't want to be told my daughter can't learn because she comes from a fatherless home or because she had corn flakes for breakfast instead of eggs."[35]

Teachers for their part were troubled by changes they perceived in their schools. In New York City, they were faced with unprecedented levels of school violence in the 1960s. In 1966, a union publication reported that 213 teachers were assaulted by students over the previous three school years.[36] The UFT and many teachers expressed outrage over unsafe conditions in schools and argued that learning could not take place in such conditions. By 1967, concern over teacher safety had reached a point that forty-six thousand teachers across the five boroughs struck over the right to expel students from their classrooms for misbehavior. More than anywhere else in the United States, teachers in New York were willing to repeatedly exercise their collective authority to contest the competing desires of parents, administrators, politicians, and local communities. It is unclear where this willingness came from: union leadership, rank-and-file discontent, or the general social unrest of the 1960s are all possibilities. Another possible answer is that the UFT could strike every few years because the support of organized labor in other industries mitigated the political fallout that striking so often would have otherwise produced.

Collective teacher authority in New York was pitted against a strong movement within the African American community for self-governance in schools. The self-governance movement wanted to assert local control over neighborhood schools that were majority African American. This local control would hopefully allow them to address a number of problems in their neighborhood schools as opposed to waiting for City Hall or the Board of Education. Through decentralization, African American activists and their allies hoped to circumvent many of the structural issues that they saw as keeping qualified teachers and African American teachers out of predominately minority schools. The decentralization effort was legally embodied in a bill before the New York State legislature that the UFT spent hundreds of thousands of dollars of lobbying money to block in the spring of 1968.[37] Because of these actions, the UFT was viewed by some in the African American community as a proxy for institutionalized discrimination. Teachers were accused of caring more about their job security than children's education. Many leaders of New York's Black Nationalist movement decried the power that the UFT wielded in shaping state policy and viewed the New York public school system as a "prison pipeline."[38]

In the 1950s and early 1960s, teachers in New York City could proudly point to their unions' support of many of the major goals of the civil rights movement. That support was possible because the major goals of the civil rights movement in the 1950s were not in direct opposition to any of the major goals held by teachers' unions. Conversely, some of the goals of African American activists in the late 1960s, such as self-governance over the schools African American children attended and who would teach in those schools, seemed to infringe on teachers' ability to determine where they would teach and the job protections they had gained after years of labor actions and so had to be opposed by the UFT.[39] This clash of ideals and interests burst into open conflict when the community-appointed principal of a high school in the Ocean Hill/Brownsville neighborhood sent termination letters to most of the school's white teachers. Shanker and the UFT backed the teachers eventually calling for three strike actions in response to contract violations and proving definitively that the teachers' union could shut down the city's schools at will. The UFT eventually won the dispute and ended the experiment in local control, but not before drawing national attention and becoming even more entangled in the racial politics of America's largest city.

Going into the 1970s, the UFT had a large body of precedent to influence its interactions with other political actors in the city, whether those actors represented the establishment or minority communities attempting to exercise political agency, other unions, or the city government. Teachers in New York City, for example, the founders of the GTA, had benefited from these negotiations but also witnessed the political fallout the UFT faced after the Ocean Hill/ Brownsville episode. The founders of the GTA understood that the UFT could be critical in achieving equality for LGB teachers and students but enlisting the help of the union on behalf of a group of educators that were morally suspect would be difficult. Engaging the UFT and other educational stakeholders in the city would require having a position to negotiate from, a sense of purpose, and the ability to engage in political actions. The founders of the GTA were experienced teachers and activists who understood that they could accomplish a lot by working with the UFT but they did not want to work for the UFT. The UFT and other educational stakeholders in the city were potential allies but allies that needed to be approached from a position of strength while maintaining a degree of separation and independence.

Beginning with the Union and Board of Education

Though GTA sources do not explicitly discuss the age of members, it becomes clear through a collective reading of these records that the initial core leadership of the group was made up of teachers who were generally less than forty years old.[40] Many of these teachers were also established as educators and had been in the profession for more than five years. It is reasonable to assert that a teacher who had spent twenty years in the closet at her middle school might be more reluctant to march in the Christopher Street Liberation Day march during the summer of 1975 or to publicly lobby the Board of Education than a thirty-year-old teacher who came of age in the political furor of the late 1960s.[41] Unsurprisingly, the two original cochairs of the GTA had backgrounds in activism and were within their first decade of teaching: Marc Rubin had been active in the GAA, and he and Meryl Friedman were both on the founding board of directors of the NGTF.

One day in 1973, while sitting in a board meeting of the NGTF, Friedman and Rubin were brainstorming "how to best organize to advance the cause of equal rights for gays and lesbians" and hit upon the idea of professional groups as being a particularly good way of moving gay and lesbian rights forward.[42] Having come to this conclusion, and both being teachers, it was natural that they would consider the possibility of starting a gay and lesbian teachers' group. Nothing came of these thoughts until the following year when Friedman, Rubin, Seth Lawrence, and Mike Brettinger were asked to come to a meeting organized by another teacher, Mike Shernoff, himself a GAA member, with a representative of the teachers' union. Their first objective was to convince the union to support the various gay rights bills that were wending their way through the labyrinth of city politics and to acknowledge that there were thousands of gay and lesbian teachers working in the city's schools.[43] Sandra Feldman was the UFT representative responsible for, what Rubin wryly described as "the uncomfortable fact that not all New York City Public School teachers are all white, heterosexual, solid-citizen types, who live in Brooklyn and Queens," and ostensibly making sure that UFT members from this broad category had a place to voice their concerns.[44] Feldman listened to the five teachers and told the nascent GTA that there would be no point in their talking to the UFT executive board at that moment. Instead, she assured them that she would "talk to people" on their behalf.[45]

Summer began, then ended, and with the return of the school year a second meeting was arranged with the UFT. It seemed that Sandra Feldman had very successfully talked to people; this meeting would not be with just any representative but with Al Shanker, the president of the UFT. Shanker was at best noncommittal about the issues raised by the GTA in this meeting. He was not opposed to the formation of a gay and lesbian teachers' group but at the same time would not support the GTA because he viewed the issues surrounding gay and lesbian teachers as too divisive.[46]

The UFT represented a wide swathe of teachers whose politics, while possibly more liberal than even the average New Yorker's, were not so liberal that the union president was willing to risk dissension in his ranks over backing gay and lesbian teachers. Shanker was also likely aware of the delicate political climate surrounding LGB teachers and was not willing to risk the public standing of his union on a widely disliked and little understood minority. So, while he admitted that there were probably thousands of homosexual teachers in his union, Shanker was not going to gamble the stability of the UFT or its public image for them. When asked by the GTA whether or not they could take out an ad in the UFT newspaper, Shanker's only reply was, "You can try."[47]

With the tacit "not disapproval" of Al Shanker, the GTA attempted to place an ad in the *New York Teacher* and were denied because the newspaper did not accept ads from outside groups seeking to recruit teachers. After a series of letters, rejections, and increasingly less plausible explanations from the UFT, lasting almost an entire year, the GTA decided that direct action was needed to engage the teachers' union leadership.[48] According to the GTA's press release, the direct action was stymied by the UFT "ducking" gay teachers: "When the gay teachers arrived at UFT headquarters they found their hopes of speaking to UFT officials in vain. Elevators stalled on lower floors preventing the teachers, TV reports, and camera crews from ascending to the newspaper office. Those that made their way up by other means found that the union official had deserted the newspaper office and retreated to a locked room, amid threats to call police."[49] The drama of this scene was likely increased by the GTA's desire for publicity, but the action did make the UFT aware that LGB teachers in the city could act collectively and politically. The GTA was a group to be negotiated with as opposed to a group that could be ignored with no consequences.

The GTA wanted to work with the teachers' union and they were willing to utilize the stance of the UFT on LGBT teachers to lobby other educational stakeholders, particularly after the UFT explicitly stated in October of 1976 that sexuality was not a relevant factor in hiring or retention of educators and made a commitment to " support the civil rights of all members, including homosexuals."[50] A similar statement from the New York City Board of Education in 1975 served as the foundation on which the GTA would build its advocacy of LGBT teachers.[51] Indeed, by 1978, Frank Machiarolla, the chancellor of New York's public schools, assured the mayor's office that "In no instance has sexuality been used as a bar for entrance into our service. In no cases are employees subject to disciplinary action of any kind on account of sexual orientation." The chancellor went on to tell the mayor that, "In addition you should know that I have received no complaints alleging the violation of any teacher's rights regarding sexual orientation. If and when I do, such matter will be handled with justice and in the equitable fashion of which you would be proud."[52]

By 1980, the GTA's relationship with the UFT had settled into what could be described as an ally kept at arm's length. The UFT was a political constant that could be negotiated with based on long-standing relationships. In contrast to the democratic cycle of elected officials at all levels of government, Al Shanker and the UFT remained a fixture in the halls of power. This made the UFT a powerful ally but also meant that if the GTA wanted to maintain independence, it also had to maintain a distance and not rely too heavily on the UFT. The UFT was in the end a heterosexual organization, like almost all groups that are not explicitly LGBT, and losing independence could entail a loss of LGB leadership. While the general support of the UFT for homosexual teachers as a group had been established in 1976, particular support from the union for specific instances of discrimination still needed to be argued for by the GTA.[53] Similarly, while the Board of Education, and the chancellor's office, and the mayor's office had signaled their willingness to be supportive, that support also had to be argued for on a case-by-case basis. The GTA needed to be in a position of independence to advocate for LGBT students and its members because a position of independence allowed it to hold the union and political actors accountable.[54] To maintain that independence, the GTA needed to build up a community of LGB teachers, a task that generations of repression would not make easy.

Creating a Community in New York City

In 1974, the membership of the GTA was five teachers, and a working relationship with the UFT remained hypothetical. The GTA needed to attract more members. The refusal of the union newspaper to publish the GTA's ad denied them an easy way to reach the city's LGB teachers. Fortunately, there were other ways of contacting LGB teachers that did not involve going through the union. The GTA could rely on other newspapers, which were less selectively liberal than the UFT publication, and placed an ad in the *Village Voice* the week after they first met with Al Shanker. This ad announced the first official meeting of the GTA and drew between forty and fifty people to a member's apartment on Fourteenth Street. What it did not attract were other teachers interested in political activism.

It was evident that most of the teachers who came to the first meeting were not interested in political action that might out them to their colleagues and administrators. Marc Rubin recalled the event saying, "we five were the only activists the group had attracted."[55] While the five activists already had a sense of mission, the other forty-five teachers in the room needed a sense of community to be mobilized as new members. The initial goal was to get teachers to come back to subsequent meetings. This basic organizational necessity was complicated by the fact that most LGB teachers in New York City were reluctant in the extreme to engage in activism or even show up at a meeting of the GTA; fifty teachers were a tiny fraction of the thousands of LGB teachers in the city.

Aside from the initial five activists, the rest of the teachers attending that first GTA meeting were primarily interested in talking about the realities of being a gay teacher with other gay teachers. They were also very concerned about the consequences of even attending the meeting. Meryl Friedman, remembering that first meeting, described the educators who came as "fifty of the most frightened people that I have ever met and the courage it took to come to that meeting is by today's standards very hard to understand."

Friedman recalled that "we didn't take last names because people were way too paranoid." As teachers walked into the meeting, they "were looking around to make sure there were no cameras and to make sure no one was going to jump out from behind a closed door."[56] In his "History of the GTA," found in one of the earliest GTA newsletters, Marc Rubin confirmed this description, saying that gay teachers were, "on the whole, an incredibly paranoid group of people."[57] While this characterization of LGB teachers might make them seem timid in hindsight, being a sexual minority in a position of public trust over children, a traditional rallying cry of antigay politicians, made the caution of these teachers understandable. Given the tremendously negative public opinion toward LGB teachers during the period, paranoia was perhaps even advisable.

As far as the teachers coming to the GTA meeting knew, there was little evidence for large numbers of LGB teachers being "out" and remaining employed. There were, however, decades of precedent for LGB teachers being terminated and professionally listed.[58] While the broader LGB movement provided examples for action and organization, the specific challenges of being an LGB teacher made both action and organization seem especially risky. These risks must have been particularly frightening for an educator in the middle or at the end of their career, who had already individually negotiated the complexities of their sexuality. The teachers who came to the first GTA meeting were not just paranoid, they were justly paranoid.

Rubin, Friedman, and the other participants in the early meetings with the UFT were exceptions to this general paranoia and had already negotiated their own sexuality and identified publicly as members of a sexual minority. For most LGBT teachers, though, just crossing the threshold of a GTA meeting was a tremendous step that was perceived as a great risk. If these understandably reticent teachers were going to advocate for themselves, let alone LGBT students, they would need to be convinced of their own security, the pressing need for advocacy, and their own ability to change the situation in New York's schools. To make these arguments, the GTA developed a practice of meeting potential members wherever they were as far as being publicly homosexual was concerned and provided all LGBT teachers with opportunities to participate in the group.

The GTA had a policy of "no judgment" toward teachers who were closeted. That lack of judgment extended to teachers who came to GTA meetings but also to the vast numbers of LGB educators in New York City who never attended a meeting. Nonjudgment entailed not asking teachers where they worked, keeping a membership list without last names, and allowing individual members to be as anonymous as they felt comfortable with. The assurance "closet rights respected" and of strict privacy were prominent throughout the GTA's flyers and publications.[59]

Fulfilling the goals of the GTA entailed getting LGB teachers to show up at the meetings, be informed, and participate in the community. This would ostensibly lead these new members to activism or to support other members of the GTA engaged in activism. Driving potential members away with rigid moral judgments would have been counterproductive for an association that aimed to organize large numbers of teachers. The GTA maintained a commitment to teacher privacy throughout the period discussed in this chapter and reiterated that commitment in interviews with the gay press. Meryl Friedman in an interview that ran in the *Advocate* in 1983 described the decision to come out as "a very private decision."[60] Educators had a right to keep sexuality private and the GTA was committed to that right to privacy.

This commitment to teacher privacy, and the "nonjudgment" that commitment entailed, presented the activist core of the GTA with a dilemma. Moralizing to the vast majority of LGB teachers in the city who were closeted would make them feel unwelcome and unwanted; no one likes a scold. On the other hand, having no stance on the need to "be out" and the benefits of being out would have undermined the raison d'être of the association; advocating for better conditions for LGB people in New York's schools.[61] Certainly, a closeted teacher could work behind the scenes toward that goal but how effective could closeted educators be while fearing they would be publicly outed? While it was not necessary to be out to benefit from, or contribute to, the activism of the GTA, it was necessary to be out to fully participate in that activism.

The GTA had to negotiate a position where they were making arguments for being openly gay at work but not passing judgment on teachers who chose to remain in the closet. The GTA viewed coming out as a process with degrees, not as a hard dichotomy between being closeted and being totally "out." The task facing the activist core of the GTA was in finding a way to present the merits of being openly LGB, both personally and at work, to their less political members in a nonconfrontational way. They accomplished this by presenting their more nuanced arguments about LGB teachers and students in writing through a monthly newsletter, often in the form of opinion pieces, rather than solely at the general meetings.

The GTA newsletter became one of the main ways that the association used to call its members to action, keep members informed, and assure potential members that political action would not cost them their teaching positions. These assurances were achieved through publishing letters from the New York City Department of Education and the UFT. These letters categorically stated that heterosexuality was not a condition for teaching or receiving support from the union because sexuality itself had no direct impact on a teacher's classroom performance.

The New York City Department of Education had repeatedly stated by the late 1970s that it had no interest in teachers' sexuality and the UFT had repeatedly claimed it would defend its gay and lesbian membership in labor disputes.[62] Both the Department of Education and the UFT asserted that they made no distinctions between heterosexual and homosexual teachers based on sexuality.[63] The eventual passage of a city ordinance protecting city employees, including teachers, from discrimination based on sexuality also provided the teachers of New York with an enviably secure position to advocate from compared to their peers in other parts of the United States.[64] The vibrant network of LGB activists and organizations that existed in New York City by the mid-1970s provided a ready source of expertise and examples that the GTA could draw on.[65] This did not make advocating for themselves or LGB students easy or even professionally safe, but the teachers of the GTA enjoyed a firmer foundation on which to build their advocacy than the vast majority of other LGB teachers in the United States.

A major argument that the GTA made in favor of coming out was that teachers would be supported when they came out by their union and by the Board of Education, with the GTA watching to make sure that support happened. While certainly optimistic in their hopes, the members of the GTA were realists in their expectations; when teachers came out in their schools, they might be met with opposition from other teachers, parents, community members, and even administrators. LGB teachers in the closet required support to counter this opposition and the fear that they would lose their jobs. The GTA could point to assurances made by the New York City Department of Education, the mayor's office, and the UFT as evidence that teachers would be supported in their decision to come out by the GTA and protected from an educational stakeholder who disapproved of homosexual educators by the GTA's allies.

In addition to well-articulated arguments about the benefits of being out and assurances that it was safe to be out, the GTA had a more concrete way of showing reticent educators the joys of exiting the closet: they knew how to throw a good party. Monthly meetings also served as social gatherings, and the GTA held events throughout the school year so LGB teachers could enjoy the company of other LGBT teachers. Holiday parties, end-of-year parties, square dances, parties on Sunday simply to have "Something to do on Sunday," and a host of other events were advertised in the GTA newsletter and through flyers. An advantage of being a teacher was ready access to copy machines.[66] Fundraisers were held for special occasions in LGBT establishments throughout the city, including at the Eagle, one of New York's gay leather bars, to benefit the GTA and local gay youth groups.[67] Far from being simple entertainment, these functions were a place for LGBT teachers to connect to one another. For teachers who were not out in their schools, the parties showed that being out was not only possible but that teachers who came out continued their lives and enjoyed themselves.

Looking back at the early years of the GTA, co-spokesperson Meryl Friedman described the benefit of being out, saying it's much harder to threaten and to scare someone and to fire someone who is out and open about who they are and is proud of who they are. Whereas if it's someone who is closeted, the fear that holds you in that closet is a weapon that is used against you all the time. And these were the people who could be manipulated and scared and fired and let go because they wouldn't fight back, and they wouldn't stand up for themselves. And so, it's a matter of convincing people that yes we can, that we were the only people that can.[68] LGB teachers required a safe space, but what safety looked like varied greatly. As a least common denominator, they all required a place where they were safe from physical and economic violence as a group.[69] Past this tier of safety, there is a divergence between teachers who wanted a space from which they could be politically active and teachers who wanted a space in which they could be socially active and professionally safe. Though a considerable number of GTA members wanted both political action and social activity, many GTA members simply wanted a place to talk to other LGB teachers.

As I discussed in chapter 1, social activity by a systemically oppressed group is often a form of political activity. The social events of the association formed part of the bedrock on which the membership of the GTA was built. The parties, events, and fundraisers served as a public face of the organization that gave the GTA broader appeal. Political action could be both effective and fun. Moreover, these social events were a part of a broader LGBT social life in New York City connecting the GTA to the larger LGBT community and raising awareness that LGB teachers were doing their part to further gay liberation and needed support in that work.

LGB teachers were not the only people in New York's schools that needed the support of the larger LGBT community. LGB students were even more vulnerable, less able to advocate for themselves, and utterly susceptible to the prejudices found in their communities. The GTA was intimately aware of these realities and from the beginning of the association saw the potential of LGB teachers to help LGB students by actively engaging those students, serving as role models, and advocating for their needs with other educational stakeholders.

Teacher Responsibility and LGB Students

Securing job protections for LGB educators was not simply about protecting their own paychecks or even their own dignity. Instead, benefiting from job protections was tied directly to their ability to protect LGB students. LGB teachers' support of their LGB students was potentially in conflict with the other authority figures in the students' lives. Families, the administration of the school, religious communities, and the community writ large were often opposed to students identifying as a sexual minority, let alone acting on that identity. The mandate of a teacher was derived in part from these other stakeholders. The authority of teachers, and their continued employment, rests on the trust that families, school administrators, and communities place in individual teachers and the profession as a whole. This complicated the ability of LGB teachers to advocate for the needs of their sexual minority students. For an individual educator to face down one of these other educational stakeholders could be perilous. But to go up against all of them by advocating something as phenomenally controversial as the rights of LGB students in the 1970s and 1980s tempted professional disaster for an individual teacher. But with job protections in place, commitments to protect LGB teachers in writing, and the support of the GTA, individual LGB teachers in New York City were better positioned to advocate for themselves and their students than almost anywhere else in the country. [70]

The leaders of the GTA had a distinct sense that what occurred in New York City could impact the rest of the country. If LGB teachers could secure better conditions in New York City's schools, other teachers around the country might be inspired to do the same. The GTA had a responsibility that was broader than just their city. They could be examples to the rest of the country. This sense of New York leadership was buoyed and vindicated by news of other LGBT teachers around the country and the world organizing to accomplish goals similar to the ones advanced by the GTA. The GTA newsletter regularly featured news from these groups and detailed the struggles of teachers as they battled their school districts through the courts.[71] Many of these court cases took years to resolve. The most extreme example of these marathon litigations was John Gish, whose activism is detailed in chapter 1. Gish appeared almost a dozen times in the newsletter over more than ten years while his case played out through the court system.[72]

These individual narratives of gay and lesbian teachers slogging through the courts after being fired stood in stark contrast to the "News from Our Friends" section on the last page of the newsletter, which detailed the activities of other gay and lesbian teachers' groups. By the end of 1978, the GTA newsletter had corresponded with LGB teachers' groups in Los Angeles, San Francisco, and Maryland and, by 1980, groups in Boston, Chicago, Portland, Oregon, and Denver. Internationally, groups in West Berlin, London, New South Wales, and Melbourne were also updating the GTA on their progress.[73] Though the number of members, length of time these groups existed, and the impact they had on their local schools varied significantly, each of these groups was also eager to discuss the goals they were pursuing, the challenges they faced, and the progress they had made. A sense of responsibility for LGB students was integral to the relationships that LGB teachers formed between one another.

The sense of teacher responsibility articulated in the pages of the GTA newsletter was heightened by the sense that LGB teachers were being forced to participate in the neglect that left LGB students at a disadvantage. An absence of LGB teachers also left heterosexual students without positive gay and lesbian examples to counteract negative stereotypes about homosexuals. Contributors to the GTA newsletter asked whether being closeted at work was more than just an act of omission but actively harmful to LGB students. One member of the GTA who taught sixth grade exclaimed, "Children are naturally curious. The continued necessity to lie because of community and school pressure is obscene. Must we lie to our students and pretend to be what we are not while preaching honesty and openness to life?"[74] Integral to this argument, and the political stance of the GTA, was the assertion that remaining in the closet, even when it was necessary to be in the closet to keep a job, was harmful to both LGB teachers and LGB students. A teacher remaining closeted might be understandable, the pressure to keep under the radar and avoid the extra scrutiny of administrators and parents was intense but could not be considered admirable as it was based in lying, actively or by omission, to students. This choice, between "out" honesty and "closeted" lies, was heightened by the GTA's portrayal of LGB students as being in great need.

Through reading the GTA newsletter it becomes clear that not only did its writers feel that LGB teachers had a responsibility to LGB students but that they had a *particular responsibility as LGB teachers to LGB students.* LGB teachers were repeatedly confronted with their own inability to help LGB students openly because a public accusation could lead to being terminated.[75] Overcoming these fears was a personal process for individual teachers to engage in. The GTA, while remaining understanding of the personal costs of engaging those fears, encouraged educators to come out for their own sake and the sake of their students.

An assertion of teacher responsibility and authority extended well beyond the educational and into areas that had long been held as the purview of a student's family. The GTA was not claiming to know how to best teach children to read or how to best prepare them for college but instead was claiming that they had the responsibility to support students whose sexuality was all too often abhorrent to their families and communities. Advocating for their right to teach and their students' right to express their sexuality and be safe in school entailed arguing that LGB teachers had a responsibility to engage in that advocacy as a matter of social justice regardless of what parents, administrators, and the local educational powers that be thought. This advocacy included the possibility that some of their students' families were ill informed or just plain wrong about their children on the level of mental health and morality.

LGB students are portrayed in the pages of GTA newsletters in a dualistic way. They are shown both as being in great need and having great potential, often in the same article. The needs that students faced by virtue of being sexual minorities existed alongside an image of these same students being empowered and engaged. Portrayals of LGB student needs were negative not because of any fault of the students but rather the systemic oppression they faced as sexual minorities. The positive portrayals of LGB students most often revolved around an active opposition by students to that systemic oppression. While the vast majority of LGBT students were unorganized, the first "gay youth" groups formed in New York City alongside their adult counterparts. Gay Youth was founded in 1970 and marched in the first Christopher Street Liberation Day parade in June 1970.[76]

The other image of LGB students in the pages of early GTA newsletters was characterized by isolation and vulnerability, but most of all neglect. At the 1978 meeting of the National Council of Teachers of English, GTA member John Zogby described the situation in a session entitled "Gay People and Gay Issues in Secondary Education," saying gay students "suffer, at times, because of the neglect of school officials."[77] The onus for action was placed squarely on gay teachers to remedy this neglect by holding schools accountable for the well-being of LGB students. However, helping even your own students, let alone taking a public position on behalf of *all* LGB students, was perceived as dangerous. The degree to which LGB teachers could advocate even for their own students was limited both by concepts of professionalism and by their fears of attack from homophobic members of the community for being "too close" to an LGB student and the ever-present "recruitment myth" that cast LGB teachers, particularly gay men, as predatory.[78] Zogby himself wrestled with the question of what was "too close" to a student in an article written for the GTA newsletter.

The year after Zogby came out as a gay man at the high school where he taught, a gay student of his named Cal came to him seeking help. Zogby, in a moment unthinkable for a teacher today but reasonable in 1976, took Cal to a diner to talk privately after school. Over many cups of coffee and cigarettes, Cal told his teacher of "how he spent many nights in the street looking for sex and companionship. He spoke of his parents' suspicion and his fear that if they 'really knew' they would throw him out of the house. They had made such threats repeatedly. As he asked me what to do, I began to think of irate parents accusing me before a board of education, calling me 'seducer,' 'pervert,' 'child molester.'" The next day at school, Cal came to see his teacher and asked if Zogby would take him in if he was thrown out of his house. Zogby refused and described that refusal as one of the most difficult decisions he had ever made. He promised to look for a place for Cal if his parents threw him out of the house and eventually effected a resolution between Cal and his family with the help of a counselor.[79]

This episode illustrates many of the challenges that members of the GTA negotiated in the 1970s and 1980s as greater numbers of students identified as sexual minorities. LGB students started coming out at their schools and made their needs known to their teachers. Zogby faced a dilemma of degree: what could he do to help Cal and when did his help cross lines of appropriateness and professionalism? What would happen to Cal if he ended up on the street or in the foster-care system? What would happen if Cal's parents called down the political furor of the Board of Education on Zogby? Countless similar situations and questions provide the context in which the job protections obtained by the GTA went from being personally beneficial and comforting to LGB teachers to utterly necessary for LGB students. When faced with the prospect of a student becoming homeless because they were gay, the support of a union and the GTA gave teachers the ability to advocate on behalf of their students with a degree of protection.

The portrayal of LGB students found in the GTA newsletter was not solely based on teachers' impressions or opinions. The GTA newsletter regularly published pieces by students themselves. These articles underscored the difficulties of being an LGB student and the need for their teachers to stand up for them. They included poetry, calls by students for administration to respect the LGB teachers at their schools, personal accounts of their experiences, and requests for GTA teachers to speak at LGB youth groups and high schools.[80] LGB teachers engaged in delineating the boundaries of appropriateness within the context of the real and often dire circumstances their students faced.

LGB teachers contended with the fact that many, if not the vast majority, of LGB students were closeted. The overwhelmingly negative stigma attached to homosexuality made seeking out students who might be lesbian, gay, and bisexual a questionable practice. Even if a teacher was not closeted and secure in their position, any approach to an individual student could be misconstrued or deemed inappropriate. Teachers had to wait for students to come to them. It is little wonder that, in the 1990s, the concepts of "safe space" and gay–straight alliances were developed for LGBT students and proved so successful.[81] Within the model of safe space, a student was assured that any adult there would be supportive. The educators involved had already weighed out, and likely attempted to mitigate, the political costs of being supportive and committed to advocacy support in the context of a national organization, the Gay, Lesbian, Straight, Education, Network (GLSEN). A gay–straight alliance enlisted the support of other students, parents, and teachers, making advocacy a collective effort centered on specific schools. As education researcher Catherine Lugg astutely notes: "Unlike the professional fields of social work and law, which began queer-positive work in the 1970s, it was not until the late 1980s and early 1990s that the pioneering work of Eric Rofes, Rita Kissen, James Sears, and Karen Harbeck began to appear in scholarly educational venues. But there was no real educational policy work that examined the lives of queer youth and US public schools until GLSEN began conducting national surveys in 1999."[82] The GTA predated all of this research and so the portrayal of LGB students found in the GTA newsletter is based primarily on the experiences and understandings of LGB teachers.

Despite the challenges facing their LGB students, it would be a mistake to think the teachers of the GTA considered LGB students helpless or hopeless. The challenges faced by their LGB students were intimately known to the teachers of the GTA; they had faced them in their own lives in even more conservative times. If anything, the GTA had an optimistic outlook regarding the future for LGB students in New York City's schools. They based this optimism on the fact that there was a community for LGB students to come out into. The LGBT community had, and arguably still has, issues surrounding access to support and resources, particularly for youth from communities of color and lower-class backgrounds who lacked many of the relative advantages of their more privileged peers, but, by the late 1970s, there were at least resources to access. LGB students in the 1970s and early 1980s were part of the first generation of Americans to even have the possibility of support from adults, and the teachers of the GTA were committed to acting on that possibility through their advocacy.

GTA advocacy for LGB students centered on holding politicians accountable for their policies, making the local community aware of the existence and needs of LGB students, and creating specific services for LGB students. The teachers of the GTA developed an understanding of what LGB students needed based on their personal experiences, their conversations with LGB students, and conversations that took place within the GTA itself. The GTA utilized this information and developed three approaches for advocating for LGB students. First, the GTA maintained a political action committee that monitored and engaged the media, politicians, unions, and the public school system. Second, the GTA organized a Speakers Bureau that allowed other organizations to request GTA members to come and speak to their group. Finally, the GTA organized a Student Services Committee that offered free tutoring at local youth centers, and worked with other organizations to raise money for LGB students.[83]

GTA Committee Activism

The GTA Political Committee saw its role evolve to include a larger variety of causes. Initially, the principal concern of the committee lay in obtaining confirmation from the New York City government, the Board of Education, and the UFT that LGB educators in the city had job protections. After these protections had been achieved, the Political Committee devoted a majority of its energies in monitoring the positions of politicians and candidates regarding LGB teachers and students.[84] They would then contact allies in the state and local government, either thanking them for their stance or asking them to reconsider their position. If appeals failed, or the opponent in question had a long-standing record of not supporting LGB issues, the Political Committee contacted their allies in the UFT and among the state's Democratic politicians to rally opposition.

The Political Committee responded with particular swiftness when Dr. Howard L. Hurwitz, a well-known opponent of LGB rights in schools, ran for the New York State Board of Regents in 1980. Hurwitz was a former Long Island City principal who had gained a reputation as a "Champion of Discipline" in the mid-1970s and became a standard bearer for conservatives in the New York City public schools.[85] The GTA encountered Hurwitz in 1978 after he had been terminated from his position in the city schools for refusing a court order to readmit a suspended student. This termination made Hurwitz a martyr and sought after as a commentator on the much-discussed failing state of schools in the city.[86]

In a local television debate with GTA members, Hurwitz stepped beyond the general conservative talking points that all gay and lesbian teachers were bad teachers and argued that "*good* gay teachers are especially threatening since they may become *preferred* role models." If gay teachers were competent educators and cared for their students, that might encourage students to admire homosexuals or, worse, experiment with homosexuality because they associated it with positive role models. In the same debate, Hurwitz also "admitted he is not aware of the needs of gay students."[87] Later, when questioned about the number of homosexuals teaching in the schools, Hurwitz claimed that "the New York School System should be shut down if ten percent of the teachers were homosexual."[88] These political positions made Hurwitz's seeking a state-wide position on the Board of Regents particularly troubling to the GTA and required an immediate response.

Letters went out to the governor, the union, and state representatives in Albany known to be supportive of LGB issues. These political stakeholders were already wary of Hurwitz's bombastic rhetoric regarding the state of New York City's public schools and willing to oppose his election in the state legislature. Hurwitz failed to unseat the incumbent, but only barely, securing a strict party-line vote. One state senator reminded the GTA, in his response to their concerns, that "The Republican legislature supported Hurwitz. The closeness of the vote was frightening."[89] The political reality of the early 1980s for LGB people was such that even in New York City, constant vigilance was required to head off conservatives in Albany and city hall.

The GTA Political Committee, in conjunction with the Media Communications Committee, actively engaged the local and national media to dispel misinformation about LGB people actively being fostered by conservative politicians and religious groups. Members of the GTA gave interviews in newspapers, magazines, radio, and television. These interviews often centered around a discussion of teachers as role models. Occasionally this media outreach involved their students being interviewed as well. A high school student being interviewed about their out gay male teacher who was a member of the GTA told CBS reporter Carol Martin that "it was important to have a gay teacher because s/he served as a role model for gay students who are often isolated in high school." The student went on to explain that, "non-gay students need to learn the truth about homosexual people and being out is the only way that homosexuality can be discussed honestly."[90] An appeal to honesty and the needs of LGB students were at the heart of the arguments made by the Political Committee when debating opponents in the local media.[91] These arguments were also utilized by the GTA Speakers Bureau in less prominent but more intimate settings.

The Speakers Bureau went into the community and advocated for LGB students and teachers with parent–teacher associations, college classes, citizens' groups, and public schools throughout New York City. While the Political Committee engaged the politically powerful, the Speakers Bureau attempted to humanize LGB teachers and LGB students to the general population of New York City.[92] A large portion of this humanizing involved making citizens aware that LGB students and teachers existed in every neighborhood and were not clustered in specific places or excluded from more conservative neighborhoods. Meryl Friedman described this as pointing out to their audiences that "when we talked about ten percent of the population being gay or lesbian it was ten percent on both sides of the desk. It wasn't just the teachers . . . you had all those youngsters, those gay and lesbian kids who deserved the right to have role models, to know that they weren't bad, that they weren't evil, and it was only through education that we were going to make this a reality."[93] By reaching communities at a local level and by educating communities at a local level, the GTA could enlist other educational stakeholders to support LGB teachers and students. Imagine being the lesbian teacher in Long Island City, Queens, in 1976 with Dr. Howard L. Hurwitz as your principal. Or being a gay student in his high school. The presence of a gay teacher association or gay youth group in the city might be comforting but having a group of citizens in Long Island City to support you would be immediately useful if Hurwitz started acting on his theories about gay teachers.

The Speakers Bureau aimed to create a greater understanding of LGB teachers and students in local communities. That greater understanding could be used to counter the negative views of other community members and educational stakeholders. Hurwitz's views were common among American school principals. A *McCall's* magazine article in 1978 titled "Should Homosexuals Be Allowed to Teach?" found that 42 percent of 1,300 principals who responded to a survey distributed nationwide by the magazine to 4,000 principals viewed homosexuality as automatic grounds for termination. While 51 percent of respondents did not agree that all LGB teachers should be fired, the survey results point to the many school administrators who believed that homosexuality and teaching were incompatible.[94] How would an LGBT teacher know which camp their administrator fell into? The risks of your principal falling into the fire-all-homosexuals school of thought made polite inquiry impossible.

The GTA utilized education to combat the view that homosexuals should not teach and to educate the public about the needs of LGB students. By sending educators out into New York City, the GTA was playing to one of its strengths. Many GTA members were accomplished public speakers and understood how to explain difficult concepts because of their profession.

The Speakers Bureau prepared lectures for community members instead of having extemporaneous question and answer sessions. These lectures were diverse in their content and included "Growing Up Gay," "Being a Gay Teacher," "Being a Gay Student," "Gay Rights in Education," and "The Gay and the Family," which indicated that LGB teachers were committed to dialogue person to person. After the prepared lecture, the floor was opened to questions. In this way, the Speakers Bureau could place evidence in front of the everyday people who elected school boards and politicians that LGB teachers were not a threat and that LGB students had specific needs that were not being met.

The GTA distributed a standardized feedback form to the audience, asking for commentary on the GTA speakers after each Speakers Bureau event. Whenever possible, a male and female GTA member presented together to be able to better address the audience and represent the diversity of the association.[95] By analyzing these surveys, individual speakers could tailor their presentation to be more effective in the future. The prospect of a better future attained through working with politicians and community groups was doubtless inspiring to the GTA, but the LGB students already in their classrooms and already facing discrimination had immediate needs. Rather than waiting for the beliefs of politicians and the goodwill of community members to manifest positive results, the GTA itself took steps to meet those immediate needs of LGB students through the Student Services Committee.

The Student Services Committee aimed to create programs that addressed LGB student needs. The needs engaged by the Student Services committee can be placed into two overlapping categories: welfare and resources. The first official action of the Student Services Committee was to print a flyer for GTA members to distribute. The flyer, printed on goldenrod paper and emblazoned with "Gay and Young," begins with the assurance, "You're not alone! Maybe you think you're the only one in the world that 'feels that way' but you're not." The flyer goes on to provide contact information for LGB students who would like to talk to a "sympathetic or gay teacher on an occasional or regular basis." The flyer also invited students to apply for a scholarship that the GTA sponsored by writing to the same address.[96] Although the Student Services Committee did not begin offering this service to students until 1982, the goal of providing counseling to LGB students had been present since the group's founding. For example, in a "Bill of Rights for Gay Teachers and Students," one of the GTA's initial documents states that the GTA "Affirms the right of gay students to non-judgmental information and counseling" in 1976.[97]

LGB students' right to nonjudgmental information remained central to the goals of the GTA between 1974 and 1985. The GTA approached providing this information from the perspective that LGB students were misinformed by the rest of society. Because of this ambient misinformation, the

GTA and LGB adults had to provide accurate information to LGB youth. This was not just a matter of adolescent self-esteem or personal empowerment. The physical welfare of students could be impacted by a lack of information: students could be bullied, physically harmed because of their sexuality by peers and family, driven into dangerous depressions by feelings of isolation and hopelessness. The stakes of misinformation were radically increased with the advent of the AIDS crisis, which was first mentioned in the GTA newsletter in January of 1983.[98] The combination of teenage sex drives, a lack of sex education, and HIV made providing nonjudgmental information to students a matter of life and death.

The GTA was not the only organization in New York City to recognize the devastating impact that the AIDS crisis could have on the lives of LGB students and actively participated in coalitions to educate both adults and youth about the disease. The committees responsible for interfacing with students and the public incorporated information about HIV and AIDS into their outreach.[99] The impact of the epidemic was deeply personal for the teachers of the GTA. John Zogby, one of the association's early members and a long-time contributor to the newspaper, died from complications caused by AIDS in the summer of 1983.[100] After the GTA held a memorial service for Zogby, they dedicated the scholarship fund they had begun the previous school year to his memory. They then worked with gay youth groups to raise money for the fund through a series of fundraisers and parties. By 1985, the Joseph E. Zogby Memorial Scholarship Fund was awarded through an essay contest distributed by GTA teachers and posted at their schools. Students were given a prompt about an issue that was pressing for LGBT youth, for example, the 1987 essay prompt was "AIDS Education: Getting the Message to Teens." [101] The scholarship provided LGBT students with the opportunity to be recognized by the GTA for their writing and also gave the GTA another way to reach out to LGB students by contacting all the students who had submitted entries.

Although the GTA was committed to LGB student welfare from its inception, there was a distinct progression in the GTA's advocacy of LGB students between 1974 and 1985, which impacted the association's capacity to realize that commitment. This progression began in the earliest documents of the GTA with political action on behalf of LGB teachers and students, extended into discussions with the community about LGB students' presence and needs, and continued with concrete services offered to LGB students by the GTA. Each subsequent step was strengthened and possibly predicated on the preceding steps. Without the political activism that assured LGB teachers a measure of job security, discussions with the community would have been almost impossible for most teachers. Likewise, without a basis of support from the political structure and the community carefully cultivated by years of discussion, providing concrete student services like counseling, tutoring, and scholarships could have been easily misconstrued as inappropriate. Having political clout and community support allowed LGB educators to help LGB students without becoming martyrs. The GTA was able to expand their advocacy because they had a position that allowed them to advocate for LGB students without losing their jobs.

The premise that schools reflect and magnify societal values while serving as a space where those values and changes are contested is a useful framework for considering the historic role of K-12 teachers in the United States.[102] Teachers, with their integral and likewise ubiquitous place at the center of schools, exist in the complex position of safeguarding social values while navigating the contested terrain of social change. All teachers are not subversive revolutionaries, just as they are not all hidebound traditionalists. However, all K-12 teachers have the potential to be subversive regarding specific social mores while at the same time being supportive of society as a whole. Teachers can simultaneously preserve and challenge the status quo through their positions at the center of education. This capacity is most apparent within historic narratives where educators were in conflict with commonly held social values, such as the effort of GTA teachers to advocate for themselves and their students in the face of widespread disapproval of LGBT people.

Educators make decisions daily about how honest they should be with their students. They balance what is permitted and deemed appropriate against what they feel is needed by their students. Teachers also make decisions about when to contest other authorities regarding their students' welfare. While education policy writ large is set by governments and administrators great and small, it is in the classroom that content is conveyed and where teachers, not politicians and principals, develop relationships with their students. Teachers ultimately decide what their students need to know and whether they are personally willing to pay the potential costs of providing that information. The GTA's advocacy of LGB students exemplifies the concern of educators in determining and acting on students' needs. The GTA's advocacy also exemplifies the idea that educators have a right to make determinations about student needs and an obligation to meet those needs. The teachers of the GTA laid claim to both the expertise needed to make these decisions and moral authority to defend their decisions.

Impact and Influence

There is no doubt that the efforts of the GTA made a significant impact on the lives of LGB teachers and LGB students in New York City. Equally significant, though, is the fact that the GTA's efforts were in full view of the public. The details of GTA advocacy and activism should be examined as a counterpoint to the defamation of LGB people by conservative politicians and religious leaders. The efforts of the GTA were in full view of the tens of thousands of closeted LGBT K-12 educators scattered across America's countless school districts. For other LGBT teachers, the GTA offered the possibility of gay and lesbian educators openly advocating for their students without the fear of losing their jobs. Conversely, to conservative Americans, the GTA was part of a cautionary tale of what could happen in every American school if homosexuals were not defeated and conservatives lost the culture wars.

The GTA was intimately aware of the precariousness of their situation; in New York by the early 1980s they had achieved protections based on negotiated agreements and local ordinances, but both of those types of protection could be canceled out by state and national laws. They were also aware of how LGBT teachers could be utilized to provide conservative politicians with a wedge issue. Members of the GTA had watched as Anita Bryant in Florida and then John Briggs in California mobilized conservatives in the late 1970s.[103] With the presidential election of Ronald Reagan and the advent of the AIDS crisis, the gains the LGBT community had made seemed under assault and required the GTA to mobilize in new ways.[104] As the political climate shifted, the GTA responded with a versatility derived from years of successful activism and advocacy.

To LGB teachers' groups across the country and across the world, the GTA was a model for how to organize and an example of what LGBT teachers could achieve. Contact with other LGB teachers' groups led to collaboration; GTA members participated in national AFT conventions with members of other LGBT teachers' groups to support the passage of resolutions condemning the Briggs Initiative and to raise awareness of LGBT teachers in the national union.[105] To LGBT groups within New York City, the activities of the GTA were evidence that K-12 LGB teachers were committed to the struggle for LGB equality and that the city's schools were viable arenas for political action and advocacy.

The central place of schools in American communities and the central role of teachers within schools offer historians an opportunity to examine the wide array of conditions that educators negotiated and how those conditions changed over time and place. This change in conditions reflects cultural shifts and developments in particular communities. The GTA's activities in New York City were an early intersection of labor, politics, and geography that provided the space for LGB teachers to openly advocate not only for themselves but also for their students.

4

California and the Image of LGB Teachers

> I knew that at any moment I could be fired but I was determined I wasn't going to go down without a fight.
> —Norman McClelland, president of the Gay Teachers of Los Angeles

This chapter will detail the foundation, activities, and accomplishments of LGB teachers' groups in California between 1975 and 1985. It will focus particularly on the two years 1977 and 1978 and the events that occurred during the campaign for Proposition 6, the so-called Briggs Initiative. Three LGB teachers' groups were active during this period: the Gay Teachers of Los Angeles (GTLA), the Gay Teachers and School Workers Coalition (GTSWC) in San Francisco, and the Lesbian School Workers (LSW) also in San Francisco. While these groups have different origins and areas of focus, they were united in 1978 by State Senator John Briggs and his ballot initiative, Proposition 6, to ban homosexuals from teaching in California's schools. This chapter will specifically focus on the opposition that California LGB teachers' groups faced. A key distinction lies in the fact that, in California, there was organized opposition to the reality of LGBT teachers. In California, ads were placed in newspapers, debates were held live on radio and television, and activists for and against Proposition 6 fanned out across the state to rally voters to their side. All of this activity occurred in the spotlight of the national media and precipitated a nationwide conversation about the plausibility of LGB teachers in American classrooms.

This chapter revolves around three sets of viewpoints and portrayals of LGB teachers that occurred in the context of the Proposition 6 campaign between 1977 and 1978. First, I examine how LGB teachers were thought of and portrayed by the state senator John Briggs and the official "Yes on 6" campaign, California Defend Our Children, as evidenced by campaign materials and other media. This examination is possible because of a wealth of documentary evidence, recorded interviews, and the media interest that followed in the wake of State Senator Briggs introducing his initiative. Second, I examine how LGB teachers' groups in California thought of and portrayed themselves through their activities and activism. Each of the three groups discussed in this chapter developed specific strategies for interacting with the public. Finally, I will examine how LGB teachers and the debates surrounding Proposition 6 were portrayed by the liberal and centrist media in California by focusing specifically on the representation of these debates in political comics. In this way, conservative and liberal representations of LGB teachers and the debates surrounding Proposition 6 can be juxtaposed against how LGB teachers represented themselves.

Political Opportunity in California

In 1975, the California legislature negated the portion of the state sodomy law pertaining to consenting adults. This also removed the mechanism by which a gay or lesbian teacher could be easily terminated from their job. LGB teachers committing consensual sexual acts with other adults were no longer guilty of a crime, and so there was no legal necessity to fire them because of moral turpitude.[1] LGB teachers in California were now in a position where termination for moral turpitude was a matter of due process, governed by negotiated agreements, instead of a summary application of antiquated sodomy laws.

State Senator John Briggs had a keen sense of political opportunity and saw the potential to propel himself to the governor's mansion on two ballot initiatives: Proposition 6, which would bar homosexuals and their supporters from California's schools, and Proposition 7, which would expand the use of the death penalty.[2] These two propositions were meant to appeal to what Nixon famously referred to as the "silent majority"; the masses of Americans who, in the wake of the liberal cultural revolution of the 1960s and in the face of wage stagnation and inflation of the 1970s, were amenable to arguments of law, order, and moral conservatism.[3]

The debate in California over Proposition 6 offers a striking look into the complexity of teachers as a symbol in American culture. For the first time in American history, the population of an entire state actively *and publicly* debated the presence and impact of LGB teachers. The activities of LGB teachers' groups in California continued after the Briggs Initiative, but, in 1977 and 1978, a tremendous amount of activity surrounding LGB teachers occurred on a scale that had not been seen before. Across California, and the entire country, people openly debated LGB teachers in a way that ten years earlier would have been inconceivable.

Schools act as cultural weather vanes and the presence of LGB educators seemed like a warning to cultural conservatives that a storm was on the horizon.[4] In many ways, cultural conservatives' attacks on LGB teachers throughout the Proposition 6 campaign reveal very little about the teachers they sought to exclude and make illegal. Conversely, though, these attacks reveal a tremendous amount about whom cultural conservatives thought should be teachers and the roles they believed California's schools and government should be playing in people's lives. LGB teachers and their allies argued that conservatives did not have a monopoly on defining a "good teacher" and were infringing on the privacy of not only LGB teachers, or even LGB people, but on the rights of all Californians by granting the state government unprecedented control over the livelihoods of citizens.

Any attempt to engage the political climate surrounding LGB teachers in California needs to grapple with the immense size and diversity of the Golden State's population. In 1970, it stood at 19,953,000 and by 1980 had grown by 16 percent to 23,667,813 people, or roughly 10 percent of the total U.S. population.[5] Because California was the most populous state, the political fringe to either the right or the left could number in the millions, larger than the population of entire states in the middle of the country. Not only was California the most populous state but, by the end of the 1970s, it was also among the most racially diverse. While the majority of Californians were white throughout the 1970s and 1980s, minority communities increased in size and distribution within the state.[6] In 1980, 31 percent of the "persons of Spanish origin" in the entire United States lived in California.[7] The state had a sizable African American population of 1.4 million centered on the Los Angeles metropolitan area and the Bay Area.[8] More than one-third of all Asian Americans, 1.3 million of the 3.7 million counted nationally for the 1980 census, lived in California.[9] Politics in California shifted in the years leading up to the 1970s, taking a rightward turn with many other states that continued into the 1980s. No single person embodied this shift more than Ronald Reagan, the state's governor between 1967 and 1975, who took his particular brand of conservativism to the White House as president in 1981.[10]

The increasing diversity of California's population and the rightward shift in state politics occurred in conjunction with an increase in the overall population. The total population of California grew significantly throughout the mid-century; between 1950 and 1980, the population jumped from 10,586,223 to 23,667,813, more than doubling in thirty years. Cities and their metropolitan areas accounted for the overwhelming majority of this population growth. The urban population in the state grew from 8,539,420 to 21,608,580 people while the rural population grew from 2,046,803 to 2,059,322 people. Over three decades urban populations grew by 253 percent while rural populations only grew by 0.6 percent; this populations shift saw rural populations go from comprising 19.3 percent of the total state population to just 9.5 percent.[11] These demographic shifts caused political power to become firmly centered on the two largest and most racially diverse metropolitan areas in the state: San Francisco and Los Angeles.[12] Because of this, LGB teachers' groups in Los Angeles and San Francisco were in a position to make the reality visible of LGB teachers to a wide swathe of Californians. The Briggs Initiative, even though it was a tremendous threat, offered them the opportunity to be seen. While the LGB teachers' groups discussed in this chapter had small memberships, the impact of their activism was greater than their membership numbers might suggest.

The political and demographic diversity of California provided fertile ground for many political ideas to be tested. In addition to this diversity, the state's use of the voter referendum and ballot initiative provided a legislative avenue that avoided the political labyrinth of the legislature in Sacramento, circumvented the veto of the governor's mansion, and enabled direct democracy. When John Briggs failed to rally support for his bills to ban LGB teachers from California schools, he had another option: he could appeal directly to the people of the Golden State.[13] That appeal rested on the ability of the Briggs campaign to present an image of LGB teachers that left little doubt in the minds of California voters that gay and lesbian teachers were not only a moral danger to children but a sign of the decay of society as a whole.

John Briggs's Presentation of LGB Teachers

It is clear from an examination of both the secondary literature and the primary sources on the Briggs Initiative that while State Senator John Briggs was repulsed by the prospect of LGB teachers, as a matter of both his religious and political beliefs, his principal interest in LGB teachers was opportunistic. Controversy over LGB teachers and the death penalty mobilized conservative voters. As a politician, Briggs was selling a particular view to the voters of California. What John Briggs actually believed, how much of his rhetoric he thought was true, is difficult to ascertain. Historian Karen Harbeck conducted interviews with Briggs in the 1990s on the topic and concluded that Briggs's "two motivating forces were a wish to be Governor and a repulsion at the idea of two men having sex together."[14]

Which of these two motivations was dominant is a matter of debate. His personal opinions and beliefs, while a driving force, may not have been the primary contributor to the vision of LGB teachers and the supposed threat they posed. Instead, Briggs was marketing a portrayal of LGB teachers in ways that he, and other supporters of Proposition 6, thought would motivate prospective voters to support the Briggs Initiative and his future career. The value of looking at the propaganda produced by the Briggs Initiative is not in whether John Briggs believed his propaganda, but in the fact that Briggs thought he could convince more than half the voters in California to vote for his proposition based on that propaganda.

Proposition 6 was possibly the most potent instance that LGB teachers were debated by large numbers of Americans. The Briggs campaign utilized every negative stereotype about gays and lesbians in their efforts to secure victory. The strategies utilized by California Defend Our Children, the official name of the pro-Proposition 6 campaign, can be broadly divided into three categories, each of which contribute to the overall image of LGB teachers and LGB people conveyed to voters. First, LGB teachers were an explicit threat against Christianity and a "decent" society. Second, LGB teachers were the spearpoint of a broader homosexual movement attempting to cement its place in American life. Third, LGB people were intrinsically predatory, and the position of LGB teachers in schools provided them with opportunities to prey on children. These three tactics created an image of LGB teachers that was revolutionary, organized, and dangerous.

It is difficult to overstate how closely Brigg's Proposition 6 campaign was tied to the rhetoric of conservative evangelical Christianity. At the most basic level, California Defend Our Children attempted to link its campaign with Christian imagery. The logo of the organization featured a cross situated in a church window. Overlaid on top of the cross were the symbols for male and female interlinked as if to shield both the cross and window behind heterosexuality. This entreaty for active defense is reiterated in the written logo of the organization. The written logo emphasizes the first letters of California Defend Our Children and can be read as both a declarative illustrating what the Proposition 6 campaign was accomplishing, "California defend our children," and as an imperative battle cry that rallied voters to the cause, "California, Defend our Children!" (See figure 4.1.)

Briggs and his allies reached out to a conservative Christian audience with letters to pastors throughout the state, asking church leaders to distribute pro-Proposition 6 materials to their congregations. These letters constructed a dichotomy between the menace of LGB teachers and the Christian community and presented LGB teachers as part of the broader decay that the religious Right was combating. In a letter to gain enough signatures to put the initiative on the ballot, Louis Sheldon, the executive director of California Defend Our Children, reminded pastors that "our battle is not against 'flesh and blood' but against those forces that are spiritually evil; therefore we need to labor twice as hard to obtain our victory."[15] Another letter, signed by Briggs himself, compared homosexuality to a host of other perceived social ills and contrasted his actions against other politicians, saying: State and federal politicians have often tolerated, and even encouraged, the moral decay which is eating at the very heart of our society. Pornography, leniency with violent criminals, public nudity, open homosexuality, prostitution and "massage parlors," filthy movies . . . it is time for God Fearing citizens to take direct action! To begin our citizen crusade against immorality, an initiative has been started to ban open and notorious homosexuals from teaching in the public schools of California.[16] Proposition 6 was portrayed as just the first step in a long crusade against "moral decay." Contained within the ellipsis following "filthy movies" were

The good influence of Godly citizens causes a city to prosper, but the moral decay of the wicked drives it downhill.
Proverbs 11:11 LB

Chairman
John V. Briggs
*California State Senator
Fullerton*

Executive Director
Rev. Louis P. Sheldon
Anaheim

Executive Committee
Bob Brill
*Member of the Board
Grant Joint Union High School District
Sacramento*

Rev. E. Cannistraci
*Pastor
Mountain View*

David Du Plessis
*International Charismatic Leader
Oakland*

Jim Ford
*President, Ford International
Irvine*

Dave Hamblin
*Vice President, Olsen Farms
North Hollywood*

Tim F. La Haye
*President
Christian Heritage College
San Diego*

Dr. G. L. Johnson
*Pastor
Fresno*

George Otis
*President, Bible Voice,
Van Nuys*

Msgr John Siebert
*St. Marys Roman Catholic Church
Fullerton*

Rev. Bill Shultz
*Pastor,
San Dimas*

Rev. Peter Unruh
*Pastor,
Oakland*

Robert Wienberger
Sacramento

Dr. Jesse Moody
*First Baptist Church
Van Nuys*

D Leroy Sanders
*Pastor,
North Hollywood Assembly of God*

Paul Toberty
*Orange County,
Businessman Developer*

Rev. Chuck Smith
*Pastor, Calvary Chapel
Costa Mesa*

Mrs. Sally Holiday
Anaheim

Dear Friend:

The children of our great state need your help now. We are very close to having the necessary 312,000 signatures to put our proposal to ban open advocates of homosexuality and openly homosexual teachers from teaching our elementary and high school children.

<u>With your help right now, we can make it. But, the deadline is upon us.</u>

Do two things for California's children right now:

1. Have 5 friends, club members, neighbors, fellow Church members, relatives or business associates sign the enclosed Defend Our Children petition who have not signed the new petition before. <u>You sign at the bottom as circulator.</u> <u>Mail this petition back in no more than three days.</u>

2. Indicate on the enclosed card how many more 5 signature petitions you could get filled if, in an emergency, we need last minute signatures to go over the top. <u>We won't need to ask you if all our supporters cooperates in getting just one petition filled</u>.

<u>Whether or not California's children are protected now depends upon you.</u>
Please have the enclosed petition completed in no more than three days.

Sincerely,

Senator John V. Briggs
Chairman, California Defend Our Children

P.S. If for some reason you can't get five signers, get as many as you can, <u>even one will help</u>. But in any case, <u>do mail your petition in three days, no more</u>.

505 E. Commonwealth, Suite G, Fullerton, California 92632
California Defend Our Children I.D. #771112 Lou Sheldon, Tr. Printed by Parker & Son, Los Angeles

FIGURE 4.1 "California Defend Our Children, Vote Yes on Proposition 6" (mailer), Fullerton, CA, 1977. (Briggs Initiative Collection, box 1, file 8, *ONE* National Gay and Lesbian Archives, Los Angeles.)

an indeterminate, and possibly infinite, number of vices and immoralities which decent citizens needed to take a stand against. The ballot initiative was a particularly powerful weapon against immorality because, rather than trusting complacent politicians, it could be wielded by citizens themselves. The politicians could be swayed by immorality, but the assembled voters of California, decent and God-fearing people, acting together would surely make the state a better place. John Briggs would lead them in this moral crusade and so ascend to power.

This begs the question: "Who was John Briggs leading a crusade against?" Surely not the small groups of LGB teachers detailed in this chapter, who combined might have numbered slightly more than a hundred teachers—hardly enough deviant tinder to ignite the fires of religious and political zeal across the most populous state in the union and not nearly enough fuel to propel Briggs into the governor's mansion. LGB teachers were, instead, symbols of the perceived moral decay that animated conservatives throughout the culture wars. Specifically, LGB teachers and the debate around them were conceived of as a front line in the contest to prevent homosexuality from being viewed as normal within mainstream public opinion.

Images of warfare and other martial metaphors are found throughout the materials produced by California Defend Our Children. A three-page fundraising letter sent to garner signatures and funds described a "large well financed movement in this country which seeks to give homosexuality society's stamp of approval. Nowhere is this movement more powerful or better organized than in California." Combating that movement could be done—"With God's help a successful campaign was waged against homosexuality in Miami"—but success could only be assured by financial contributions and political support from California's churches.[17]

The same letter goes on to explain that in Miami, "Wealthy homosexuals and their supporters had raised hundreds of thousands of dollars to stop us. They funded a slick, high priced advertising campaign designed to distort the issue and confuse voters." The readers of this letter are left to wonder how much money this organization of wealthy homosexuals could raise in California because, "homosexuals often brag that they are strongest in California and that they can't be defeated here. They are wrong. If we defeat them here our cause for morality can and will sweep the nation."[18] If homosexuals were not defeated in California, the opposite could be true; they might gain ground across the United States to the detriment of children and their families.

The intense rhetoric used to describe the "organization" that was financing opposition to Proposition 6 was firmly rooted in the myth of the homosexual as a predator intent on destroying families and recruiting children. To help potential supporters understand the peril that children across California faced, California Defend Our Children often enclosed excerpts from media outlets detailing protesters confronting Briggs throughout the state. One photo that was particularly favored for this purpose first appeared in the *Los Angeles Times* and showed Briggs being confronted by "a representative of the homosexual community" in San Francisco. Here was one of the men trying to lead the children of California into immorality. In the postscript of fundraising letters, potential supporters of Proposition 6 were directed to look at attached articles and "take a look at the man in the Times photo who is wearing an earring and fingernail polish. Ask yourself this question, 'Is this the sort of man I want teaching my children?'"[19] Another mailer featured this image under the headline: "Homosexuals Are Raising Millions to Defeat Us. Normal, Decent Californians Must Act or THEY Will Defeat Us."[20]

Other materials produced by California Defend Our Children were explicit in linking LGB teachers to sexual abuse of children regardless of whether educators of any sort were involved in said abuse. A particularly vicious example of this association was a trifold mailer that reproduced supposed headlines and portions of articles from across the country to prove the need for Proposition 6. Fifteen scandalous headlines, with titles ranging from "Former Scoutmaster Convicted of Homosexual Acts with Boys" to "Stricter Laws Asked; Senate Shown Movie of Child Porn" are displayed over a footer reading, "There Is No 'Human Right' to Corrupt Our Children." Of the fifteen headings featured, only three deal with teachers and just one of those three reports alleged child abuse. The lack of explicit connection to teachers was irrelevant because the rest of the mailer had very little to do with LGB teachers and instead focused on general gains made by the gay and lesbian community. For example, a list of goals that had reportedly been agreed upon in 1972 by the National Coalition of Gay Organizations featured prominently on the first section of the mailer. First on the list was, "Repeal of all laws governing the age of consent."[21] Through these unprovable attacks, homosexual teachers were portrayed as a particularly pernicious symptom of a much larger social disease.

State Senator Briggs and California Defend Our Children excelled at making arguments about LGB teachers based not on evidence but instead on appeals to "common sense" in the context of larger fears about the moral decay in society. By appealing to broad prejudices against homosexuals, Briggs did not need to rely on concrete facts about gay and lesbian teachers or gay and lesbian people. Instead, the image of LGB teachers portrayed by the "Yes on 6" campaign relied on the assumption that the majority of people were "decent" and part of that decency entailed a visceral disgust toward homosexuals. In many ways, a vague image of a predatory gay man in a hypothetical classroom was more useful to California Defend Our Children than the concrete reality of Hank Wilson teaching his second-grade class in San Francisco or Norman McClelland going over multiplication tables with students in Los Angeles.

The actual educational practices of LGB teachers were fairly unremarkable because they were indiscernible from the educational practices of their heterosexual colleagues. Long division and charts of the solar system taught by homosexual teachers did not provide the emotions needed to conjure up widespread moral panic. The Proposition 6 campaign relied on sensationalism and outrage, and, as we will see, the LGB teachers' groups found in California in the late 1970s were not terribly sensational. An ill-defined group of social deviants was easier to portray as a source of corrupt societal ills than a few groups of gay and lesbian teachers trying to avoid the choice between persecution and the closet. With the advent of the Briggs Initiative already existing, LGB teachers' groups in California's two largest urban areas pivoted to face the new threat of Proposition 6 and worked to take control of the narrative surrounding LGB teachers.

The Gay Teachers of Los Angeles

Writing LGBT history is a relatively new endeavor with the first academic works of history on gay, lesbian, bisexual Americans being written in the 1980s and early 1990s.[22] For a substantial portion of that endeavor, Los Angeles and its LGBT communities were often overlooked in favor of the more obvious, and easily studied, LGBT communities in San Francisco.[23] Because of these factors, research on Los Angeles's LGBT history has been produced by a handful of historians and the impact of Los Angeles's LGBT community on the American LGBT movement as a whole has only been examined in detail by those same few historians.[24] Lillian Faderman and Stuart Timmons give readers a comprehensive overview of this history in their book, *Gay L.A.: A History of Sexual Outlaws, Power Politics, and Lipstick Lesbians*. Faderman and Timmons discuss the distinct gay male and lesbian communities as they developed and the specific challenges they faced. Of particular note in this research is the tracing of the LGB communities in Los Angeles into the early twentieth century by examining how the politics of different periods impacted these communities.[25]

Los Angeles already had a decades-long history of LGB activism and publications by the early 1970s. *ONE Magazine* (1953), the publication of the Mattachine Society, and the *Advocate* (1967), the longest running LGBT publication in the United States, were both based out of Los Angeles.[26] Los Angeles, in the postwar period leading up to the 1970s, offered the anonymity of a large urban center and the draw of the motion picture industry centered on Hollywood with its long-standing connections to, if not acceptance of, gay men.[27] The growth of Los Angeles, and its economy, throughout the middle of the twentieth century offered young men and women from across the country significant opportunities for gainful employment.[28] Among these opportunities was a swiftly growing school district that was fast becoming one of the largest in the country and almost always in need of teachers.

Because of this need, when Norman McClelland graduated with his master's degree and could not find work, he found a job prospect on a bulletin board at his university; the Los Angeles Unified School District was recruiting male preschool teachers. The school district was particularly interested in male teachers to provide role models for children from "single-parent homes." McClelland got the job and, much to his surprise, found that he enjoyed the work and its benefits. He would go on to have a teaching career that spanned thirty-three years. McClelland also volunteered at the Gay Community Center. In 1976, he was leading a discussion group and noticed that many of the men that were coming to his group were also teachers and wanted to talk about issues directly related to their profession. He concluded that there was a disconnect occurring between the educators and everyone else and that "the non-teachers in the group had no idea what they were talking about ... emotionally and working with kids and the feeling that you could be fired at any time." In response to this need, McClelland decided to "establish a group where gay and lesbian teachers could come and talk to each other and get some support," and founded the GTLA in June 1976.[29]

McClelland was out in his personal life but not at the school where he taught. For much of his first year as leader of the GTLA, he maintained a separation between his sexuality and professional life. The GTLA met once or twice a month, and McClelland continued teaching. This separation of the personal and professional was practical for him and seemed to be satisfactory, if not ideal, until State Senator John Briggs announced his intentions of putting Proposition 6 on the 1978 ballot.[30] McClelland understood that most of the teachers coming to GTLA meetings were not in a position to come out publicly but that there needed to be a public face for the gay and lesbian teachers of Los Angeles. He was particularly offended by the broad reach of the Briggs Initiative. It was not just teachers who were affected but any employee in a school who "advocated" for homosexuals.[31] Specifically, the Briggs Initiative proposed that, "Public homosexual conduct means advocating, soliciting, encouraging, or promoting of private or public homosexual activity directed at or likely to come to the attention of school children or and/or other employees."[32] This ill-defined portion of what was overall a loosely written proposition ensured that when McClelland decided to look for support against the Briggs Initiative, he readily found allies.

After deciding that he was going to come out publicly as a gay teacher, McClelland immediately went to the offices of the United Teachers of Los Angeles (UTLA).[33] McClelland was unaware of the position of the state teachers' union or the AFT regarding gay and lesbian teachers going into his initial meeting with the union but reasoned that the union was "very liberal" and "could not let that thing go unchallenged because there was too much at stake with civil rights of teachers and that if something like that went through it could break the union."[34] He also recalled later that, "if the proposition went through I would be the first person to be fired in the state," and that the backing of the union would be a tremendous asset. He met with UTLA president Hank Springer and explained that the Briggs Initiative, "Was not just a threat to gay teachers but to all teachers." Springer spoke to the union's board about supporting gay and lesbian teachers to spur them into action and pointed out that McClelland would have the opportunity to speak to the assembled union if he was elected as one of the 250 representatives of the UTLA House of Delegates. Not only did McClelland get elected as a representative, but so did three other members of the GTLA. The GTLA used these positions to successfully introduce anti-Briggs resolutions within the union at the local and state level.[35]

The GTLA participated in two lawsuits against the Briggs Initiative. The first, an effort to prevent the Briggs Initiative from being placed on the ballot, failed.[36] A second lawsuit, organized with the GTSWC of San

Francisco to immediately challenge the constitutionality of the Briggs Initiative and to seek an injunction against the enactment of the ballot initiative, was successful. McClelland became an unofficial spokesperson for LGB teachers in the local media appearing on radio and television shows and being interviewed for local newspapers and came to the attention of Briggs himself.

Briggs began claiming that McClelland said there were five thousand gay teachers in Los Angeles. McClelland noted in his interview for this study that, "if there were five thousand gay teachers, I knew about two dozen of those five thousand." He also pointed out that this false quote, meant to exaggerate the supposed peril of LGB teachers, backfired when the media seized on the number and began questioning what the Los Angeles Unified School District would do if they were forced to fire five thousand teachers from already difficult-to-staff schools.[37] Briggs's arguments were filled with, at best, questionable numbers and assertions. For example, in an interview with the *LA Times*, he claimed that, "The teaching profession is terribly attractive to homosexuals.... A third of San Francisco's teachers, 20 to 30 percent of Los Angeles teachers, are homosexual." In the same interview, Briggs claimed that LGB teachers were more dangerous to civilization than communism because, "Homosexuality . . . is like a creeping disease, where it just continues to spread like a cancer throughout the body—and the body in this case being society."[38] In the face of being compared to a terminal illness, and during a political campaign that would have legally mandated their firing, the other members of the GTLA became if anything more important.

Longtime GTLA member and secretary Peter Englander remembered the GTLA's activities as being social and supportive. While the Briggs Initiative certainly shifted the activities of the association toward political actions, the social and supportive aspects of the association were if anything enhanced by that politicization.[39] Englander wrote the group's monthly newsletter, the *Cheery Chalkboard*. He saw the newsletter as an opportunity to extend the support of the GTLA to a larger audience and was the major force behind its three-year run. At its height, the *Cheery Chalkboard* had a distribution of around eighty subscribers and offered the GTLA the opportunity to connect to other like-minded LGB educators and teachers' groups across the country. Like the GTA in New York City, the GTLA was careful to not push members into coming out or being politically active, even during the Briggs Campaign.[40]

There was a sense among GTLA members that the city they lived in was still fairly conservative as far as gays and lesbians were concerned. This conservatism made political caution a necessity during the 1970s. In his interview for this study, McClelland explained the political realities faced by GTLA members, saying, "We were never more than 18 or 19 people, we were really very tiny . . . it was a very closeted community here. It was not like San Francisco where people could be really out."[41] Part of the reticence that some of the GTLA members felt may be attributable to the complicated intersectionality between race and sexuality experienced by teachers. For the minority of GTLA members who were not white, coming out as a gay or lesbian teacher was complicated significantly by the added risk of also being targeted as a racial minority.[42] At the risk of oversimplification, a gay African American male teacher was almost invariably in a more precarious position than his white gay counterpart and so, when weighing the costs of being politically active or even out at school, had added risks to consider.[43] The willingness of members of the GTLA as a group to commit to political actions during the Proposition 6 campaign was likely impacted by the size of the group, its racial diversity, and the political climate of Los Angeles, which was perceived by GTLA members as being conservative.

McClelland was an outlier because of his willingness to be publicly outspoken in the face of the Briggs Initiative.[44] Looking back on his activism, he denied ever wanting to be political but instead thought that he had been pushed to act by the Briggs Initiative and the fact that "nobody else was speaking out and I said, 'Well I'm going to endanger my job' because these teachers were suffering and someone has to be a face." He also remembered that gay teachers in the union who were not members of the GTLA avoided being associated with him because of how closeted they were. At union meetings, "I would see this migration. I would be on one end and suddenly this migration of teachers, that I knew were gay, would suddenly migrate to the other side of the room as though just being on the side of the room that I was on would identify them as queer. It was an interesting time." Indeed, the teachers that stayed on the same side of the room with McClelland were ones whose sexuality was unmistakably "straight" and who were also secure enough in their teaching positions and liberal politics to not be threatened by his activism.[45]

The size of the GTLA and the perception that GTLA members held of Los Angeles made working through the teachers' union an understandable choice. Teachers' unions were natural allies of LGB teachers, and in many ways were the only politically potent institutions that LGB teachers in Los Angeles had access to. The LGB community in Los Angeles lacked the necessary political power and expertise to combat a statewide ballot initiative. Broad political organizing in Los Angeles for LGB rights was in many ways a product of combating the Briggs Initiative. While there had been political activity before Proposition 6, the threat of the Briggs Initiative mobilized gays and lesbians as a community in a way that the city and Southern California had not seen before.[46]

Evidence of the newfound power of the LGB community in Los Angeles could be seen in its dealings with law enforcement and the city's politicians. In the early and mid-1970s, the LGB community in Los Angeles still mistrusted the police, remembering decades of arrests and bar raids, but, by the end of the decade, the relationship had shifted significantly.[47] After organizing for the Briggs Initiative, gay men and lesbians did not "deorganize" but instead maintained and developed political influence in the city. When faced with a problem involving the police, Rev. Troy Perry, the minister of a large LGB church and founder of the Metropolitan Community Church, spoke of being able to "pick up the phone and call Peggy Stevenson. She chairs the Police and Fire Committee. We don't own her, but she's a good friend." When asked where the political power of Los Angeles's gay community had come from, many gays claimed credit went to "Anita Bryant and State Senator John Briggs," who had inspired gays and lesbians in California, and throughout the country, to embrace political action within already existing structures of power to gain recognition of their civil rights.[48]

The defeat of John Briggs and the slow but steady integration of the LGB community into the politics of the city had a direct impact on the GTLA. Eventually, the GTLA shifted away from political activity for its members and became a social group meeting for dinners. Geographically, the location of the official organization also shifted in the early 1980s to the far eastern suburbs of Los Angeles, where the political climate was more conservative and LGB teachers, particularly lesbian teachers, felt a need for the support of an organized group.[49] Members of the GTLA in Los Angeles continued to meet for dinner as friends once a month and many went on to have decades-long careers in local schools where their sexuality and being teachers had personally become significantly less of an issue.[50]

The Gay Teachers and School Workers Coalition of San Francisco

The GTLA grew out of a discussion and support group meeting in Los Angeles's gay community center. By contrast, LGB teacher activism in San Francisco began as a focus group within a broader LGB political organization whose stated goal was gay liberation. In Los Angeles, gay teachers were spurred into political action by the Briggs Initiative; in San Francisco, the founders of the Gay Teachers Caucus were already political activists.[51] Hank Wilson, Tom Ammiano, and Paul Lanzo were all members of the Bay Area Gay Liberation (BAGL) in 1974. They were also all teachers in the San Francisco Unified School District. Members of BAGL had organized a number of special interest caucuses to pursue activism in specific contexts. BAGL members had established a Latino caucus and a women's caucus. When Ammiano, Wilson, and Lanzo realized there were a number of teachers in BAGL, the Gay Teachers Caucus was formed.[52] Lanzo left teaching soon after the initial formation, but Ammiano and Wilson remained central to the Gay Teachers Caucus. In 1977—it is unclear exactly when—the Gay Teachers Caucus changed its name to the Gay Teacher and School Workers Coalition.[53] It is clear that the group was acting independently of BAGL before this name change. They did, however, maintain a close working relationship with BAGL that would prove instrumental in their activism.[54]

The GTSWC had its first major victory in June 1975 when it forced the city's Board of Education to adopt a "gay anti-bias" policy through a series of political actions.[55] Initially, the GTSWC and longtime lesbian activists Del Martin and Phyllis Lyon had received assurances that the board would vote on adding sexual orientation to the district's nondiscrimination policy but were outraged when the board adjourned its meeting without voting on the issue. In response, the GTSWC covered the Castro with leaflets announcing a demonstration at the next Board of Education meeting. Ammiano and Wilson entered that meeting at the head of three hundred demonstrators singing, "When the Gays Go Marching In," blowing whistles, standing on tables, and not allowing any business to occur until the issue of the anti-gay-bias policy was addressed.[56]

This action was not limited to LGB activists but also included community members enlisted by the GTSWC. Tom Ammiano was a politically active teacher before taking up the issues of LGB teachers. Ammiano was

142 • Not Alone

well connected to the local community and had supported families at his school as they worked to make education in the community better for their children. Allies he had made during his time as a teacher proved to be integral to pressuring the board to act. His school had a significant population of Spanish-speaking families and African American families who were politically active and able to help in the support picket. Ammiano recalled in a 1995 interview that these parents were "black and brown and they were trying to get a moratorium on IQ testing because of the cultural bias. And I helped in community actions around that, and then, I think everyone knew I was gay, but then in '75 I said I was gay, and then I went to them, and they knew me, and I said to them, 'Well I've been helping you, could you partake in this demonstration?' And a bunch of them did, they wrote letters and participated in the march."[57] The school board agreed to take up the issue at the next meeting two weeks later.

Jackie Blount describes this demonstration and the political acumen of the GTSWC, which lobbied individual members of the school board behind the scenes to break what they knew would be a tied vote.[58] Working in conjunction with BAGL, the GTSWC blanketed the gay bars in leaflets announcing a support picket of the meeting: "Every gay bar had signs. Our jobs were on the line. . . . We wanted our community to know that this was going to be voted on, we needed their support and we expected their support. Our goal was to make sure that every gay person in the city knew that this was going to happen." Hundreds of people came in support of the GTSWC.[59]

Unexpected support came from board member Tom Reed, a Catholic priest and Jesuit, who had for years been principal of a local Catholic high school.[60] While he was principal, a group of young men who called themselves the "Queer Hunters Club" attacked a teacher from their school at the local train station, robbed him, and left him unconscious on the tracks. The teacher was run over and killed that night. Reed recounted this story at the council meeting and, minutes later, the resolution to add sexual orientation to the nondiscrimination policy passed unanimously.[61] Their victory in 1975 led to Wilson and Ammiano being appointed to the city's Human Rights Commission on the Youth and Education Committee. Sitting on these committees gave the GTSWC the opportunity to work with other communities and build stronger relationships with their allies. For example, Wilson recalled working with the African American community on the issue of student suspensions, which were concentrated at schools with large minority student populations and seemed racially biased.[62]

Two years later, Hank Wilson also volunteered to spend three weeks in the summer of 1977 working against Anita Bryant's Save Our Children campaign in Florida as part of a contingent of teachers from San Francisco. This trip was prompted by Wilson's belief "that this would have a ripple effect across the country." Even though Bryant was victorious, Wilson thought in hindsight that the loss in Florida was a net gain for the LGB movement, saying, "but at that time people had not met, people had not experienced, we didn't have the talk shows, we didn't have a lot of that stuff that we have now, we hadn't seen live lesbians or live self-acknowledged gay people. This was like a quantum leap for us to be visible in a new way. Anita Bryant did us a wonderful service, I mean in the sense of raising us to a visible level. She also caused a lot of kids to commit suicide." Wilson based this assertion on the jump in teen suicide and the reality that this was the first time that gay people were in the news but there was no voice to counter Bryant because the LGB movement was still in its infancy. [63] Instead, the only voice that LGB youth heard was Anita Bryant sorrowfully explaining why such immoral people needed to be kept out of Florida's classrooms.

A few months later, in 1978, when Proposition 6 was being debated throughout their home state, Wilson, Ammiano, and other members of the GTSWC engaged in directly talking to voters about Proposition 6. Understanding that winning a few extra votes in San Francisco was not the most productive use of their time, they organized carpools to suburban and rural towns throughout Northern California and set up card tables in shopping mall parking lots to meet voters. Wilson believed that it was Californians' personal experience of seeing gay and lesbian people that could chip away at Briggs's support in conservative areas one voter at a time.[64] Members of the GTSWC went on radio talk shows, appeared in newspaper articles about Proposition 6, and even debated Senator Briggs on television.[65] The publicity they achieved was a product of their efforts: it was not sanctioned or encouraged by the coalition of organizations mounting statewide campaigns against the Briggs Initiative.

Wilson and Ammiano each recalled that leaders of the statewide campaign against the Briggs Initiative were not eager to include them in statewide actions. Wilson thought this reluctance stemmed from how unrepentantly public he and Ammiano were about their sexuality. That openness made them an unwanted variable in the carefully crafted message the "No on 6" campaign was trying to convey; that the battle was about the rights of teachers in general, not gay teachers in particular.[66] Staying on message led many organizations to keep the leaders of the GTSWC at arm's length; for example, they were not invited to participate in a press conference with "educational leaders" who opposed the Briggs Initiative. The GTSWC only found out about the conference after it had happened.[67]

Ammiano felt that there was a class element at play in his exclusion and that his working-class background, combined with his homosexuality "threatened people more than say a middle-class person; and even during the Briggs campaign some people shied away from and tried to find straight people who were sympathetic rather than have a gay teacher because it looked 'biased.'"[68] The "No on 6" campaign was looking for polished speakers who would not intimidate or alienate voters, and openly gay teachers from San Francisco apparently did not meet their standard.

After the defeat of the Briggs Initiative, membership in the GTSWC dwindled, but the organization continued to make progress in areas of LGB-friendly curriculum and initiated a Gay and Lesbians Speakers Bureau in the public schools. The GTSWC continued to lobby for the rights of gay teachers and students until the early 1980s when the AIDS crisis focused the activism of the LGBT community in San Francisco toward the epidemic.[69] Tom Ammiano would go on to run for a seat on the San Francisco School Board in 1980 but did not win the election. In 1988, he ran again for the school board, spending just twelve dollars on his campaign, running explicitly on LGB issues, and garnering sixty thousand votes. He lost a second time. Two years later in 1990, he ran a third time and was successful, becoming the first openly gay school board member in city history.[70] He went on to have a long career as an elected official, winning a seat on the city Board of Supervisors and eventually becoming a state senator. Hank Wilson founded a succession of LGB organizations and initiatives, including housing and caring for formerly homeless people living with AIDS during the height of the epidemic.[71]

The Lesbian School Workers and Coalition Activism

The GTSWC faced a schism late in the fall of 1977. A number of lesbian teachers decided to split from the gay male leadership of GTSWC and start an explicitly female group. The reasons behind this split are unclear. Sara

Smith, in her dissertation "Organizing for Social Justice," observes that the politics of the LSW in San Francisco were very similar to those of the Gay School Workers of San Francisco, with a few notable exceptions, which will be discussed later in this section. Smith also notes that the split from the GTSWC was natural and amicable; indeed, one member of the LSW claimed that it was hardly a "split" at all.[72] Rather, it seems that a large portion of the female members of the GTSWC decided to focus their activism in other directions and felt that an independent group would enable that shift in focus. Tom Ammiano remembered the impetus to have a lesbian group as "part of the fabric of the time, that it was more attractive to the lesbians to have their own group."[73]

There is no indication in the primary sources or oral histories that were examined in this study that the departure of the lesbian contingent was anything but on the best of terms. In fact, when the split occurred, the new group took with them a portion of the money that the GTSWC had gained through a grant from the Vanguard Foundation the previous year.[74] Despite the amicable nature of their departure, for a relatively small group like the GTSWC to lose between ten and twenty committed activists, just as the campaign against the Briggs Initiative was escalating, would have been significant.

A possible explanation for the founding of the LSW may be that the feminist politics of much of the lesbian community in California at the end of the 1970s—"the fabric at the time" that Ammiano alluded to—favored separatism as a way of ensuring that issues specifically impacting women were addressed through leadership by women. A statement by the Lesbian Caucus in the GTSWC's first newsletter succinctly explained the specific challenges facing lesbians: "As lesbians we work under the double oppression of being women and being gay, and so a group of us has come together to focus on a Lesbian-Feminist approach to these issues."[75] The use of the agglutinative "Lesbian-Feminist" is telling and indicates an articulation of lesbian oppression as being inextricably an oppression of women and rooted in gender disparity, rather than solely based on sexuality.[76]

Faderman and Timmons in *Gay L.A.* point out that, by the 1970s, many of the lesbian activists who had been involved in the Gay Liberation Front and Gay Center opted to move their activism and support to the Women's Building, a left-oriented feminist community center, having concluded that they had more in common with straight women than gay men. Highlighting the political diversity within the lesbian community, Faderman and

146 • Not Alone

Timmons observe that, in Los Angeles earlier in the decade, "Both 'gay women' and 'lesbian feminists' believed by 1971 that 'the women had to do it for themselves.' Until huge crises arose later in the decade that demanded that gay men and lesbians work together against a common enemy collaboration with gay men became minimal. But not only did they split from the men; 'gay women' and 'lesbian feminists' split from one another."[77] It seems that a similar dynamic was in play among the LGB teachers in San Francisco. Within this context of "identities that came to be defined ever more finely (or narrowly)," it is perhaps more remarkable that the women who would form the LSW had initially decided to try to be a part of a group of mixed-gender LGB teachers in the first place.[78] That willingness to work with gay male teachers may have been further evidence of how threatening the Briggs Initiative was to lesbian teachers rather than a political shift.[79] It is not surprising that many of the female members of the GTSWC eventually decided to form a separate group in keeping with the central place given to self-determination within feminist ideology.

The LSW were in many ways more inclusive of other minority groups than the GTSWC, despite their separatism. The LSW did not make a clear distinction between their activism as women and their activism as lesbians. According to the LSW, lesbian activism was feminist activism; any group of marginalized people that included women were potential allies, not out of political expediency, but because of shared experiences between women. The other LGB teachers' groups in California could not make a similar connection because they were founded by, and primarily attracted, male members. The LSW reached out to other groups that shared their political values through the common experience of working for women's rights. They took up the causes of those allied groups as a matter of solidarity and because the LSW had an overarching concept of oppression. The most obvious manifestation of the LSW coalition politics can be seen in their activism against Briggs's death penalty proposition, Proposition 7 .[80]

Broadly speaking, the LSW were more focused on working within the community rather than serving as representatives of gay and lesbian teachers to media outlets or in the context of debates with conservative supporters of Briggs. The community focus of the LSW, unlike the GTLA or the GTSWC, who were focused on working with unions and through the media, also lead to another distinguishing characteristic of the group. The LSW were more focused on educating the communities they interacted with than the GTSWC or the GTLA. In addition to dances, fundraisers, and theatrical productions, they developed a slideshow to teach the community about the dangers of Briggs's two initiatives.[81]

The specifics of their slideshow reveal a tremendous amount about the politics of LSW and how they presented themselves to the public. The LSW saw their activism as being part of the broader social justice initiatives of the Left and viewed oppression of racial minorities, women, LGB people, and other marginalized groups as being part of greater oppression. The script of the slideshow is six pages long and provided presenters with text and musical prompts to accompany almost three dozen images.

The slideshow begins by asking the audience to question the validity of what is being taught in California's schools. It goes on to explain why Briggs and social conservatives had an interest in what was occurring in schools by positing that there was universal interest in seeing schools succeed, and Briggs was taking advantage of the fact that,

> Everyone is concerned about what is happening to our children and how our schools are preparing them for life. This is why Briggs is focusing this initiative on gays working in schools; rather than gays working as clerks, nurses, telephone operators, etc. The schools are the place where children are taught to take their so-called proper place in society. Those who define proper define what and how our children learn.[82]

This opening emphasizes both the importance of schools and what the LSW perceived as a major problem with schools. Schools prepared students for life, which is necessary, but prepared them in a way that predisposed them to specific discriminatory roles.

The next two slides reiterate these themes and feature scenes of patriotism in the schools and "lies" that are taught to children every day. The list of falsehoods conveyed to students include:

> Most kids will grow up to be on welfare and unemployment.
> White men are the only people who have ever done anything important.
> Kids who don't speak English are stupid.
> Your Parents don't really care about you if they don't dress you well.
> Girls don't need to get jobs because they'll get married.
> Boys will support their families.[83]

Starting a slideshow about defending schools and teachers from Proposition 6 with a list of all the untrue things that students learn in schools might seem counterproductive, but this strategy makes sense in the political context of the Bay Area, one of the most liberal regions of the country. Beginning in this manner firmly established the LSW's critical stance on issues of race, immigration, gender, and class. The tenor of the rest of the slideshow was set by acknowledging at the beginning of the slideshow that schools had a default political stance. The default political stance of education maintained a status quo that was discriminatory. Because of this, the inherent potential of schools to effect positive change in society was not being realized but could be realized through political activism. By showing they were willing to acknowledge the flaws in mainstream education, the LSW was assuring their audience that *they* were not a part of the problems facing education and would work to fix those problems, starting with Proposition 6.

The next slide links Briggs to the lies that children are taught in schools. Briggs's "defense of families" extended only to the families that met a narrow definition. Keeping with the LSW's emphasis on women's issues, the presenter pointed out that Briggs's idea of correct family life demanded that:

The woman must be
1   Totally dependent financially on her husband
2   The sole source of emotional nurturance for the entire family
3   Sexually on call to her husband's desires
4   In general, the self-sacrificing caretaker of everyone's life except her own.[84]

The presenter went on to describe how this scenario left women powerless and excluded any family that did not ascribe to the nuclear ideal that John Briggs was attempting to champion. According to the LSW slideshow, priority to nuclear families as the ideal was particularly detrimental to "Third World Peoples" and poor people for whom "being able to rely on an extended family and community has meant survival and the ability to resist oppression in a day-to-day way."[85] John Briggs is portrayed as standing in the way of the progress made by the women's movement in the past few decades, even as he attempted to increase the use of the death penalty and infringe on the rights of LGB teachers.

The final slides of the show reiterate that Briggs was a troubling part of a larger effort by social conservatives to undo the work of marginalized groups to combat the social oppression they faced. Gay liberation and the women's movement are placed within the context of a series of historic efforts toward equality:

> This time of rapid growth for women's and gay liberation movements grew out of an era of social change. The struggles of Third World People set the tone and led the way. The Civil Rights movement and the Black Power movement which grew out of it voiced the demand for Liberation. The resurging Native American movement fought to regain control of stolen lands and resources. As these and other Third World people developed their movements across the U.S., the successful struggle of the people of Vietnam for their independence had a profound effect on the people of this country.[86]

The presenter went on to explain that the collective success of all these groups had prompted the conservative backlash they were now experiencing, and that "As all of these struggles continue to build, the gains that were made in the '60s and early '70s are now being attacked and cut back." The efforts of State Senator John Briggs "exemplified" this backlash with each of his propositions targeting a marginalized population: Proposition 6 was directed at gays and lesbians and Proposition 7 at African Americans and Latinos. Briggs was "not a lone crusader" but was instead, "a small part of the reactionary forces growing nationwide." Just as Briggs was a small part of a series of "reactionary attacks," the LSW saw their fight against Briggs as meeting a small part of an "urgent need for all of us to support each other in fighting them."[87] Countering a nationwide conservative assault required a nationwide liberal coalition.

The three LGB teachers' groups discussed in this chapter were significant parts of the coalition to defeat the Briggs Initiative. In Los Angeles and San Francisco, they were visible to the public and active in countering the portrayal of gay and lesbian teachers that was spread by State Senator John Briggs and his campaign to ensure that Proposition 6 passed. For LGB teachers and their allies in the rest of the state, the GTLA, GTSWC, and LSW represented the possibility of LGB teachers organizing to defend the rights of not just sexual minorities but all educators. What occurred during the debate over Proposition 6 was not just the empowerment of LGB teachers, it was an unprecedented empowerment of LGB teachers in the face of an equally unprecedented public assault on their livelihoods, moral character, and basic humanity.

Causes of Proposition 6's Defeat

Three fears led to the defeat of the Briggs Initiative in 1978: eroding freedom of speech, loss of the separation of church and state, and the foreboding that, if Proposition 6 succeeded, Briggs's crusade would expand nationwide.[88] Ultimately, Briggs reached too far when he targeted *support of homosexuality* as part of the initiative. Proposition 6 not only went after LGB teachers but anyone working in a school who was "imposing, supporting, or promoting of private or public homosexual activity."[89] This overreach presented a weakness for opponents of Proposition 6 to attack. It was not only the substance of Proposition 6 that inspired outrage but also how the "Yes on 6" campaign was conducted.

Briggs himself produced seemingly limitless fodder for his opposition. Opponents of Proposition 6 did not focus on the reality of LGB teachers but instead highlighted the assault that the Briggs Initiative was mounting against free speech and the separation of church and state. The goal for mainstream opponents of Proposition 6 was not to show why LGB teachers ought to be allowed to teach, or that LGB teachers were as competent as their heterosexual counterparts, but, instead, to portray the efforts to legislate morality as being un-American and the tactics used by Briggs as outrageous to reasonable Californians.[90] While the debate over the Briggs Initiative raged, political comics that ran in newspapers throughout California bluntly illustrate the incredulity that Briggs inspired in 1978.

Central to these comics is a mistrust of Briggs standing in judgment over others. These political comics portrayed attacking LGB people as attacking democracy itself. The most graphic of these comics features the state senator as an undersized medieval knight bearing a shield designating him, "Saint Briggs." The religious overtones of Briggs's actions are evident; he is shielded by his "sainthood," though his crusade has some unexpected casualties. Saint Briggs stands over the fallen form of Lady Liberty, who has been impaled with a sword labeled "Prop 6" while Uncle Sam covers his eyes to avoid seeing the carnage (see figure 4.2). Briggs himself appears confused by what had occurred and breaks the fourth wall explaining to readers, "Oops . . . I thought it said 'lesbian.'" Briggs does not appear concerned that he has slaughtered Liberty, only befuddled that he has made a mistake. Readers are not asked to think about the morality of homosexuals in this comic. They are asked whether John Briggs should be wielding a sword capable of toppling the embodiment of American democracy.

California and LGB Teachers • 151

FIGURE 4.2 "Oops... I Thought It Said 'Lesbian,'" *Press Democrat*, October 26, 1978, Santa Rosa, CA. (Briggs Initiative Collection, box 3, file 1, *ONE* National Gay and Lesbian Archives, Los Angeles.)

LGB teachers are conspicuously absent as visible characters from these critical political comics. Instead, Briggs features as the central figure in many political cartoons, heightening the already prevalent association between him and Proposition 6. Some comics feature teachers, but these contain few identifying characteristics, caricatures, or stereotypes based on gender norms or appearance, that would satirically designate a teacher as homosexual. When teachers were featured in opposition comics, they were almost invariably shown as being put in an awkward, if not hypocritical, position by Proposition 6 and John Briggs. One comic in the *Sacramento Bee* featured an aghast female elementary school teacher looking on as State Senator Briggs, clutching the American flag, leads her class in a modified version of the Pledge of Allegiance: "one nation under God, indivisible, with liberty and justice for all but gays." The students look at one another in confusion as if to underscore the cartoonist's point that even elementary school children know that the U.S. Constitution could not allow such blatant

FIGURE 4.3 "Repeat After Me," Renault, *Sacramento Bee*, 1977–1978. (Briggs Initiative Collection, box 3, file 14, *ONE* National Gay and Lesbian Archives, Los Angeles.)

discrimination (see figure 4.3). The sexuality of this teacher is not evident, or important; what is evident is her horror at what has coopted her classroom and taken center stage: Senator Briggs showing the students how to be "decent" Americans.[91]

A cartoon in the *San Francisco Sentinel*, an LGB weekly, warned that what could happen to teachers could happen to other professionals as well.

FIGURE 4.4 "It's Just Not Our Problem," *Sentinel*, July 27, 1978, San Francisco. (Briggs Initiative Collection, box 3, file 4, *ONE* National Gay and Lesbian Archives, Los Angeles.)

The teacher in this comic is locked in a stockade while a doctor and lawyer raise their hands, explaining that, "It's Just Not Our Problem." Over their shoulder, a dump truck is about to pour a load of "Arkansas" on all of their heads while, in the distance, smoke carrying the word "Briggs" rises, warning of even more dangers on the horizon (see figure 4.4). The illustrator of this comic pointedly invokes the moral superiority of Californians over less enlightened Americans and links Briggs to the bigotry of southern states. Implicit in this comic was both an accusation of hypocrisy and an argument that complacency was foolish. Were Californians of good conscience willing to sit idle as others were persecuted? If they were unwilling to take a stand against Proposition 6, could they expect others to come to their aid? This comic warned that if Californians would not speak up for teachers, even gay and lesbian teachers, who were being unjustly targeted, then they could expect other groups to be targeted soon after Proposition 6 passed. To an LGBT audience, the warning against complacency took on a greater significance, in essence telling readers that, "They will come for you too." The comic predicted that discrimination, once unleashed and given legal sanction, would not be content with gay and lesbian teachers but would instead target other groups like a landslide gaining momentum as it raced downhill.

Politicians legislating the morality of Californians struck many in the state as uncomfortably close to McCarthyism. The memory of the Red Scare, with its "fact-finding panels" and long-standing lists, was still potent in 1978. When the *Los Angeles Times* published a cartoon featuring John Briggs coming "Out of the Closet" wearing a suit of McCarthyism and holding a bucket of tar labeled "Prop 6," it sent a very clear message to the paper's readers: gays and lesbians would be tarred with the same brush that supposed communists were in the 1950s (see figure 4.5).[92] This comic pointed out that Californians had all too recently witnessed the tactics that Briggs was engaged in and knew where following in Joseph McCarthy's footsteps would lead. The genius of this comic, and many of the comics critiquing Briggs and Proposition 6, lay in their simplicity. The reader is left to determine exactly what State Senator Briggs is going to do now that he has come out of the closet, but it is clear that a victory for Proposition 6 would revive a style of political persecution that few people remembered fondly.

As election day approached, the thought of Briggs being victorious invoked even darker persecutions than the Red Scare in the minds of some political cartoonists. Ken Alexander, a longtime political cartoonist and editor for the *San Francisco Examiner*, captured the ambiguity of the Briggs Initiative and its potential impact in his September 12 illustration.[93] The comic features a man—who he is, or whether he is a teacher, is unclear—seated under a spotlight with his back to the reader (see figure 4.6). He is under interrogation by a group of four looming figures, hooded like members of the Ku Klux Klan, who are labeled "Prop 6." As he leans away from his inquisitors, they assure him, "You have nothing to worry about, my friend . . . as long as you can explain that lavender shirt." This mixture of humor and gravity raises one of the talking points of opponents of Proposition 6: exactly how would the state of California determine who was a homosexual teacher? The text of Proposition 6 referenced putting together committees at a local level to determine whether or not accusations about a teacher's homosexuality were credible.

Out of the Closet

FIGURE 4.5 "Out of the Closet," *Los Angeles Times*, September 22, 1978. (Briggs Initiative Collection, box 3, file 3, *ONE* National Gay and Lesbian Archives, Los Angeles.)

The Ku Klux Klan hoods and robes of the panel facing the person under interrogation in this comic might be an exercise in comedic license, but the situation it portrayed was serious. Teachers and school workers being interrogated to determine their sexuality and fitness to teach would occur if Proposition 6 passed. California in the 1970s was a politically diverse state: what would the local committees charged with rooting out gay teachers look like in the conservative rural portions of the state? Conservatives had enough clout in California politics that Reagan had been elected to two terms as governor. This comic plays on the unease that being judged invoked in its

'You have nothing to worry about, my friend... as long as you can explain that lavender shirt'

FIGURE 4.6 Ken Alexander, "Prop 6," *San Francisco Examiner*, September 12, 1978. (Briggs Initiative Collection, box 4, file 8, *ONE* National Gay and Lesbian Archives, Los Angeles.)

readers and the fear that the judgment mandated in Proposition 6 would be a license for extreme invasions of privacy. The argument made by this comic was straightforward. Even if you thought homosexuality was immoral and the thought of gay teachers was disconcerting or, worse, disgusting, did that mean your child's teachers should be subject to a bureaucratic inquisition?

Political comics produced in response to the Briggs Initiative articulated arguments in a way that was easy to understand and had broad appeal. One argument that opponents of Proposition 6 raised centered on how the Briggs Initiative would erode teacher authority. The Briggs Initiative would make it more difficult for teachers to be impartial in grading and administering discipline because it could provide students and their parents with a way of applying leverage to those decisions. This argument is illustrated in a comic that features three middle school students threatening their teacher (see figure 4.7). As two male students look on, the female student leans disrespectfully on her teacher's desk and makes a proposition reminiscent of a mob

California and LGB Teachers • 157

GIVE US STRAIGHT "A's" OR WE'LL TELL THE SCHOOL BOARD YOU'RE A FILTHY QUEER

FIGURE 4.7 Hedaian, "Give Us Straight A's," 1978. (Briggs Initiative Collection, box 4, file 8, *ONE* National Gay and Lesbian Archives, Los Angeles.)

movie: "Give us straight 'A's' or we'll tell the school board you're a filthy queer." This comic raises several pressing questions for the reader. How could teachers manage behavior in their classrooms and maintain discipline if their students could accuse them of homosexuality and get them fired?

Confronted with the choice between being strict, or even fair, and facing one of the investigatory panels that the Briggs Initiative would mandate, which would a teacher choose? How "straight" did an educator have to act to be beyond suspicion? The idea of a teacher being extorted by their students was of course laughable, but it was a laughable possibility that could become a distressing reality if Proposition 6 passed. The appeal of an argument to individuals or groups of people is a difficult thing to gauge, but even a simple argument could be appealing.[94]

The activism of teachers is missing from these comics, but that absence is in keeping with the strategy of mainstream liberals and centrists to defeat the Briggs Initiative. Teachers are portrayed by this coalition as a group that is being acted upon, not politically active. Rather than being politically powerful, teachers are threatened with blackmail, inquisition, and the specter of McCarthyism. Where are the activist teachers working through their unions to defeat Proposition 6? Where are the LGB teachers' groups detailed earlier in this chapter? Ultimately those activist teachers did not fit well into the mainstream arguments that these cartoonists illustrated to their readership. The idea of activist teachers might have fit with a liberal conception of educators but did not fit nearly as well with a more conservative or even centrist idea of teachers as nurturers and civil servants. Opponents of Proposition 6 were attempting to convince the middle of the electorate to vote against the Briggs Initiative by appealing to the way those voters conceived of teachers and schools as symbols of fairness and order, not by arguing for the acceptance of homosexual teachers.

Proposition 6 and the Teacher as Symbol

The arguments presented in political comics by newspapers who opposed the Briggs Initiative throughout the state had very little to do with LGB teachers as individuals. Instead, they showed how Briggs was attacking teachers as a whole and, through teachers, one of the fundamental aspects of America: freedom of speech. LGB teachers were protected by this rhetoric not because they were part of a sexual minority but in spite of the fact that they were part of a sexual minority. From the perspective of liberal and centrist political stakeholders, conducting a witch hunt in schools was degrading to all parties concerned. The *Los Angeles Times* editorial board summed up this stance in a scathing and brief op-ed titled, "Dignifying Rumor and Innuendo."

The editorial board of the *Los Angeles Times* tore into the Briggs Initiative, opening their analysis with a blunt assessment of the threat posed by Proposition 6 and the people who supported it, saying, "The proposal is so repugnant to basic American freedoms that we'd prefer to ignore it altogether. But since people seeking to limit those freedoms often carry the day while the other side isn't looking, we must flatly say we oppose Proposition 6." Aside from the conversation being simply distasteful, the board contended that "Proposition 6 is so vaguely worded that it would subject teachers to sweeping accusations on baseless charges, it would dignify rumor and innuendo. Proposition 6 would place these weapons in any child's hands—weapons that could be used to harass any teacher who is disliked." The editorial board did not deny that there were homosexual teachers, or even that those homosexual teachers might be a problem. Instead, they denied that there was any need for a law targeting those teachers: "There always have been and no doubt always will be homosexual teachers. The question is not sexuality, but behavior in the classroom with students. On the books already are laws that protect students from being molested by teachers, homosexual or heterosexual. On the books already are laws to permit the dismissal of teachers for moral turpitude."[95] The editorial board of the *Los Angeles Times* was not supporting LGB teachers as members of a sexual minority. It was advocating due process and supporting teachers as a group of professionals. Proposition 6 had introduced an unnecessary conversation about California's schools, exposing the very children Briggs was supposedly defending to a repugnant topic that was already covered by the state's laws.

Many of the liberal opponents of the Briggs Initiative were interested in defending LGB teachers because not defending them would degrade the overall value of schools and teachers. Allowing such degradation in California's schools would, in turn, open up basic civil liberties, like freedom of speech and freedom of association, to further attacks by conservatives. Opponents of Proposition 6 did not have to approve of LGB teachers or homosexuality; they just had to disapprove of Briggs and his brand of fearmongering more than they disapproved of gay teachers.

The official rebuttal to Proposition 6, signed by the California Federation of Teachers, the police commissioner of San Francisco, and a Los Angeles supervisor, which appeared in the official 1978 *California Voters Pamphlet*, exemplifies this line of reasoning. Making liberal use of capital letters, these public figures contended that: SENATOR BRIGGS suggest that all of our social ills—drugs—violence—immorality—will be eliminated by his elixir—PROPOSITION 6. THIS IS RIDICULOUS! Shifting the burden of curing society's ills to our teachers is unwarranted and unfair. SENATOR BRIGGS and his followers would have you believe that teachers are promoting homosexuality in the classroom. THIS IS RIDICULOUS. Any teacher who did so would be fired, and we have the laws to do so right now.[96] According to these officials, Briggs was a snake oil salesman peddling false cures for make-believe ailments and should be firmly rejected.

In *Fit to Teach*, historian Jackie Blount summarizes the stance of many Californians that voted against Proposition 6, concluding that, "In the final analysis, many voters in California did reject Proposition 6 because it threatened free speech rights. It would have provided a point of entry through which further restrictions on basic rights might pass. Although many Californians did not particularly like the thought of LGBT persons, they also recognized that this measure would have taken away rights from a targeted group of persons."[97] African American voters were particularly aware of the dangers represented by singling out of a group of Americans for punitive laws and opposed the Briggs Initiative more strongly than any other racial demographic.[98] It is difficult, if not impossible, to determine whether the majority of "No" votes against Proposition 6 were motivated by a desire to defend LGB teachers or a desire to defend freedom of speech. It is significantly less difficult to make the argument that many, if not most, of the "Yes" votes for Proposition 6 were motivated by apprehension and fear over the presence of LGB teachers in California schools. Many voters were convinced by Briggs's arguments but not enough to carry the day.

Briggs based his arguments on threatening the symbolic value that Americans attached to teachers and particularly on the symbolic value that many conservative Americans attached to teachers as maintainers of social and moral norms. In many ways, Briggs and his supporters evidenced a greater faith in the ability of teachers to impact their students' moral development than his opponents did. The unprovable accusations that Briggs made—for example, "One-third of San Francisco's teachers are homosexual. I assume that most of them are seducing young boys in toilets"—were based on more than just the disgust that voters felt when considering pedophilia.[99] Briggs's arguments drew their power from the idea of the symbolic value of both teachers and schools being violated and from the fear that conservatives were losing control of the places where their children were educated. Americans in general, and conservatives in particular, were sensitive to these arguments precisely because they placed so much value in schools. This added tremendously to the dramatic appeal of Briggs's arguments.

When Briggs claimed that "Your rights as a parent, a citizen, and a taxpayer, are under attack," he based that claim on two unproven assertions. First, that there was a "coalition of homosexual teachers and their allies." Second, that this coalition was somehow omnipresent enough and powerful enough to attack the rights of citizens, taxpayers, and parents across the state of California. Whether he personally thought that such a group existed is not nearly as important as his ability to convince 41.6 percent of voting Californians that LGB teachers were a threat to the rights of parents and the safety of children. To protect children from "the symptoms of moral decay all around us," parents needed to be able to rely on the morality of teachers who "spend more time with our children than we do."[100]

In his official explanation of why Proposition 6 was needed, Briggs argued that only with the help of schools could parents hope to avoid having their children "hooked on hard drugs, sex and violence glorified in the mass media, gang wars, casual premarital sex among teenagers, and all the rest."[101] But how could schools be relied on if they harbored the obvious immorality of homosexuals? How could parents have faith in their students' teachers if some of them might be gay? If schools tolerated such deviants, then the potential of education to guide the morality of young Californians would not only be called into question but could be co-opted by a "coalition of homosexual teachers and their allies."

According to this logic the only way for conservative citizens to again have faith in California's schools, the only way the symbolic value of teachers could be maintained, was through rigorously policing the morality of K-12 teachers and purging the ranks of educators already in the schools. Proposition 6 would have given school administrators the ability to do just that, while trampling all over the civil rights of educators throughout the state.

Briggs appealed to a commonly held belief that a teacher by default impacted the moral growth of the students they came in contact with, saying, "We know that the example of an admired teacher can influence an impressionable young mind more than a library full of books. If that teacher respects the essential decencies of American life, he can set the feet of our youngsters on the path of moral responsibility, but if that teacher questions the most elementary truths of our society, his influence can lead to tragedy."[102] This *argumentum ad populum* rested, like all such logical fallacies, on presenting debatable points as simple, common sense. There was no proof that a teacher had greater influence than a library of books, but Briggs's argument did not require proof, only an appeal to what he assumed was a majority opinion. His argument also rested on a division of the electorate on the issue of Proposition 6 between the "We" who possessed the common sense necessary to understand the tremendous impact that a teacher had and everyone else, who for whatever reason lacked the sense to see what should be obvious about the dangers of homosexual teachers.

In the face of this rhetoric, LGB teachers and their allies found themselves arguing against the assertion that teachers preeminently influence the moral growth of students. While Briggs argued that influence occurred regardless of the actions of a teacher, his opponents held a more nuanced view. Teachers certainly could influence their students, but this influence was mitigated by innumerable factors and was ultimately individual.

In one debate with the state senator, San Francisco City Council member Harvey Milk wryly responded to Briggs's claims that students would want to be homosexual if exposed to LGB teachers saying, "If it were true that children mimicked their teachers, you'd sure have a helluva lot more nuns running around."[103] Briggs argued in absolutes, any student in contact with any homosexual teacher could and would be influenced into a degenerate lifestyle by that contact. His opponents did not have to respond to particulars because Briggs's arguments were so generalized. Opponents of the Briggs Initiative did not have to argue that LGB teachers had a positive influence on students. Instead, they could rebut Briggs and the rhetoric of California Defend Our Children simply by claiming that the influence of teachers on their students was variable and limited.

John Briggs and California Defend Our Children portrayed Proposition 6 as drawing a line in the sand against moral decay. Their liberal and centrist opponents saw Proposition 6 as cutting a swathe through the rights of Americans and the first step down a slippery slope of government-sanctioned prejudice. LGB teachers' groups in Los Angeles and San Francisco saw a direct threat to their livelihoods and a threat to the livelihoods and dignity of all gay and lesbian Americans. In the face of that dire threat, they made the argument that they were people. While this seems like a simple assertion, it ran counter to the efforts of Briggs to portray LGB teachers as sinister projections of a homosexual cabal working through local schools to corrupt California's communities. Emphasizing the humanity of LGB teachers also ran counter to efforts of the mainstream opposition to Proposition 6, which tried to keep the debate focused on Briggs and his incendiary tactics.

Despite the efforts of Briggs to paint them as the vanguard of moral decay and the reluctance of their allies to include them more fully in statewide debates, LGB teachers' groups achieved at least three significant accomplishments during the debate over Proposition 6. First, they ensured that the presentation of LGB teachers to the people of California was in part determined by LGB teachers themselves through engaging directly with the media and local communities. In the state's two largest urban areas, coverage of LGB teachers' groups provided people living in San Francisco and Los Angeles with information and an intimate view of LGB teachers who were willing to go on the record despite the possibility of losing their jobs if Briggs was successful. LGB teachers' groups in San Francisco and Los Angeles built on their earlier accomplishments and political alliances, helping to ensure that major population centers in the state, and their elected officials, remained steadfastly opposed to Proposition 6.

LGB teachers' groups achieved a second accomplishment through their successful interaction with other LGB organizations across California. In the mid-1970s, these interactions with gay teachers were among the first that LGB groups had with members of their community organizing around a specific profession. After Proposition 6, LGB Californians could not help but be aware that there were LGB teachers in their state who were working not only for their job security but for the continued advancement of the LGBT community. The battle over Proposition 6 fixed the attention of the LGBT community on schools, adding them to the list of institutions where discrimination against LGBT people needed to be actively and continuously contested.

The third accomplishment that LGB teachers achieved in the context of the Briggs Initiative was rallying the state's teachers' unions to defend both the civil and negotiated rights of their LGB members. The California Federation of Teachers has had a nondiscrimination clause regarding homosexuals since 1969 but it was not until the Briggs Initiative posed a threat to all of California's teachers that the statewide union acted on that policy and defended LGB teachers as a class rather than on a case-by-case basis. The threat of Proposition 6 and the activism of LGB teachers forced liberal organizations and labor unions to take a political stand when they might otherwise have simply ignored LGB teachers.

Collectively, these accomplishments qualitatively shifted the conversation about LGB teachers in California. Before the debate over the Briggs Initiative, conversations about the value of LGB teachers, the impact of being homosexual on the process of education, or even the presence of gay and lesbian teachers, occurred without the input of LGB people. Specifically, before the debate around Proposition 6, these conversations took place without input from LGB teachers themselves. Before the Briggs Initiative, when conservatives in California said that gay male teachers were pedophiles, there were few, if any, gay male teachers willing to argue against them. When conservatives claimed that having a lesbian teacher in the classroom would lead female students into a degenerate lifestyle, there were few, if any, lesbian teachers to publicly disprove that argument. After the defeat of the Briggs Initiative, not only were there LGB teachers willing to defend their rights, there was also a statewide precedent for such a defense being successful that included thousands of straight allies. This success would serve as a positive example for future efforts to secure LGBT rights not only in California, but throughout the entire country.

Conclusion

Recurring Themes

Four themes are found throughout the historical narratives detailed in this study: professionalism, community, negotiation, and the portrayal of LGB teachers. I have focused each of the preceding chapters on one of these themes to develop them, but it is important to stress that these themes do not stand alone but are instead intertwined. Between 1970 and 1985, the first LGB teachers' groups formed in places where these four themes could support one another. To conclude this study, I will discuss the ways these four themes are apparent in each chapter, the connections between these themes, and the ways that they reinforced one another.

Professionalism as a guiding principle and goal appears throughout each of the chapters in this study. LGB teachers attempted to expand the boundaries of professionalism to encompass LGB teachers. Within both the NEA and the AFT, national debates over what qualified as professional behavior for K-12 educators occurred at many, if not all, national conventions. By the end of the 1960s, the NEA had shifted from an organization in which educational administrators determined what constituted professionalism to an organization where K-12 teachers determined what professional behavior looked like. This shift expanded debates within the NEA and focused them on the needs and experiences of classroom teachers. When John Gish appeared in 1972 at the annual meeting with the politics of the

166 • Not Alone

gay liberation movement and represented a silent mass of LGB educators, he found a receptive audience. Discussions about teacher sexuality and teacher professionalism revolved around the boundaries between the privately acceptable and the publicly acceptable. That boundary was not static but instead moved based on the local political context, which evolved at different rates in different places.

Because the boundary between the personal and the private shifted both over time and geographically, privately acceptable behavior for a K-12 educator and publicly acceptable behavior for a K-12 educator varied dramatically from place to place. This shifting boundary is particularly apparent when considering the early history of LGB teachers' groups based in American cities. In New York City, LGB teachers coming to the first meetings were among "the most frightened group of people" that GTA cofounder Meryl Friedman had ever seen.[1] The cause of that fear was the thought that they might have crossed the boundary between public and private in an irrevocable way: that by crossing the threshold of a GTA meeting, they had removed themselves from the professionally acceptable space of the closet into an undefined and perilous space that could cost their livelihoods because it was deemed unprofessional by some educational stakeholders. As American society, in some places, became more accepting of homosexuality between 1970 and 1985, LGB teachers in those places successfully contested their exclusion from the category of "professional."

In each of the three cities discussed in this study, the meaning of professionalism was negotiated through the efforts of a community of LGB teachers and their allies working in conjunction to expand professional behavior to include gay, lesbian, and bisexual teachers. The ability to negotiate, the right of teachers to determine what constituted professional behavior, was a prerequisite for the formation of LGB teachers' groups. It is striking that all the LGB teachers' groups discussed in this study formed in places where the tradition of K-12 educators discussing and negotiating professionalism occurred in the context of organized labor unions.[2] LGB teachers within the NEA and AFT were operating in teacher-centered organizations; there was no question about whether teachers had a say in what constituted professional behavior. LGB teachers' groups in New York, Los Angeles, and San Francisco all had the benefit of a tradition of teachers' unions in their cities actively negotiating what was expected of a teacher.

The first LGB teachers' groups formed communities in places where other teachers' groups, like unions and special interest groups within unions, were politically active. They formed in places where teachers actively participating in negotiation about diverse political issues was not only a possibility but also had a long history. In these politically viable spaces, there was no question about whether teachers had the right to advocate for their political beliefs; the debate instead revolved around which political beliefs were worth advocating for. LGB teacher activism was modeled on the collective activism of other groups of teachers from historically oppressed groups such as women's caucuses and African American caucuses, which were the largest and most active interest groups in urban- and national-level teachers' unions. LGB teachers were schooled in the art of negotiation by the examples set by this history of teacher negotiation and, as cited throughout this study, their own participation in that history of negotiation.

LGB teacher activism was also derived from the bubbling activism of the LGBT movement in the early 1970s. Each of the groups discussed in this study had leaders with a history of involvement in the broader gay liberation movement. In New York, both Meryl Friedman and Marc Ruben were involved with the NGLTF; in Los Angeles, Norman McClelland facilitated discussion groups at the city's gay and lesbian community center; John Gish founded the initial NEA Gay Caucus after being involved with the New York Gay Activist Alliance; and, in San Francisco, Tom Ammiano and Hank Wilson were active members of the BAGL. LGB teachers' groups were a projection of gay liberation politics into the arena of education and drew inspiration from the successes of gay and lesbian activists in other spheres. The tactics utilized by LGB teachers' groups between 1970 and 1985 can be seen as a combination of traditional union tactics and the tactics of LGBT political groups. It is difficult to separate these two sources of influence into distinct strands because they are so thoroughly woven together throughout these histories.

LGB teachers and allies brought a significant degree of political savvy to the table. They understood the politics of their local school districts and teachers' unions and they devised strategies to achieve their goals based on those understandings. They also understood which educational stakeholders they could form alliances with. LGB teachers displayed a remarkable degree of political acumen in the context of national teachers' unions, pushing through numerous proposals and amendments despite the fact that in both the NEA and the AFT they lacked an official caucus for the fifteen years that this study is primarily concerned with. LGB teachers in cities capitalized on the benefits of forming advocacy groups that could change tactics as the local political climate shifted. In many respects, the success of LGB teachers' groups, the degree to which they were able to better conditions for LGB teachers and students, was determined by their ability to negotiate with other educational stakeholders.

That negotiation was itself predicated on the way that LGB teachers and their groups portrayed themselves to other educational stakeholders. LGB teachers had to prove that they were a group that could be negotiated with. They did this by clearly articulating goals that were palatable to other educational stakeholders and by evidencing a level of political sophistication that made avoiding LGB teachers' demands difficult, if not impossible. This pattern is clearly visible in the initial negotiations between LGB teachers in San Francisco and New York with their local school boards. As part of their initial efforts, LGB teachers' groups in both cities approached the school boards with demands and, when those demands were not taken seriously, organized very public political actions to force the school board to take them seriously. With their credibility established, LGB teachers' groups could then work with their respective city governments and school systems to ensure greater equity for themselves and LGB students.

A similar process occurred in national-level teachers' unions. These unions were as a whole liberal but the large democratic bodies of the NEA and the AFT also initially had to be convinced of the presence of LGB teachers in their ranks and the legitimacy of the demands made by LGB teachers. LGB teachers and their allies made the case for the legitimacy of their goals and their rights as union members year after year, eventually gaining the majority opinion in both national teachers' unions. Negotiating with school boards and teachers' unions secured institutionally powerful allies for LGB teachers' groups that could then be used to bolster their legitimacy to the broader public. Those allies were integral to lobbying politicians and, in California, combating the Briggs Initiative, which would have barred LGB people and their allies from the state schools.

Central to each of the previous three themes is the portrayal of LGB teachers. The fifteen years between 1970 and 1985 entailed dramatic shifts both in how LGB teachers were portrayed and who portrayed them. How LGB teachers were portrayed went from being overwhelmingly negative and often pathological in the 1970s to the possibility of a positive portrayal fifteen years later. This shift in portrayal was predicated on an equally prominent shift in who was portraying LGB teachers and LGB people in general.

Before the rise of widespread and militant self-advocacy by LGBT activists in the late 1960s, the portrayal of LGB people was principally pathological and criminal. When the general public considered homosexuality, it was in the context of mental illness and criminal activity. LGB people were portrayed as diseased criminals who could spread their lifestyle to other people. Homosexuality was not just mentally but also morally pathological from the perspective of a majority of Christian denominations. Before 1970, LGB people were almost universally portrayed by mental health professionals, religious leaders, and law enforcement as abnormal and deviant. Opponents of LGB teachers like California State Senator John Briggs had been raised within this worldview and developed their beliefs about the inherent deviance of LGB people, without input from LGB people themselves.

The distinction between being acted on and being actors, on having political agency versus being political scapegoats, is crucial to understanding the relevance of LGB teachers' groups. LGB teachers' groups portrayed themselves. They took control of their own image. The first LGB teachers' groups showed the rest of the country that it was possible to not only be discussed but to lead the discussion. This possibility of leadership by teachers elevated not only the LGBT community but the potential of all teachers to create change.

Further Research

Any historical inquiry that deals principally in primary sources and examines a relatively unexplored area of history will raise nearly as many questions as it answers. This study is not an exception to that truism. In the course of writing this study, a number of topics that require further research became apparent. Four areas of inquiry warrant attention from historians in the future: the intersectionality of race and sexuality for LGB teachers, the history of transgender teacher activism, the histories of other LGB teachers' groups active between 1970 and 1985, and the histories of LGB teachers' groups active in other countries, would be viable as topics of distinct historical inquiries.

It is readily apparent from a reading of this text that, while this study is not solely an examination of the activism of white teachers, it is primarily an examination of the activism of white teachers. There were people of color in the LGB teachers' groups discussed in this study, but there is no evidence that those teachers were in leadership positions or comprised a significant percentage of the general membership. The achievements of LGB teachers' groups between 1970 and 1985 certainly impacted LGB teachers from racial minorities regardless of their participation in those LGB teachers' groups. Many of the core activists in these LGB teachers' groups expressed a commitment to working with communities of color and saw the struggle for LGB rights as part of a broader civil rights movement in the United States. But it is unclear from this study why there appears to be a distinct absence of people of color from many of the historical narratives detailed in this study. This study also only briefly discusses the intersectionality of race and sexuality as it relates to LGB teacher activism. An in-depth study of this intersectionality could revolve around the impact of race on LGB teacher activism and would be a valuable contribution to the historical understanding of teachers more broadly.

Similarly, the historical narratives examined in this study are silent with regards to the presence and/or activism of transgender teachers who may have been involved in the LGB teachers' groups examined in this study. The primary sources examined for this study and the oral histories collected do not indicate such a presence, but this may be a case of transgender teachers being unidentified or remaining silent about their gender diversity as a matter of personal safety and professional necessity. It is entirely possible that transgender teachers did contribute to LGB teachers' groups between 1970 and 1985 and that those teachers intentionally remained silent about their gender diversity. Another possibility is that the nomenclature and conversation surrounding transgender people, particularly in the 1970s, was not advanced or prevalent enough to be included in the primary sources examined for this study. These possibilities are purely speculative. As such, an inquiry into the activism of transgender teachers and their presence in LGB teachers' groups is sorely needed and would be a significant feature in any discussion of LGBT teacher activism after the 1980s.

As mentioned in the introduction, this study only examines the histories of six of the eleven known LGB teachers' groups active between 1970 and 1985 in the United States. The remaining five groups: located in Boston, Baltimore, Denver, Chicago, and Portland, Oregon, were each excluded from this study because of the scarcity of primary sources available detailing their activities. Of these five groups, the Boston Area Gay and Lesbian School Workers and the Gay Teachers of Maryland are likely the most accessible topics for future research. Jackie Blount briefly details the activism of

Eric Rofes, the Boston group's founder and principal organizer, in her book *Fit to Teach* and provides a timeline of LGB teacher activism in New England.[3]

The Gay Teachers of Maryland left a small series of newsletters that appear in several archives and could be the basis for a historical inquiry.[4] While these sources were not numerous enough to include these two groups in this study, it is possible that more sources are available and would contain enough information to construct viable history. More challengingly, the LGB teachers' groups in Denver and Portland, Oregon, appeared in the research conducted for this study only in references, while the group in Chicago is evidenced by only a single document. Further research would be needed to determine whether more information on these groups is available and to what degree the histories of these groups add to the broader history of LGB teachers' groups.

While this study has been concerned solely with the formation and activism of LGB teachers' groups in the United States, the activism of LGB teachers was not limited to the United States. As mentioned in chapter 3, there is evidence of LGB teachers' groups in Great Britain, Germany, and Australia. These groups, which were based in London, Berlin, Melbourne, and Sydney, were in contact with the GTA of New York.[5] Whether there was a larger network of international contact between LGB teachers' groups is unclear and would require research in the countries in question. Much of the historical narrative concerning American LGB teachers' groups is centered on the system of local control that dominates education in the United States. The rest of the Anglosphere utilizes a centralized system of control over the education system. The impact of this difference of central control versus local control on the organization and goals of international LGB teachers' groups is unclear and would require in-depth research to make a comparison. Similarly, the LGB teachers' group in Berlin presents a potentially interesting subject of research considering the bifurcation of Berlin between communism and democracy. How did having a totalitarian regime literally blocks away affect LGB teachers' activism as they pursued their goals?

Finally, there is significant research that remains to be done on the activism of LGB teachers directly after the period that is covered by this study. The late 1980s and 1990s saw already existing LGB teachers' groups shift their activities to meet the changing political and educational needs of LGB teachers and students. In particular, the foundation and eventual national scope of GLSEN in 1990 was a significant shift in the scope of advocacy for LGBT people in K-12 schools.[6] Local chapters of GLSEN within a state, and eventually at the national level, could coordinate their efforts to create change in ways that earlier LGB teachers would have found astonishing. The efforts of the NEA LGB, and eventually LGBT, caucus continued throughout the 1990s and this group remains active today. Likewise, the AFT LGBT caucus received official recognition in 1990 and is still in existence today. The histories of these national-level LGBT teachers' groups and their development have the potential to illuminate the changes that have occurred surrounding LGB teachers and students in the past thirty years.

Collective Impact

Between 1970 and 1985, the number of educators active in LGB teachers' groups never numbered more than a few hundred. The three groups in California all had less than a hundred members at their height. The New York GTA distributed their newsletter to a few hundred subscribers, but their membership also seems to have hovered around a hundred. Until the AFT had an official caucus in 1990, it is impossible to determine exactly how many teachers participated in pushing through the numerous resolutions passed by that union. The NEA LGB caucus's membership numbers are likewise difficult to determine.[7] The exact membership numbers of any of the LGB teachers' groups are difficult to pin down. The reason for this lack of clarity is simple; for the entire fifteen years that this study discusses, these groups often kept secret membership lists to protect the identities and livelihoods of their members or did not keep a membership list at all.

Carol Watchler, leader of the NEA LGB caucus, recalled the need for anonymity, even in the late 1980s, particularly for members in parts of the country where "people did not even want to think about being out in that school district because of a great fear of the kind of repercussions that could lead to for either staff or the community."[8] One incident that stood out to Watchler involved regional contact information in the NEA LGB caucus newsletter. The caucus newsletter had volunteers that would list their phone numbers in the newsletter and be willing to be called at home to answer questions. Getting a volunteer for the southeast of the country was particularly challenging, but eventually a teacher stepped up. Years later that teacher told Watchler "that when she saw her name in that newsletter, even though that newsletter probably wouldn't be seen by hardly anyone who wasn't involved in the caucus, it was a major shake."[9] Even a teacher who volunteered to be public about being a member was apprehensive; it is difficult to imagine the emotions of a completely closeted teacher approaching an LGB teacher meeting for the first time.

The impact of LGB teacher activists and their allies, accomplished between 1970 and 1985, was impressive from a purely quantitative standpoint. In 1980, 77.9 percent of all teachers were members of the NEA and 9.9 were members of the AFT. Collectively these two unions represented the vast majority of American K-12 educators either in collective bargaining as a union or as a professional association lobbying for the interests of K-12 educators at the local, state, and federal levels.[10] By 1980 these national organizations were on the record as being in support of workers' rights for LGB teachers. While the majority of national labor unions avoided engaging in the question of workplace discrimination based on sexual orientation, national teachers' unions led the way in putting in place policies that defended their LGB members. Because the majority of teachers in the United States belonged to the NEA or AFT, this meant that K-12 education as an economic sector could be impacted by these policies.

I have been cautious throughout the chapters dealing with the AFT and NEA when discussing the ability of resolutions passed at a national level to impact the lives of individual teachers at the local school board level. That is not because I believe that there was such an impact but is difficult to quantify that impact as it was reflected individually in the thousands of school districts with AFT and NEA negotiated contracts. A study that focused on those locally negotiated contracts or on individual teachers utilizing negotiated agreements to contest sexuality-based discrimination would be needed to make such a quantification. From a purely qualitative perspective, the first handful of LGB teachers' groups showed that it was possible for small groups of dedicated activists to achieve protections for LGB teachers and LGB students. There is a tremendous difference between the possibility of success with precedent and the possibility of success without precedent. When John Gish entered the convention hall in Atlantic City to lobby for LGB teachers in 1972, he had exactly one example of success to convince other educators to join his fledgling gay teachers caucus. Featured front and center on the vibrant pink flyers he passed out was the news that the school board in Washington, D.C., had just passed a nondiscrimination clause for gay teachers working in the nation's capital (see figure C.1). Gish's efforts in turn led

Resolution Passed May 23, 1972 by

District of Columbia Board of Education

The District of Columbia Board of Education, after discussion and consideration, hereby recognizes the right of each individual to freely choose a life style, as guaranteed under the Constitution and the Bill of Rights. The Board further recognizes that sexual orientation, in and of itself, does not relate to ability in job performance of service.

Therefore it is resolved that henceforth it shall be the policy of all departments and services of the educational system under the jurisdiction and control of the District of Columbia Board of Education to promote a policy of non-discrimination in hiring, employment, promotion, tenure, retirement, and/or job classification practices, within such jurisdiction and control, relative to the sex or the personal sexual orientation of any individual(s) regardless of past, present, and/or future status of such individual(s).

FIGURE C.1 John Gish, Flyers: "Resolution Passed," 1972. (*Access*: Barbara Gittings and Kay Tobin Lahusen Gay History Papers and Photographs, Manuscripts and Archives Division, The New York Public Library, New York, NY, B 93 F 9.)

to successes on which other LGB teacher activists could base their activism. As LGB teachers' groups in cities across the country accomplished different goals, they in turn provided ever more local examples that LGB teachers could be successful in defending their rights to employment and their LGB students' rights to a nondiscriminatory education.

The success of LGB teachers' groups also showed heterosexual colleagues and administrators that treating LGB teachers equitably would not cause the sky to fall. The NEA and AFT did not suddenly lose all respectability. Presidential candidates still appeared at NEA conventions and politicians of all stripes still sought the endorsement of the teachers' unions at local, state, and national levels. The city governments of Los Angeles, New York City, and San Francisco were not inundated with a flood of lawsuits from irate parents or the negative press of dozens of gay and lesbian teachers being arrested for child abuse; their bureaucratic worlds kept turning. The contention that supporting LGB rights in schools would cause a political firestorm had incrementally less credibility with the passage of each LGB positive union resolution and city ordinance.

That is not to say that there was no backlash—the Briggs Initiative and the Helm's law both pushed back against the progress of LGB rights—but rather that the backlash was not universal, and the political cost was not nearly as high as the doomsayers predicted. The arguments that undergirded

Conclusion • 175

a significant portion of the opposition to LGB teachers and students lost potency in ever larger numbers of school districts because the advent of openly gay and lesbian teachers did not result in an educational cataclysm. The progress of LGB teachers' groups was fueled by the fact that, with every teacher who came out and continued doing their job, it became more difficult to demonize LGB teachers or students. Likewise, every school district that adopted nondiscrimination policies that included LGB teachers added to the difficulty of opposing such policies.

While social conservatives might be appalled by these developments, the vast political middle of society slowly began to understand that LGB teachers had no discernible negative impact on the process of education. That slow realization has not been even or apparent in all places and, as such, debates over the appropriateness and morality of LGB teachers continues to this day, but the progress started by LGB teachers' groups in the 1970s continues. Until recently, LGBT teachers faced a patchwork of union protections, local statutes, state laws, and administrative prerogatives that determine which geographic spaces are safe to be open about one's sexuality and which spaces remain unsafe.

The Supreme Court ruling *Bostock v. Clayton County, Georgia* on June 15, 2020 was a landmark case for LGBTQ workers' rights. In this ruling, conservative Supreme Court Justice Neil Gorsuch writes, "An employer who fired an individual for being homosexual or transgender fires that person for traits or actions it would not have questioned in members of a different sex. Sex plays a necessary and undisguisable role in the decision, exactly what Title VII forbids. Those who adopted the Civil Rights Act might not have anticipated their work would lead to this particular result. But the limits of the drafters' imagination supply no reason to ignore the law's demands. Only the written word is the law, and all persons are entitled to its benefit."[11] This ruling is an answer to the legal complexity that LGBTQ workers have faced and represents progress to an amazing degree. But a Supreme Court ruling is not legislation, and the shifts in the membership of the Supreme Court could lead the court to revisit the rights of LGBTQ workers. All progress can be contested and must be guarded.

Even if *Bostock v. Clayton County, Georgia* remains precedent for decades, the narratives that have been explored in this book make clear the challenges that LGBT teachers still face. The ability to defend one's rights is contingent on time, money, and personal willingness. In the case of the Supreme Court recognizing an overarching protection for LGBTQ workers under

Title VII, the time to contest a firing, the financial resources to do so in court, and the personal willingness to take on an employer are all realities with which other groups of minorities protected under Title VII are all too familiar. *Bostock v. Clayton County, Georgia* fundamentally alters the calculus that LGBT teachers need to engage in when deciding to work in a school and a particular community, but the calculus remains dominated by the same question: "Will they think I shouldn't be a teacher?"

During the 1970s and 1980s, places where LGB teachers could be out were like isolated islands that had been newly pulled out of a sea of discrimination by the efforts of LGB teachers and their allies. Today we have a Supreme Court ruling applicable across the country and we have entire states that have nondiscrimination laws offering LGBT teachers some measure of protection. But until every state passes such legislation or there is a federal law that makes it illegal to discriminate on the basis of sexuality and gender expression, LGBT teachers will continue to be at a significant disadvantage in American schools.

Between 1970 and 1985, LGB teachers' groups and their allies confronted the precedent of generations of discrimination and for the first time secured a place for openly lesbian, gay, and bisexual people in American schools. LGB teachers could argue for the educational rights of their students and the employment rights of other LGB teachers from these spaces of security. The activism of LGB teachers' groups from 1975 to 1980 laid the foundations of local laws and union protections secured through collective bargaining that LGBT teachers today utilize to defend their employment rights and the education rights of their LGBT students. The activism of LGB teachers' groups also served as a powerful example to LGB teachers and their allies in politically conservative communities that it was possible to change the boundaries of what was acceptable for teachers.

In 1970, it was practically impossible for a K-12 educator in the United States to be openly gay, lesbian, or bisexual; however, by 1985 it had become possible. The possibility of being open and remaining a K-12 teacher existed in relatively few places, but that possibility was achieved through the efforts of LGB teachers' groups and their allies. Members of early LGB teachers' groups had an audacity of imagination that was remarkable; confronted with generations of oppression, overwhelmingly negative public opinion, and no certainty of success, these educators risked their livelihoods to work for a better future. LGB teachers were not merely the beneficiaries of changing social norms around sexuality but, instead, actively changed social norms in individual school districts and through their unions.

Those changes set the stage for statewide nondiscrimination laws and a K-12 education system in which firing a teacher for being a lesbian is not a standing policy but is instead a matter of debate—a debate in which LGBT teachers are active participants. LGBT teachers continue to face challenges to their right to be in the classroom and continue to fight for their LGBT students' right to a safe and equitable education. LGBT teachers and their allies can draw inspiration and hope from the history and success of early LGB teachers' groups as they pursue these goals today.

Acknowledgments

This book would not have been possible without the support of my family, friends, and colleagues. My husband Jordan not only has been a constant inspiration but agreed to marry me in the middle of this project—a testament to love if ever there was one. My best friend Dave arranged my first interview for this project and convinced me it was worth pursuing. My friends have collectively read a dozen versions of this work and are no doubt breathing a sigh of relief that it is completed. Don't worry; my next book is well underway and I'll need you all again soon.

This work has taken seven years and throughout that time I have been guided by an amazing group of scholars who I can't thank enough. Ethan Hutt, my PhD adviser, has been unfailing in his generosity. Ebony Terrell Shockley and Campbell Scribner both sat on my PhD committee and their insights and faith in my work have been steadfast and tremendously kind. Karen Graves also sat on my committee and her research, along with Jackie Blount's work, served as an inspiration for this book. My colleagues in the History of Education Society have been with me during every step of this project, offering the constructive criticism needed to turn a collection of research papers into a single volume.

A small legion of librarians and archivists across the country were unfailingly helpful in conducting this research. Their intimate knowledge of the collections under their care increased the efficiency and quality of my research by at least a magnitude. I would especially like to thank Vakil Smallen at George Washington University, Michael Oliviera at *ONE* Archives,

Daniel Golodner at the Walter P. Reuther Library, and the staff of the LGBT Community Center National History Archive in New York City who all answered innumerable emails and pointed my search for primary resources in the right direction.

Finally, I am grateful beyond words to the LGBT educators and our allies whose histories are recounted in these pages. Their courage and foresight were nothing short of remarkable. This is the first time many of the educators I interviewed for this book were contacted about their involvement in LGB teachers' groups. I can only hope that I have done them justice and that their history will inspire today's educators to be equally bold in their activism.

Notes

Introduction

Epigraph: "Apple Banner Energy Transformed," *Gay Teachers and School Workers Coalition Newsletter* 1, no. 1 (August/September 1977): 1, Lesbian School Workers Collection, box 1, file 1, June Mazer Lesbian Collection, Los Angeles, CA.

1 Catherine Lugg's *US Public Schools and the Politics of Queer Erasure* illustrates the complexities of constructing a historical narrative involving LGBTQ (lesbian, gay, bisexual, transgender, and queer) teachers. Lugg's research presents a compelling account of the different ways that LGBTQ teachers and students have been silenced in American schools. Unfortunately, LGB teachers' groups are not discussed by Lugg until the advent of PFLAG (Parents and Friends of Lesbians and Gays) in the 1990s, leading the reader to erroneously conclude that the erasure that Lugg discusses was all encompassing up to that point. Queer erasure was expansive and persistent through the 1970s and 1980s, but it was not absolute. This study will provide multiple examples of LGB teachers' groups that actively contested their erasure and were anything but silent in the face of oppression. By examining the oral histories of teacher activists, their allies, and the archival evidence of LGB teachers' groups, we can examine exceptions to the systemic oppression that Lugg discusses in detail. See Catherine Lugg, *US Public Schools and the Politics of Queer Erasure* (New York: Palgrave Pivot, 2015), chap. 3.
2 Jackie M. Blount, *Fit to Teach: Same-Sex Desire, Gender, and School Work in the Twentieth Century* (Albany: State University of New York Press, 2006), 108, 135.
3 Blount, *Fit to Teach*, 108, 3–4.
4 Karen Graves, *And They Were Wonderful Teachers* (Urbana: University of Illinois Press, 2009), xii–xiv.
5 Craig M. Loftin, *Masked Voices: Gay Men and Lesbians in Cold War America*, SUNY Series in Queer Politics and Cultures (Albany: State University of New York Press, 2012), chap. 6.

182 • Notes to Pages 8–11

6 Lugg, *US Public Schools*, 49–54.
7 For examples of this first wave of historical research on LGBT teachers, see William J. Letts IV and James T. Sears, eds., *Queering Elementary Education: Advancing the Dialogue about Sexualities and Schooling* (Lanham, MD: Rowman & Littlefield, 1999); Karen M. Harbeck, ed., *Coming Out of the Classroom Closet: Gay and Lesbian Students, Teachers, and Curricula* (New York: Haworth Press, 1992); Rita M. Kissen, *The Last Closet: The Real Lives of Lesbian and Gay Teachers* (Portsmouth, NH: Heinemann, 1996); Rita M. Kissen, "Voices from the Glass Closet: Lesbian and Gay Teachers Talk about Their Lives" (Presentation, Annual Meeting of the American Educational Research Association, Atlanta, GA, April 12–16, 1993), https://files.eric.ed.gov/fulltext/ED363556.pdf; Karen M. Harbeck, *Gay and Lesbian Educators: Personal Freedoms, Public Constraints* (Malden, MA: Amethyst, 1997).
8 For examples of LGBT histories detailing specific cities, see Gary L. Atkins, *Gay Seattle: Stories of Exile and Belonging* (Seattle: University of Washington Press, 2011); St. Sukie de la Croix, *Chicago Whispers: A History of LGBT Chicago before Stonewall* (Madison: University of Wisconsin Press, 2012); Marc Stein, *City of Sisterly and Brotherly Loves: Lesbian and Gay Philadelphia, 1945–1972* (Philadelphia, PA: Temple University Press, 2004).
9 Jim Downs, *Stand by Me: The Forgotten History of Gay Liberation* (New York: Basic Books, 2016). For another exemplar study that traces the relationship between the LGBT community and other institutions and movements, see Emily K. Hobson, *Lavender and Red: Liberation and Solidarity in the Gay and Lesbian Left* (Oakland: University of California Press, 2016). Hobson traces the founding debates of gay liberation politics through the organizations and groups where those conversations occurred and then connects the results of those debates to political realities, like U.S. involvement in Nicaragua, and the AIDS crisis.
10 Downs, *Stand by Me*, chap. VII.
11 For example, Eisenbach's research in *Gay Power: An American Revolution* does not reference schools, LGBT teachers, or labor unions, see David Eisenbach, *Gay Power: An American Revolution*, repr. ed. (New York: Da Capo, 2007).
12 Tom Ammiano, "My Adventures as a Gay Teacher," in *Smash the Church, Smash the State! The Early Years of Gay Liberation*, ed. Tommi Avicolli Mecca (San Francisco: City Lights, 2019), 40–42.
13 Miriam Frank, *Out in the Union: A Labor History of Queer America* (Philadelphia, PA: Temple University Press, 2014), xxiii–xxv.
14 Tiemeyer presents the complicated relationship between gay men and the airline companies they worked for as mitigated by labor unions, which were successful in lobbying for gay flight attendants with varying degrees of success. Despite this variability, the presence of a union appears to be beneficial throughout his study, particularly in the context of the AIDS crisis during the 1980s and 1990s. See Philip James Tiemeyer, *Plane Queer: Labor, Sexuality, and AIDS in the History of Male Flight Attendants* (Berkeley: University of California Press, 2013), 46, 56–58, 106, 110, 217–218, 223–224.
15 Miriam Frank's scholarship on the subject of LGBT people in labor unions represents almost the entirety of research on the topic. Her work has focused for decades on collecting and examining oral histories. Frank, *Out in the Union*, 7,

84–87, 120–122. An exception to the general lack of research on LGBT people in the labor movement is Allan Bérubé's work on the Marine Cooks and Stewards Union in the 1930s and 1940s, which remains unpublished but was compiled into a video lecture posthumously by D'Emilio and Friedman. Allan Bérubé, "'No Red-Baiting! No Race-Baiting! No Queen-Baiting!': The Marine Cooks and Stewards Union from the Depression to the Cold War," (online lecture produced by John D'Emilio and Estelle Freedman, Outhistory.org, 2016), http://outhistory .org/exhibits/show/no-baiting/red-race-queen.

16 For examples of teachers' unions engaged in local-level politics, see Jonna Perrillo, *Uncivil Rights: Teachers, Unions, and Race in the Battle for School Equity* (Chicago: University of Chicago Press, 2012); Jon Shelton, *Teacher Strike! Public Education and the Making of a New American Political Order* (Urbana: University of Illinois Press, 2017). For examples of teachers' unions engaged in state-level politics, see Don Cameron, *Educational Conflict in the Sunshine State: The Story of the 1968 Statewide Teacher Walkout in Florida* (Lanham, MD: R&L Education, 2008); Dennis Gaffney, *Teachers United: The Rise of New York State United Teachers* (Albany: State University of New York Press, 2007); Steve Kink, *Class Wars: The Story of the Washington Education Association 1965–2001* (Federal Way, WA: Washington Education Association, 2004). For biographies and autobiographies of teacher union leadership, see Don Cameron, *The Inside Story of the Teacher Revolution in America* (Lanham, MD: R&L Education, 2005); Richard D. Kahlenberg, *Tough Liberal: Albert Shanker and the Battles over Schools, Unions, Race, and Democracy*, Columbia Studies in Contemporary American History (New York: Columbia University Press, 2007).

17 For concise statistics of the NEA and AFT over the twentieth century, see Marjorie Murphy, *Blackboard Unions the AFT and the NEA, 1900–1980* (Ithaca, NY: Cornell University Press, 1992), 277, Table 6.

18 Murphy, *Blackboard Unions*, 110; Cameron, *Inside Story*, 25–30.

19 Murphy, *Blackboard Unions*, 196–208.

20 Wayne J. Urban, *Gender, Race, and the National Education Association: Professionalism and Its Limitations*, Studies in the History of Education (New York: Routledge Falmer, 2000), 73, 212, 255–256.

21 Urban, *Gender, Race*, xviii–xx, 254–257, 260–262.

22 The groups in Denver and Portland are evidenced only through references in other LGB teachers' groups publications. As detailed later, the Chicago group is evidenced by a single flyer and a single reference in a gay newspaper. The Boston group generated a larger number of primary sources, but those sources require a separate analysis as part of the collection of long-time LGBT activist Eric Rofes.

23 The other teachers' group that had a regional, and arguably national, scope was the American Teacher Association. This professional association was historically African American and, as detailed later in this study, merged with the National Education Association and its affiliates on a state and national level over the course of the 1960s and 1970s.

24 National Education Association of the United States, Research Division, *Status of the American Public School Teacher, 1980–1981* (Washington, DC: NEA, Research Division, 1982), 67, Table 49.

25 For discussions of the impact of the AIDS crisis on the LGBT community and the pivot toward the AIDS crisis in LGBT activism, see Ann Cvetkovich, *An Archive*

184 • Notes to Pages 15–25

of Feelings: Trauma, Sexuality, and Lesbian Public Cultures (Durham, NC: Duke University Press, 2003), 156–160, 160–162, 167–202; Steven Seidman, *The Social Construction of Sexuality*, 2nd ed. (New York: W. W. Norton, 2009), 69, 78, 196. Seidman argues that eventually after the AIDS crisis had peaked in the late 1980s, the experiences of LGBT persons throughout the crisis refocused the movement on civil rights such as marriage. Marc Stein, *Rethinking the Gay and Lesbian Movement* (New York: Routledge, 2012), 141–145, 151–155. Marc Stein titles the period from 1981 to 1990 as "The Age of AIDS" and argues that AIDS-related activism completely superseded other political activism, including efforts to secure employment rights, during this period.

26 Blount, *Fit to Teach*, 158–159, 183–184.

Chapter 1   The National Education Association

Epigraph: A. Hoffman, "Out of the Closet, Into the Class," *Washington Post, Times Herald 1959–1973*, July 3, 1972, Style People the Arts Leisure.

1 National Education Association, *A Voice for GLBT Educators*, National Education Association Archives, Gelman Library, George Washington University, Washington DC, 2.

2 Blount, *Fit to Teach*, Introduction.

3 For a succinct analysis of the gendered roles of teachers throughout the twentieth century, see Jackie M. Blount, "Spinsters, Bachelors, and Other Gender Transgressors in School Employment, 1850–1990," *Review of Educational Research* 70, no. 1 (March 1, 2000): 83–101.

4 This chapter extends three years beyond the general time frame of my study. The reasons for doing this, and placing this chapter at the beginning of this manuscript, are twofold. First, the NEA did not recognize a LGB caucus until 1987 and so a hard stop at 1985 would exclude this extremely important development from this study. Second, by first presenting what was accomplished in the NEA by LGB teachers without a caucus and then presenting what was accomplished after the foundation of a caucus, it is possible to illustrate the value and utility of having a formal organization in comparison to the accomplishments of coalitions of individual LGB educators and their allies.

5 Riis Beach is a "local" gay beach for New York City on the southern shore of Long Island, and an alternative to the more expensive and distant Fire Island. It had been a gathering place for gay men for decades.

6 The specifics of Gish's motivations and early involvement are based on an interview conducted with the author for this study. It is the only such interview Gish has given regarding his activism. See John Gish, interview by author, August 12, 2015, recording, author's collection.

7 Gish, interview.

8 Gish, interview.

9 Gish, interview.

10 This ability to utilize organizations for protection is in distinct contrast to earlier experiences of individual LGB teachers in Florida during the Cold War. See Graves, *And They Were Wonderful Teachers*, 50–97.

Notes to Pages 25–29 • 185

11 Stuart Biegel, *The Right to Be Out: Sexual Orientation and Gender Identity in America's Public Schools* (Minneapolis: University of Minnesota Press, 2010), 59–77, 226 n. 1.

12 Blount, *Fit to Teach*, 116–120.

13 Murphy, *Blackboard Unions*, 277, Table 6.

14 For an examination of the efforts of organized labor to organize and maintain unions in the American South during the 1970s, see Anna Lane Windham, *Knocking on Labor's Door: Union Organizing in the 1970s and the Roots of a New Economic Divide* (Chapel Hill: University of North Carolina Press, 2019), 213–254.

15 For state-level NEA histories, see Gaffney, *Teachers United*; Kink, *Class Wars*.

16 For example, the 1973 convention had just over nine thousand representatives; the same article claimed the NEA membership in 1973 stood at 1.4 million. Evan Jenkins, "N.E.A. Convention to Weigh Merger," *New York Times*, July 1, 1973.

17 Even after the NEA began functioning as a teachers' union, actively negotiating contracts and engaging in collective bargaining/workplace arbitration, it officially used alternate nomenclature such as "walkouts" instead of strikes, much to the exasperation of more union-oriented NEA members. See Cameron, *Inside Story*, 45, 77.

18 Urban, *Gender, Race*, 182, 255–258.

19 Urban, *Gender, Race*, 32–34, 170–172, 178–179.

20 For a discussion of this lack of prestige as it relates to reform and educational policy, particularly in New York City, see Diana D'Amico Pawlewicz, *Blaming Teachers: Professionalization Policies and the Failure of Reform in American History* (New Brunswick, NJ: Rutgers University Press, 2002).

21 For a treatment of the lobbying efforts of American school teachers in the early twentieth century, see Dana Goldstein, *The Teacher Wars: A History of America's Most Embattled Profession*, repr. ed. (New York: Anchor, 2015), chap. 4.

22 Wayne J. Urban, *Why Teachers Organized* (Detroit: Wayne State University Press, 1982), 173.

23 Joseph A. McCartin, *Collision Course: Ronald Reagan, the Air Traffic Controllers, and the Strike That Changed America*, repr. ed. (New York: Oxford University Press, 2013), 9.

24 Cameron, *Inside Story*, 39.

25 Wayne J. Urban, *More Than the Facts: The Research Division of the National Education Association, 1922–1997* (Lanham, MD: University Press of America, 1998), 77, 100, 109.

26 Murphy, *Blackboard Unions*, 227–231.

27 This of course would have not been possible as the political movement from which Gish derived his inspiration and tactics blossomed in the wake of the 1969 Stonewall riots, but this is nonetheless an interesting thought experiment, which illustrates how swiftly power shifted within the NEA during this period.

28 The reasons for the passage of this ordinance remain unknown. Karen Harbeck notes that the measure passed with "little apparent fanfare" and that the cities of St. Paul, Minnesota, Eugene, Oregon, and Wichita, Kansas, "soon followed suit." See Harbeck, *Gay and Lesbian Educators*, 236–237.

186 • Notes to Pages 29–35

29 *National Education Association Records of the Representative Assembly* (Washington, DC: NEA, 1972), 131.
30 Gish, interview.
31 Gish, interview.
32 Hoffman, "Out of the Closet."
33 *Records of the Representative Assembly*, 131.
34 *Records of the Representative Assembly*, 288.
35 "Teacher Sick or Board," *Advocate*, August 16, 1972, box 4, file 87, Advocate Subject Records, *ONE* National Gay and Lesbian Archives, Los Angeles.
36 Gish, interview.
37 For an account of efforts for African American worker's rights as part of and integral to the civil rights movement, see Nancy MacLean, *Freedom Is Not Enough: The Opening of the American Work Place* (New York: Sage; Cambridge, MA: Harvard University Press, 2006). As part of the women's rights movement relating specifically to working rights, see Dennis A. Deslippe, *Rights, Not Roses: Unions and the Rise of Working-Class Feminism, 1945–80* (Urbana: University of Illinois Press, 1999).
38 *Records of the Representative Assembly*, 18–19.
39 Myron Lieberman, "The 1973 NEA Convention: Confusion Is King," *Phi Delta Kappan* 55, no. 1 (1973): 3–89.
40 Gaffney, *Teachers United*, 124–127.
41 Wolfgang Saxon, "Elizabeth Koontz, 69, Dies: Led Teachers' Union," *New York Times*, January 8, 1989.
42 For example, white teachers in South Carolina formed the short-lived Palmetto State Teachers Association. See Jon Hale, "Desegregating and Merging the Southern Teacher Associations, 1963–1979" (Presentation, America Education Research Association Conference, San Antonio, TX, April 2014).
43 Urban, *Gender, Race*, 218.
44 Urban, *Gender, Race*, 189–200, 256–257.
45 Robert H. Terte, "NEGRO TEACHERS FAVOR N.E.A. LINK: But National Group Qualifies Its Support for Merger 'Glaring Lack' of Negroes Formed as Protest," *New York Times*, August 4, 1963, 71; Thelma D. Perry, *History of the American Teachers Association* (Washington, DC: National Education Association, 1975), 327.
46 National Education Association of the United States, Research Division, *Status of the American Public School Teacher, 2000–2001* (Washington, DC: NEA, Research Division, 2003), 91, Table 70.
47 Blount, *Fit to Teach*, 181 fn. E.I.
48 The gendered nature of teaching in the United States was not limited to public schools but extended into religious schools as well. This was most notably and widely the case in the Catholic school system's utilization of nuns as educators. See Michael P. Caruso, *When the Sisters Said Farewell: The Transition of Leadership in Catholic Elementary Schools* (Lanham, MD: R&L Education, 2012), chap. 1.
49 NEA, Research Division, *Status*, 77, Table 56.
50 For a detailed history of women attaining these administrative positions despite systemic obstacles, see Jackie M. Blount, *Destined to Rule the Schools: Women and the Superintendency, 1873–1995*, SUNY Series in Educational Leadership (Albany: State University of New York Press, 1998); Clarence Taylor, *Reds at the*

Blackboard: Communism, Civil Rights, and the New York City Teachers Union
(New York: Columbia University Press, 2011), 276–278.

51 The work options available to women were complicated by race, class, and geography. For example, African American women in the segregated South were further limited in their work prospects by the intersectionality of their circumstances. Conversely, wealthy white women with the advantage of college had more options. Women from the working classes historically worked outside the home. For discussions of these and other intersectionalities in twentieth century America, see Dorothy Cobble, *Dishing It Out: Waitresses and Their Unions in the Twentieth Century* (Urbana: University of Illinois Press, 1991); Deslippe, *Rights, Not Roses*; Stephanie J. Shaw, *What a Woman Ought to Be and to Do: Black Professional Women Workers during the Jim Crow Era*, Women in Culture and Society (Chicago: University of Chicago Press, 1996), chaps. 4, 5, 6.

52 Alice Kessler-Harris, *Out to Work: A History of Wage-Earning Women in the United States* (New York: Oxford University Press, 1982), 300–301.

53 Sara M. Evans, *Tidal Wave: How Women Changed America at Century's End* (New York: Free Press, 2003), 134, 136–138.

54 Evans, *Tidal Wave*, 161.

55 Windham, *Knocking on Labor's Door*, 49, 54–57, 72–73.

56 Paul Johnston, *Success While Others Fail: Social Movement Unionism and the Public Workplace* (Ithaca, NY: ILR Press, 1994), 7–8, Figures 1.1 and 1.2, 15–18.

57 In this regard, I disagree with Wayne Urban's assertion that because the driving force behind the unionization of the NEA appeared to be male high school teachers, the association shifted dramatically and "the attention paid to women teachers appeared to diminish drastically." I would argue that, instead, goals that had not been historically associated with teaching, high wages, collective bargaining, and prestige became sought after by teachers in the NEA. Urban posits that the three themes of race, gender, and professionalism as concerns in the NEA ebb and flow with one of them being ascendant at a given point in history at the expense of the other two. Instead, I propose that the NEA expanded its idea of professionalism away from being "anti-union" to encompassing the welfare of a broader and more diverse membership in the 1970s which included women, racial minorities, and, as detailed in this chapter, LGBT teachers. See Urban, *Gender, Race*, xviii—xx.

58 Shelton, *Teacher Strike!*, 112, 152, 69–70, 116, 178, 184, 107–108.

59 Shelton, *Teacher Strike!*, 8.

60 In the early twentieth century, it was common for male teachers to receive a higher salary; even after gender was no longer used as a determining factor, this difference in salary was maintained de facto because high school teachers, the majority of male teachers worked and continue to work in high schools, received a higher salary than elementary school teachers. For the particulars of this system and its eventual shift to a salary schedule based on years of service and academic degrees in New York City, see Taylor, *Reds at the Blackboard*.

61 For a historical comparison of teachers' salaries relative to other economic sectors, see Murphy, *Blackboard Unions*, 276, Table 5.

62 Murphy, *Blackboard Unions*, 277, Table 6; NEA, Research Division, *Status*, 64–65, Figure 12.

63　Lillian Faderman, *The Gay Revolution: The Story of the Struggle*, repr. ed. (New York: Simon & Schuster, 2016), 403; Frank, *Out in the Union*, 76–81; Evans, *Tidal Wave*, 232–235.

64　Harbeck, *Gay and Lesbian Educators*, 234–242.

65　Jane Stern, interview by author regarding LGBT activism and the NEA, October 31, 2014, recording, author's collection.

66　Stern, interview.

67　Respectively New Business items: 75, 64, 67 / 13, 22, 76 / 41, 84, 9. See *Records of the Representative Assembly, 1974*, 68–69, 92–93.

68　*Records of the Representative Assembly, 1974*, 129.

69　Jackie Blount, *Fit to Teach*, 112–120.

70　*Records of the Representative Assembly, 1974*, 129.

71　*Records of the Representative Assembly, 1974*, 130.

72　*Records of the Representative Assembly, 1974*, 131.

73　Richard Rubino, interview by author, November 11, 2013, recording, author's collection.

74　Rubino, interview.

75　National Education Association, *A Voice for GLBT Educators*, 2.

76　Examples of the importance of exclusive LGBT social space can be found in various contexts during the twentieth century and have been discussed by historians. See, respectively, Allan Bérubé, *Coming Out Under Fire: The History of Gay Men and Women in World War II* (Chapel Hill: University of North Carolina Press, 2010); Lillian Faderman, *Odd Girls and Twilight Lovers: A History of Lesbian Life in Twentieth-Century America* (New York: Columbia University Press, 2012); John Howard, *Men Like That: A Southern Queer History* (Chicago: University of Chicago Press, 1999).

77　Exclusion within the LGBT community and constituent parts of the LGBT community, gay male culture for example, is well documented. I am not making a claim that all members of the LGBT community have been equally welcomed but am instead claiming that the creation of LGBT-specific social spaces was a necessary component of community building and activism based in identity politics.

78　Martin B. Duberman, *Stonewall* (New York: Plume, 1994), 181.

79　Downs, *Stand by Me*, 17–28; Marc Santora, "Orlando to Turn Pulse Nightclub into a Memorial," *New York Times*, November 9, 2016, https://www.nytimes.com /2016/11/09/us/orlando-pulse-nightclub-memorial.html.

80　For a discussion of the development and importance of LGB dances as a space of organizing and the reaction of the local community in Lawrence, Kansas, see Beth L. Bailey, *Sex in the Heartland* (Cambridge, MA: Harvard University Press, 1999) 183–187.

81　Other "invisible" minorities can be seen in the case of teachers who have religious backgrounds who were discriminated against and who therefore chose to not make their religions known professionally. Historically this would most notably include Jewish Americans and, given the political climate since 9/11, Muslim Americans with members of said religious communities possibly being identified as part of the Christian majority by default.

82　For a masterful analysis of the federal government defining homosexuality and revealing homosexuals through definition in the process of immigration, see

Margot Canaday, *The Straight State: Sexuality and Citizenship in Twentieth-Century America* (Princeton, NJ: Princeton University Press, 2011), chap. 6.

83 Similar off-site and secret parties for gay men occurred during the 1970s at the American Psychiatric Association Convention. Such parties were crucial to the declassification of homosexuality as a disorder and are detailed in Jack Drescher and Joseph P. Merlino, *American Psychiatry and Homosexuality: An Oral History* (New York: Harrington Park Press, 2007), 51, 85.

84 New York (1972) pioneered the merger of state-level NEA/AFT affiliates in the 1970s. State and local unions sent delegates to both conventions. LA Unified, as one of the largest school districts in the country, had a significant delegation within the larger California delegation. *Records of the Representative Assembly, 1972*, 15–16.

85 Jeff Horton, interview by author, February 15, 2015, recording, author's collection.

86 Horton, interview.

87 Horton, interview.

88 This group will be detailed in Chapter 4.

89 Mary Futrell, interview by author, November 11, 2014, recording, author's collection.

90 Sandy Harrison and Peter Larsen, "Horton Declares He Is Homosexual," in "Out and Elected in the USA: 1974–2004," ed. Ron Schlittler, *Daily News*, October 12, 1991, http://outhistory.org/exhibits/show/out-and-elected/1991/jeff-horton.

91 Steve Lopez, "After 40 Years in L.A. Schools, This Outspoken Teacher Gives the LAUSD His Final Grade," *Los Angeles Times*, June 7, 2017, http://www.latimes.com/local/california/la-me-lopez-horton-06072017-story.html.

92 Carol Watchler, interview by author, June 19, 2015, recording, author's collection.

93 Watchler, interview.

94 Moving into the 1990s, the Gay and Lesbian Caucus focused more intensely on student rights in parallel with the newly formed Gay, Lesbian, and Straight Educator Network (which eventually became known by the acronym GLSEN). Watchler continued to advocate for LGBTQ educators and students, eventually serving as the cochair of GLSEN's Central New Jersey organization.

95 Eric Marcus, *Making Gay History: The Half-Century Fight for Lesbian and Gay Equal Rights* (New York: HarperCollins, 2002), 245.

96 The classic work on the political climate surrounding the early HIV/AIDS epidemic during the early and mid-1980s is Randy Shilts, *And the Band Played On: Politics, People, and the AIDS Epidemic* (New York: St Martin's Griffin, 2007), 507.

97 While this process has generally been described as a coming together of the LGBT community against a common threat, recent scholarship has complicated this narrative. For a discussion of this, see Deborah B. Gould, "The Shame of Gay Pride in Early AIDS Activism," in *Gay Shame*, ed. David M. Halperin and Valerie Traub (Chicago: University of Chicago Press, 2009), 234–236.

98 For a comprehensive study of ACT UP that pays particularly close attention to the arguments utilized by the group and the role of emotion in those arguments, see Deborah B. Gould, *Moving Politics: Emotion and ACT UP's Fight against AIDS* (Chicago: University of Chicago Press, 2009); Marcus, *Making Gay History*, 246.

99 *Records of the Representative Assembly, 1987*, 304.

100 *Records of the Representative Assembly, 1987*, 305.

190 • Notes to Pages 50–57

101 *Records of the Representative Assembly, 1987*, 306.
102 For examples of the wide range of legislative responses to AIDS in one state, see Jean Griffin and Daniel Egler, "20 Bills Set Sights on AIDS: State Legislation Even Aims at Those Planning to Wed," *Chicago Tribune (1963–current file)*, March 20, 1987, sec. 1.
103 "Education Board Proposes AIDS Testing in School," *Atlanta Daily World (1932–2003)*, May 19, 1987; Cohn D'Vera, "Fairfax AIDS Proposal Criticized: Teachers Union Wants More Protection for Other in School Policy," *Washington Post (1974–current file)*, January 15, 1988.
104 The Briggs Initiative was a ballot initiative proposed in 1978 that would have banned LGB teachers from employment in California and also subjected current LGBT teachers and their allies to termination. The fourth chapter of this study will discuss the Briggs Initiative and its impact on the California LGBT community, including three LGBT teachers' groups in that state.
105 *Records of the Representative Assembly, 1978*, 275.
106 Blount, *Fit to Teach*, Introduction.
107 Futrell, interview.
108 Virginia Education Association, "VEA: Our History," August 16, 2017, https://www.veanea.org/about/history/.
109 The degree to which the NEA or its state and local affiliates lived up to this commitment to protect the educational rights of minority students was of course variable. It is important to note, however, that by the mid-1980s, those commitments to minority students were explicitly stated in official policy and were being actively pursued.
110 Futrell, interview.
111 *Records of the Representative Assembly, 1988*, 22–24.
112 Miriam Frank places the first mentions of transgender rights in labor agreements in the 1980s with the agreement to add "change of sex" to the list of protected classes. It is unclear on which date this contract went into effect, given the citation used. See Frank, *Out in the Union*, 2, citation 6.
113 *Records of the Representative Assembly, 1988*, 228.
114 *Records of the Representative Assembly, 1988*, 228–229.
115 *Records of the Representative Assembly, 1988*, 229–231.
116 *Records of the Representative Assembly, 1988*, 233.
117 C-42, C-43, C-44, see *Records of the Representative Assembly, 1988*, 231–232.
118 Discussion of mandatory testing for HIV was common between 1988 and 1992, with groups being proposed for testing including immigrants, doctors, K-12 students, and criminals. For examples, see Robert Bears, "Problems Seen in Reagan Testing Plan," *New York Times*, June 3, 1987; Martin Gerry and Martin Hornbeck, "Dealing with the AIDS Threat in Maryland Public Schools," *Washington Post*, January 17, 1988; Altman K. Lawrence, "AIDS Testing of Doctors is Crux of Thorny Debate," *New York Times*, December 27, 1990; Leslie Werner, "Mandatory Testing Urged," *New York Times (1923–current file)*, May 1, 1987.
119 *Records of the Representative Assembly, 1988*, 245–247.
120 There are instances of LGBT activism within the NEA at the state level prior to 1987. Most notably, the composite NEA/AFT state teachers' union of California was active in the Briggs Initiative campaign of 1978. The principal scholarship on

this activism can be found in Sara R. Smith's dissertation work on rank-and-file teachers' activism and unions in California. This topic will be discussed more fully in chapter 3. For a list of labor organizations active in opposing the Briggs Initiative, see Sara R. Smith, "Organizing for Social Justice: Rank-and-File Teachers' Activism and Social Unionism in California, 1948–1978" (PhD diss., University of California, Santa Cruz, 2014), 402.

121 "NEA Gay, Lesbian, Bisexual, Transgender Caucus | Nea-Glbtc.org," September 16, 2017, http://www.nea-glbtc.org/.

122 This process of creating and defining new categories of acceptable persons within a polity, or, in the case of this study, within a profession, is discussed in detail by Margot Canady in the context of various departments and official policies within the federal government. A similar study could be conducted regarding LGBT teachers though a large portion of Canady's argument rests on the fact that federal policy is applied nationally. It may be that a study detailing the eventual policy acceptance of LGBT teachers in a country with a centralized education system, such as France, would have greater utility. See Canaday, *Straight State*.

Chapter 2   The American Federation of Teachers

Epigraph: American Federation of Teachers, *Proof of 1979 Convention Proceedings*, August 1979, 176, box 51, file 2 of 9 "1979 Convention," AFT Series Part II, Walter P. Reuther Library, Wayne State University, Detroit.

1 For the first executive order, which will be discussed in detail later in this chapter, see American Federation of Teachers Executive Council, *Resolution 18*, December 1970, AFT Unprocessed Publications, Walter P. Reuther Library, Wayne State University, Detroit. For the initial formation of a LGBT AFT caucus, see Paul Thomas, "Letter from Paul Thomas to Al Shanker re: Foundation of AFT Gay Teachers Caucus," August 8, 1988, AFT President's Office, Albert Shanker Records, box 12, file "Gay and Lesbian Caucus," Walter P. Reuther Library, Wayne State University, Detroit. See also Frank, *Out in the Union*, 120–123; Gerald Hunt, ed., *Laboring for Rights: Unions and Sexual Diversity across Nations*, Queer Politics, Queer Theories (Philadelphia: Temple University Press, 1999), 64 fn. 8.

2 Miriam Frank in *Out in the Union* includes the AFT in her timeline of queer union history but, aside from this mention, and Jackie Blount's brief discussion of the AFT in *Fit to Teach*, the subject of sexuality and LGBT teachers in the national-level AFT remains unexamined. The two major labor histories on national-level teachers' unions, Wayne Urban's *Gender, Race, and the National Education Association* and Marjorie Murphy's *Blackboard Unions*, do not examine the issues surrounding LGBT teachers and organized labor. The most notable research examining teachers' unions and LGBT teachers/rights is Sara R. Smith's study, "Organizing for Social Justice," which will be discussed in detail in Chapter 4 and which is primarily concerned with the California Federation of Teachers and not the national AFT.

3 Murphy, *Blackboard Unions*, 277, Table 6.

4 Murphy, *Blackboard Unions*, 215–216.

5 For example, in 1972, the Chicago Teachers Union, one of the largest AFT locals, was entitled to send 233 delegates but sent only eighty: in 1973, it was entitled to 235

192 • Notes to Pages 63-68

and sent only 105, or less than half of the possible number. See Martha R. Bethel, "CTU Blues," *Chicago Defender (Daily Edition) (1973–1975)*, April 4, 1973.

6 It should be noted that, to date, since Al Shanker in 1974, no one has been elected to the presidency of the AFT without being deeply involved in the UFT and specifically with the leadership of the UFT.

7 For a history of the New York State United Teachers and the role of the UFT in the state level union, see Gaffney, *Teachers United*.

8 Louis Weiner, interview by author regarding LGBT teacher activism in the AFT, January 17, 2015, recording, author's collection.

9 For a comprehensive treatment of Shanker, his influences, and actions, see the biography by Kahlenberg, *Tough Liberal*.

10 Weiner, interview.

11 Each of these locals had spent the previous two years involved in the racial unrest and reform movement on California college campuses. These actions were followed closely by the *Stanford Daily*, the Stanford University newspaper. For examples of actions by the San Jose State local 1362, see David Packard, "Crises May Reignite on Area Campuses," *Stanford Daily*, January 6, 1969. For San Francisco State University Student Workers local 1928, and more broadly the strike actions of San Francisco State University Professors local 1352 from 1968 to 1969, see Smith, "Organizing for Social Justice," chap. 2.

12 Sara Smith points out that the California Federation of Teachers had passed an even more progressive series of pro-gay resolutions beginning in 1969 and extended through the 1970s to opposing the Briggs Initiative. It is apparent from Smith's analysis that the politics of the California Federation of Teachers were significantly more liberal than the AFT throughout the period covered in this study. See Smith, "Organizing for Social Justice," 436.

13 Weiner, interview.

14 AFT Executive Council, *Resolution 18*.

15 Frank, *Out in the Union*, xxiii–xxv.

16 This was a central feature of a number of court cases involving LGBT teachers in the early 1970s dealt with. See Biegel, *Right to Be Out*, 132–133, 226. This is precisely the argument that Karen Graves makes in describing the reasons why members of the Florida NAACP (National Association for the Advancement of Colored People) and faculty members at the University of South Florida were successful in fending off the Johns Committee in the late 1950s and early 1960s through public hearings. Homosexual teachers were denied the ability to go public, because publicity would have the same result as private persecution, losing your teaching job, with the added cost of public humiliation. In effect, combating the government required an organization and community support; LGBT teachers caught up in the Johns Committee had neither. See Graves, *And They Were Wonderful Teachers*, chap. 3.

17 The level of commitment made by the American labor movement to minority rights is a matter of debate and represents a spectrum of positive and negative interactions as varied as unions themselves. I am not making an argument about the efficacy or degree of that commitment, but, instead, describing the ways in which activists writing the 1970 proposal positioned their own struggle within the broader struggle for civil rights, and the belief of those same activists that labor unions had a historic commitment to civil rights. By their passing of the

Notes to Pages 69–72 • 193

resolution, the Executive Council indicated that the majority of its members did not disagree with this position.

For a discussion of the complex role(s) that unions played in the inclusion of women and people of color in the American workplaces, see MacLean, *Freedom Is Not Enough*.

18 American Federation of Teachers, *Resolution 9: Convention Proceedings (Abridged)*, August 1973, box 97, file 31, AFT Educational Issues Department Records, Walter P. Reuther Library, Wayne State University, Detroit.

19 Biegel, *Right to Be Out*, 55.

20 Biegel, *Right to Be Out*, 56. Biegel makes the argument that *Morrison* was not, strictly speaking, a gay rights case. He bases this on Morrison's refusal to reveal his sexuality. While this is true from a strictly legal stance, it is clear that, at the very least, others, for example, the authors of the 1973 AFT resolution discussed here, did in fact see this case as being a matter of gay rights. In a similar manner to John Gish (see chapter 1), Morrison and/or his counsel likely understood that the ability to win a case depended on his showing that his opponents had violated a broadly held protection, in this case the "panoply of legal protections," that Justice Tobriner asserted surrounded a person's employment, rather than appealing to questionable sympathies surrounding homosexuality.

21 Biegel, *Right to Be Out*, 57, 229.

22 This turn toward a right to privacy, as a way of ensuring the protection of an activity/group not necessarily supported by majority opinion, was in keeping with a broader legal trend in the 1960s that extended into the 1970s and beyond. See *Griswold v. Connecticut*, *Loving v. Virginia*, and *Roe v. Wade* for examples.

23 AFT, *Resolution 9*.

24 The convention was widely covered by the press, but the major story was the ousting of President David Selden in favor of Albert Shanker rather than any of the numerous resolutions passed and a possible merger with the NEA. See Thomas Carey, "Shanker Wins AFT Presidency Ousting Incumbent David Selden," *Washington Post (1974–current file)*, August 22, 1974; David Pike, "Boston Teachers Gain Strength at National Union Convention," *Boston Globe (1960–1986)*, August 26, 1973; Richard E. Prince, "AFT Restates Willingness to Merge with Rival NEA," *Washington Post*, August 25, 1973.

25 In Miriam Frank's timeline of queer activism in American unions, after the AFT and NEA, the next national union to include LGB people in significant policies, like employment protections, was the American Federation of State, County and Municipal Employees in 1983. This was itself a public sector union and the significance of the first three national unions to actively recognize and support LGB members being public sector unions is an area that requires further study. Also in 1983 the AFL-CIO added sexual orientation to its nondiscrimination policy but the origins of this activism remains unexplored. See Frank, *Out in the Union*, xiii–xviii; Smith, "Organizing for Social Justice," 380. In a similar fashion, the history of gay and lesbian activism within professional organizations such as the American Librarian Association, another site of early activism, is needed to construct a fuller narrative of the efforts of LGBT activists to shift the climate of the American workforce in the 1970s. For an example of research focusing on a professional organization, see Drescher and Merlino, *American Psychiatry and Homosexuality*.

194 • Notes to Pages 73–80

26 American Federation of Teachers, *Resolution 5: Rights of Individuals to Personal and Political Preferences, 1977 Convention Report*, August 1977, box 97, file 31, AFT Educational Issues Department Records, Walter P. Reuther Library, Wayne State University, Detroit.

27 Frank, *Out in the Union*, 86.

28 Frank, *Out in the Union*, 47.

29 The national response to Anita Bryant's "Save Our Children" campaign included a number of gay and lesbian teacher activists from San Francisco volunteering in Florida over the summer of 1977 to work in opposing the repeal campaign. This included Hank Wilson, who was one of the founders of the first LGBT teachers' groups in San Francisco, which will be discussed in chapter 4. See Frank, *Out in the Union*, 88.

30 Kahlenberg, *Tough Liberal*, 207; Faderman, *Gay Revolution*, 336–354.

31 Frank, *Out in the Union*, 88–89.

32 See Blount, *Fit to Teach*, 131–136, 133 fn. 98.

33 It may be the case that the AFT did respond to Bryant's campaign with the 1977 resolution, but because there is no record of the motivations of the authors of the resolution or a verbatim transcript of the floor proceedings in the material reviewed for this study, it is impossible to do more than speculate about this possibility.

34 The actions of the state and local teachers' unions in California in response to the Briggs Initiative will be discussed in chapter 4.

35 See Blount, *Fit to Teach*, 143–145; Faderman, *Gay Revolution*, 366–393.

36 For examples of coverage of the Briggs Initiative by the national press, see Muriel Dobbin, "Teachers are Target," *Sun (1837–1991)* (Baltimore), May 30, 1978; Grace Lichtenstein, "Laws Aiding Homosexuals Face Rising Opposition around Nation," *New York Times (1923–current file)*, April 27, 1978; Mary McGrory, "In Calif., a Bid to Clear Schools of Homosexuals," *Boston Globe (1960–1986)*, June 7, 1978; Victor F. Zonana, "California Is Roiled by a New Initiative, Over Homosexuals," *Wall Street Journal (1923–current file)*, October 10, 1978.

37 American Federation of Teachers, *Resolution 6: Opposition to Briggs Initiative 1978 Convention Report*, August 1979, box 97, file 31, AFT Educational Issues Department Records, Walter P. Reuther Library, Wayne State University, Detroit.

38 For an analysis of the specific debates that occurred during the passage of the 1978 resolution, see Smith, "Organizing for Social Justice," 440–442.

39 AFT, *Proof of 1979 Convention Proceedings*, 207.

40 Smith, "Organizing for Social Justice," 322.

41 Smith, "Organizing for Social Justice," 175.

42 AFT, *Proof of 1979 Convention Proceedings*, 176.

43 AFT, *Resolution 9*.

44 AFT, *Proof of 1979 Convention Proceedings*, 177.

45 AFT, *Proof of 1979 Convention Proceedings*, 177, 180.

46 AFT, *Proof of 1979 Convention Proceedings*, 181.

47 AFT, *Proof of 1979 Convention Proceedings*, 182–183.

48 AFT, *Proof of 1979 Convention Proceedings*, 184.

49 AFT, *Proof of 1979 Convention Proceedings*, 190–191.

50 AFT, *Proof of 1979 Convention Proceedings*, 193–203.

51 AFT, *Proof of 1979 Convention Proceedings*, 207–208.

Notes to Pages 80–85 • 195

52 American Federation of Teachers, *1979 Convention Promotional Materials*, 1979, AFT President's Office, Albert Shanker Records, box 10, file "Convention 1979 1 of 2," Walter P. Reuther Library, Wayne State University, Detroit.

53 American Federation of Teachers, *Job Discrimination Resolution, 1979 Convention Report*, August 1979, box 97, file 31, AFT Educational Issues Department Records, Walter P. Reuther Library, Wayne State University, Detroit.

54 As discussed in the first chapter of this study, the rise of teachers' unions throughout the 1970s, coupled with the decline of private sector unions, made teachers' unions particularly visible. For the reasons behind, and political impact of, this greater visibility, see Shelton, *Teacher Strike!*

55 Fejes's work is a notable examination of the initiatives in question and the campaigns both for and against them. It is particularly strong in its review of periodicals and news media. There is a significant oversight in this work, however, that may be the cause of Fejes's neglect of the agency of LGB teachers or even their straight teacher allies in his narrative. Despite his work being published in 2008, Fejes does not cite the relevant literature on LGBT teachers; Blount (2000, 2006), Graves (2007), and Harbeck (1997). Moreover, his focus almost explicitly on published media to the exclusion of other primary sources makes finding the voices and actions of teachers in his narrative difficult. Fred Fejes, *Gay Rights and Moral Panic: The Origins of America's Debate on Homosexuality* (New York: Palgrave Macmillan, 2008).

56 AFT, *Job Discrimination Resolution, 1979.*

57 Faderman, *Gay Revolution*, 564–580.

58 Biegel, *Right to Be Out*, 226.

59 Joshua Dressler, "Gay Teachers: A Disesteemed Minority in an Overly Esteemed Profession," *Rutgers Camden Law Journal* 9, no. 3 (1978): 399, 405–415, 438–440.

60 Joshua Dressler, interview by author regarding early legal scholarship on LGBT teachers, March 23, 2015, recording, author's collection.

61 Richard S. Amato, "Letter to UFT Vice President George Altomare re: GAA Displeasure with UFT 'Silence,'" May 26, 1971, United Federation of Teachers Records, box 120, file 13, Gay Teachers Association, Tamiment Library and Robert F. Wagner Labor Archives, New York University, New York.

62 For example, see the NGTF letter to the AFT notifying Shanker of Oklahoma State Teacher's union Complacency: Jean O'Leary and Bruce Voeller, "Letter to Albert Shanker re: Opposition to the Briggs Initiative," April 7, 1978, AFT President's Office, Albert Shanker Records, box 87, file 19, NGLTF, Walter P. Reuther Library, Wayne State University, Detroit.

63 Jean O'Leary and Bruce Voeller, "Letter to Albert Shanker re: Helm's Bill and OK State Teachers' Unions," March 31, 1978, AFT President's Office, Albert Shanker Records, box 87, file 19, NGLTF, Walter P. Reuther Library, Wayne State University, Detroit.

64 Harry Culver, "Unions Neutral on Gay Bill," *Oklahoma Journal*, February 9, 1978; Clifford Rosky, "Anti-Gay Curriculum Laws," *Columbia Law Review* 11, no. 6, https://columbialawreview.org/content/anti-gay-curriculum-laws/.

65 Harbeck, *Coming Out*, 129–130 fn. 29–31; Blount, *Fit to Teach*, 159–160.

66 O'Leary and Voeller, "Helm's Bill."

67 Culver, "Unions Neutral on Gay Bill."

196 • Notes to Pages 85–92

68 C. F. Bryden and Lucia Valesk, "Letter Requesting Join Action against Helm Law," February 9, 1981, AFT President's Office, Albert Shanker Records, box 87, file 19, NGLTF, Walter P. Reuther Library, Wayne State University, Detroit.

69 For a detailed account of the litigation against the Helm's law, see Joyce Murdoch and Deb Price, *Courting Justice: Gay Men and Lesbians v. the Supreme Court* (New York: Basic Books, 2002), 253–260.

70 Neither the appellate court nor the Supreme Court saw any legal issue with the firing of teachers for being homosexual. So while the NGTF's victory saw the portion of the Helm's bill that allowed for termination due to advocating homosexuality, the court case did not rule the entire law unconstitutional. See "Board of Ed. v. National Gay Task Force, 470 U.S. 903 (1985)," March 12, 2018, https://supreme.justia.com/cases/federal/us/470/903/; "Nat. Gay Task Force v. BD. of Educ. of City etc., 729 F.2d 1270 (1984) | 2d127011796," March 12, 2018, https://www.leagle.com/decision/19841999729f2d127011796.

71 Blount, *Fit to Teach*, 159–160.

72 Larry Gold, "Memo from Larry Gold to Albert Shanker RE: AFL-CIO Amicus Curiae Brief in Oklahoma City Board of Education v. NGTF," December 5, 1984, AFT President's Office, Albert Shanker Records, box 87, file 19, NGLTF, Walter P. Reuther Library, Wayne State University, Detroit.

73 Lawrence Poltrock, "Letter to Mr. Simms/ACLU re: Filing Amicus Curiae Brief in Oklahoma City Board of Education v. NGTF," December 26, 1984, AFT President's Office, Albert Shanker Records, box 87, file 19, NGLTF, Walter P. Reuther Library, Wayne State University, Detroit.

74 "Draft Document Regarding AFT Response to Oklahoma City Board of Education v. NGTF," December 1984, AFT President's Office, Albert Shanker Records, box 87, file 19, NGLTF, Walter P. Reuther Library, Wayne State University, Detroit.

75 "Draft Document Regarding AFT Response."

76 "Draft Document Regarding AFT Response."

77 Blount, *Fit to Teach*, 123–124; Harbeck, *Coming Out*, 243.

78 Philip Hager, "Justices Affirm Ruling Upholding Gay Teachers' Rights," *Los Angeles Times*, March 27, 1985.

79 *National Gay Task Force v. Board of Education of the City of Oklahoma City, Oklahoma*, U.S. 470 U.S. 903 (1985).

80 Murphy, *Blackboard Unions*, 196–200. For a comparison to the NEA, see Michael John Schultz, *The National Education Association and the Black Teacher: The Integration of a Professional Organization* (Coral Gables, FL: University of Miami Press, 1970).

81 Murdoch and Price, *Courting Justice*, 253.

Chapter 3   The Gay Teachers Association of New York

Epigraph: Marc Rubin, "History of the Gay Teachers Association," *Gay Teachers Association Newsletter* 1, no. 1 (January 1, 1978): 3, NYPL LGB Periodicals Collection, box 147, New York Public Library Manuscript Division.

1 Portions of this chapter have previously been published in *Teachers College Record* and are used with permission. See Jason Mayernick, "The Gay Teachers Association of NYC and LGB Students: 1974–1985," *Teachers College Record* 122, no. 9 (2020): 1–30.

Notes to Pages 93–97 • 197

2 Mayernick, "Gay Teachers Association."

3 The GTA of New York City (hereafter GTA of NYC) changed its name in the late 1980s to the Lesbian and Gay Teachers Association as a reflection of shifting nomenclature in the broader LGBT community. This name shift seems to have occurred between 1990 and 1991. See Lesbian and Gay Teachers Association, *LGTA Newsletter* 14, no. 4 (June 1991), *ONE* Subject Files Collection, box 3, file "GTA," *ONE* National Gay and Lesbian Archives, Los Angeles.

4 Neil Miller, "Out of the Classroom Closet," *Boston Phoenix*, November 11, 1979, 4–5, *ONE* Subject Files Collection, box 3, file "GTA," *ONE* National Gay and Lesbian Archives, Los Angeles.

5 Audacity in the face of the New Right, "moral majority," and Christian Right is a defining characteristic of gay and lesbian activism in the 1970s and early 1980s. Marc Stein notes the challenges of LGB activism between 1973 and 1981, saying, "In this context, there were significant setbacks for gay and lesbian activism, but the movement's accomplishments in these years are notable in part because they occurred in such difficult circumstances." It should be noted that the initial organization of groups of LGB teachers took place in the context of what Stein titles "The Era of Conservative Backlash," illustrating that LGB teachers' groups achieved their goal in the context of conservatives rallying nationally against LGB people. Marc Stein, *Rethinking the Gay and Lesbian Movement* (New York: Routledge, 2012), 3.

6 The arguments of conservatives regarding the presence of LGB teachers in K-12 classrooms is discussed in detail in chapter 4.

7 Which was the stance that the vast majority of Christian denominations took in the 1970s and 1980s, to the extent that LGBT Christians in many cases founded their own denominations and splinter groups within larger organizations to lobby for change. For a history of one such denomination, the Metropolitan Community Church, and its impact, see Downs, *Stand by Me*, chap. 2.

8 This is of course a generalization, but it is a useful despite the obvious exceptions that occur.

9 For GTA newsletter, see *Gay Teachers Association Newsletter*, NYPL LGB Periodicals Collection, box 147—Melbourne 3, no. 3: 3; New South Wales 4, no. 2: 4; London 3, no. 2: 4/3, no. 7/8: 3; West Berlin 2, no. 7/8: 3, New York Public Library Manuscript Division.

10 Out of these seven groups, only one, the Maryland group, did not occur in an urban area. Instead, the Maryland group was centered on suburban Howard County, which is equidistant between Washington, DC, and Baltimore. See Gay Teachers of Maryland, *Gay Teachers of Maryland Newsletter* 3, no. I. (1981), 1–4, Human Sexuality Collection, file "Gay Teachers of Maryland Newsletter," Cornell University Archives, Ithaca.

11 For discussions of the connections between LGBT people, particularly gay men, and cities, see Robert Aldrich, "Homosexuality and the City: An Historical Overview," *Urban Studies* 41, no. 9 (2004): 1719–1737; Kathy Weston, "Get Thee to a Big City: Sexual Imaginary and the Great Gay Migration," *GLQ: A Journal of Lesbian and Gay Studies* 2, no. 3 (January 1, 1995): 253–277. For a focus on lesbians in a smaller American city, see Elizabeth Kennedy and Madeline Davis, *Boots of Leather, Slippers of Gold: The History of a Lesbian Community* (New York: Penguin Books, 1994).

198 • Notes to Pages 98–100

12 This is of course not a suggestion that urban Americans did not react to deviant behavior—they did and often violently—but rather that the amount of deviance required to provoke a widespread reaction was significantly greater than in other settings. Likewise, I am not claiming that all American cities were liberal in their social mores: Chattanooga was not Los Angeles. I am saying that they were liberal in comparison to the local alternatives; the opportunities for anonymity and even tolerance in southern cities was far greater than in the small towns that surrounded it. For a discussion of this aspect of regionally important urban areas in the American South, see Howard, *Men Like That*.

13 Chicago Gay Teachers Association, *Gay Teachers News* I, no. I.1 (Winter 1973): 3, LGB Periodicals Collection, box 147, New York Public Library Manuscript Division.

14 There is one article in the *Chicago Gay Crusader* referencing the Chicago GTA marching in the 1973 Pride Parade, *Chicago Gay Crusader* I, no. I.1 (May 1973): 1, William B. Kelley papers, Gerber/Hart Library and Archives, Chicago.

15 Chicago Gay Teachers Association, *Gay Teachers News*, 2; NYPL LGB Periodicals Collection, box 147, New York Public Library Manuscript Division.

16 Tracy Baim, *Out and Proud in Chicago: An Overview of the City's Gay Community* (Evanston, IL: Agate, 2009), 199. Baim claims that there was a gay teachers' group founded in Chicago in 1969 but does not provide a source for this information for the purposes of further research. Baim also does not cite the existence of the 1972–1974 Chicago Gay Teachers Association, which may or may not be distinct from the earlier group.

17 For a comprehensive treatment of the political development of the LGBT community in Chicago, see Timothy Stewart-Winter, *Queer Clout: Chicago and the Rise of Gay Politics* (Philadelphia: University of Pennsylvania Press, 2016).

18 Chicago Gay Teachers Association, *Gay Teachers News*, 2.

19 As we will continue to see throughout this study, debunking the recruitment myth was a universal concern for LGBT teachers' groups precisely because it was among the most common accusations leveled against LGBT people and because LGBT teachers were in close proximity with young people. For a discussion of the impact of this myth, see Fejes, *Gay Rights*.

20 Chicago Gay Teachers Association, *Gay Teachers News*, 2.

21 George Chauncey, *Gay New York: Gender, Urban Culture, and the Making of the Gay Male World, 1890–1940* (New York: Basic Books, 1995), 277.

22 Chauncey, *Gay New York*, 226, 227–230, 349–350.

23 See Charles Kaiser, *The Gay Metropolis: The Landmark History of Gay Life in America* (New York: Grove, 2007); Bérubé, *Coming Out Under Fire*.

24 Faderman, *Odd Girls*, 149; Martin Meeker, *Contacts Desired: Gay and Lesbian Communications and Community, 1940s–1970s* (Chicago: University of Chicago Press, 2006), 83.

25 For a discussion of the political activities of the Daughters of Bilitis in various American cities, including New York, see Marcia M. Gallo, *Different Daughters: A History of the Daughters of Bilitis and the Rise of the Lesbian Rights Movement* (New York: Carroll & Graf, 2006), 150, 213.

26 For a first-person account of the Stonewall riots told from multiple perspectives, see Duberman, *Stonewall*.

Notes to Pages 100–104 • 199

27 Note for a discussion of the broad impact of labor on culture in New York City, see Joshua B. Freeman, *Working-Class New York: Life and Labor since World War II* (New York: New Press, 2000).

28 Taylor, *Reds at the Blackboard*, 42, 36–37.

29 Clarence Taylor claims that the appeal of the UFT, and its direct precursor, the Teachers Guild, lay in the fact that they did not tackle broad social issues but instead focused narrowly on the issues that concerned teachers as professionals. The UFT was born out of this appeal to an apolitical advancement of teachers' issues by merging the Teachers Guild with the High School Teachers Association. See Taylor, *Reds at the Blackboard*, 296–299.

30 The importance of the New York City local, the UFT, to the AFT as a whole is difficult to overstate. In effect, the New Yorkers became the single largest power block in the AFT and as such set/approved the national agenda, and UFT support became crucial for anyone seeking national office in the AFT. Outvoting the UFT required coalitions of other large locals acting in conjunction; the complexity of such coalitions and their political cost likely explains their rarity particularly after Al Shanker became AFT president in 1974. This relationship and its impact is discussed in chapter 2, which details LGBT activism in the AFT.

31 Murphy, *Blackboard Unions*, 215–217, 277.

32 For an exhaustive discussion of the role that other unions played in supporting the UFT see David Selden, *The Teacher Rebellion* (Washington, DC: Howard University Press, 1985). This work is autobiographical and written by a former AFT president and, as a whole, details the evolution of the AFT from the 1950s to the 1970s. It is one of the only memoirs detailing the inner working of the AFT and UFT, the role that labor played in supporting the AFT, and the impact labor politics had on the leadership of the AFT. The NEA is recounted in a similar fashion in Cameron, *Inside Story*, which illustrates the inner workings of the NEA during the same period and is also an autobiographical account by a union "insider."

33 Jerald Podair, *The Strike That Changed New York: Blacks, Whites, and the Ocean Hill-Brownsville Crisis* (New Haven, CT: Yale University Press, 2004), 14–15, 165–166, 206–207.

34 Perrillo, *Uncivil Rights*, 124.

35 Podair, *Strike*, 62.

36 Perrillo, *Uncivil Rights*, 126–127.

37 Daniel H. Perlstein, *Justice, Justice: School Politics and the Eclipse of Liberalism* (New York: Peter Lang, 2004), 7.

38 Perlstein, *Justice, Justice*, 125.

39 Podair, *Strike*, 116–117.

40 When I use the designation "core leadership," I am not speaking of official positions; the only official positions in the GTA were cochairs/co-spokespersons who served as public spokespersons. The GTA itself was remarkably egalitarian in its lack of formal organization. Instead, I am referring to the individuals who appeared in the newsletter as organizers and authors over and over, taking on unofficial leadership roles and, perhaps more tellingly, allowing their names to appear in print.

41 Though of course this is a generalization; Marc Rubin came out publicly as a gay teacher after many years as a professional educator.

200 • Notes to Pages 104–108

42 Meryl Friedman, interview by author regarding LGBT teacher activism in New York City, August 29, 2016, recording, author's collection; Rubin, "History," 3.

43 Blount, *Fit to Teach*, 124; Gene Maeroff, "Homosexuals Declare Right to Teach; Assert Sexual Orientation Is Irrelevant: Students Not Told Preferences Already Set," *New York Times*, May 20, 1974; Rubin, "History," 2–3.

44 Rubin, "History," 2.

45 Already experienced in 1974, having accompanied Al Shanker as an aide during the Ocean Hill/Brownsville conflict six years earlier, Sandra Feldman would go on to a long career within the UFT and eventually rise to be president of both the UFT and the national AFT from 1997 to 2004. While it is difficult to speculate about the impact of her early negotiations with the GTA on her leadership it is clear that she was an early and ardent ally of the LGBT community and LGBT teachers in particular. See Joseph Berger, "Sandra Feldman, Scrappy and Outspoken Labor Leader for Teachers, Dies at 65," *New York Times*, September 20, 2005, https://www.nytimes.com/2005/09/20/nyregion/sandra-feldman-scrappy -and-outspoken-labor-leader-for-teachers.html.

46 For a discussion of Shanker and his impact on American education as a whole, see Kahlenberg, *Tough Liberal*.

47 Note this account is contained in Marc Rubin's recounting of the history of the GTA. Rubin, "History," 2.

48 Marc Rubin and Meryl Friedman, "Letter from GTA to NYSUT re: Refusal to Run Advertisements 4/11/76," April 11, 1976, Lesbian and Gay Teachers Association of New York (hereafter LGTA of NY) Collection, box 2, file 147, LGBT Community Center National Archives, New York.

49 GTA of NYC, "UFT Ducks Confrontation with Gay Teachers," April 14, 1976, LGTA of NY Collection, box 2, file 147, LGBT Community Center National Archives, New York.

50 Albert Shanker, "Letter from Albert Shanker to Meryl Friedman re: UFT Resolution on Homosexual Teachers," October 6, 1976, LGTA of NY Collection, box 2, file 147, LGBT Community Center National Archives, New York.

51 Frank Arricale, "Letter from Frank Arricale to Meryl Friedman re: BOE Stance on Homosexual Teachers," January 24, 1975, LGTA of NY Collection, box 2, file 147, LGBT Community Center National Archives, New York.

52 Frank Machiarolla, "Letter from NYPS Chancellor Machiarolla to Mayor Koch: Copy," November 8, 1978, LGTA of NY Collection, box 2, file "Support Statement—Teachers," LGBT Community Center National Archives, New York.

53 Shanker, "Albert Shanker to Meryl Friedman."

54 Meryl Friedman and Marc Rubin, "Letter from GTA to City Council Members Introducing GTA," March 6, 1975, LGTA of NY Collection, box 5, file 151, LGBT Community Center National Archives, New York.

55 Rubin, "History," 2.

56 Friedman, interview.

57 Rubin, "History," 2; Blount, *Fit to Teach*, 123–125.

58 Craig Loftin details the correspondence of gay male teachers to *ONE* magazine evidencing their awareness of both the persecution they personally faced as gay teachers and the widespread nature of that persecution in the 1950s and 1960s decades before LGB teachers organized professionally. Loftin, *Masked Voices*, chap. 6.

Notes to Pages 109–111 • 201

59 "The Pleasures and Politics of Being Out," *Gay Teachers Association Newsletter* 2, no. 4 (April 1, 1978), NYPL LGB Periodicals Collection, box 147, New York Public Library Manuscript Division.

60 Peter Friedburg, "New York's Gay and Lesbian Teachers and Youth," *Advocate* (August 4, 1983), *ONE* Subject Files Collection, box 3, file "Teachers," *ONE* National Gay and Lesbian Archives, Los Angeles.

61 GTA of NYC, "A Bill of Rights for Gay Teachers and Students," LGTA of NYC Collection, box 1, file 2, LGBT Community Center National Archives, New York.

62 Thomas Hobart, "Letter from NYSUT Informing GTA of Passage of Resolution Affirming Right of Homosexuals to Union Protections," September 7, 1976; Albert Shanker, "Letter from UFT to GTA re: Resolution on Rights of Homosexual Teachers," October 6, 1976. Both letters are from LGTA of NYC Collection, box 2, file 90, LGBT Community Center National Archives, New York.

63 Frank Arrincale, "Letter re: BOE Stance on Homosexuality and Teaching 1/24/75," *Gay Teachers Association Newsletter* 1, no. 2 (February 1, 1978): 1, NYPL LGB Periodicals Collection, box 2, file 90, New York Public Library Manuscript Division.

64 Meryl Friedman, "Moving Right Along," *Gay Teachers Association Newsletter* 1, no. 2 (February 1, 1978): 1, NYPL LGB Periodicals Collection, box 147, New York Public Library Manuscript Division.

65 For example, in the case of teacher Sallie Hernon, the GTA and the New York Civil Liberties Union worked with the UFT to see Hernon rehired after her termination in October 1976 due to discussing homosexuality in a class she was teaching. GTA of NYC, "Press Release RE: Reinstatement of Sallie Hernon 5/19/78," LGTA of NYC Collection, box 2, file 176, LGBT Community Center National Archives, New York.

66 See, respectively, GTA of NYC, "Come Celebrate Gay Pride/End of Term" (flyer), LGTA of NYC Collection, box 2, file 146, LGBT Community Center National Archives, New York; GTA of NYC, "Nothing to Do on Sunday?" (flyer), LGTA of NYC Collection, box 2, file 146, LGBT Community Center National Archives, New York; GTA of NYC, "GTA Square Dance" (flyer), Marc Rubin Collection, box 1, file "GTA," LGBT Community Center National Archives, New York.

67 GTA of NYC, "Dance at the Eagle" (flyer), LGTA of NYC Collection, box 2, file 147, LGBT Community Center National Archives, New York.

68 Friedman, interview.

69 The most recent and comprehensive treatment of the creation of safe and specifically urban spaces by and for the LGBT community in the 1970s is Hanhardt's *Safe Space: Gay Neighborhood History and the Politics of Violence.* Hanhardt focuses on the shifting politics of LGBT neighborhood groups and the relationship of their actions to concepts of race and gay space. LGBT neighborhoods were conceived as distinct spaces by LGBT activists and in light of perennial violence against LGBT people by the 1970s some groups eventually formed armed neighborhood patrols. For the purposes of this study, it is important to note that both New York and San Francisco are discussed in depth by Hanhardt and in both cities she illustrates that fears of violence and the ensuing mobilization by the LGBT community had distinct racial and class-based elements. See Christina B. Hanhardt, *Safe Space: Gay Neighborhood History and the Politics of Violence* (Durham, NC: Duke University Press Books, 2013).

202 • Notes to Pages 112–115

70 For a legal analysis of the conditions faced by LGB teachers nationally in the late 1970s, as understood at the time, and the first treatment of gay and lesbian teachers in an academic journal, see Dressler, "Gay Teachers," 399.

71 "Gay Teacher Sues in Texas," *Gay Teachers Association Newsletter* 3, no. 1 (January 1, 1980): 1, NYPL LGB Periodicals Collection, box 147, New York Public Library Manuscript Division; "News from Our Friends: John Gish," *Gay Teachers Association Newsletter* 1, no. 6 (June 1, 1978): 4, NYPL LGB Periodicals Collection, box 147, New York Public Library Manuscript Division.

72 "Teachers Freedom of Speech Upheld in New Jersey," *Gay Teachers Association Newsletter* 4, no. 7/8 (September/October 1, 1981), NYPL LGB Periodicals Collection, box 147, New York Public Library Manuscript Division. Gish's case was appealed to and denied consideration by the Supreme Court. See Murdoch and Price, *Courting Justice*, 241–243.

73 For initial appearance of these groups in the GTA newsletter see *Gay Teachers Association Newsletter*, NYPL LGB Periodicals Collection, box 147, New York Public Library Manuscript Division—Los Angeles 1, no. 1: 4; San Francisco 1, no. 1: 4; Massachusetts 1, no. 7/8: 4; Maryland 1, no. 10: 4; Denver 2, no. 2: 4; Boston 2, no. 2: 4; Portland, Oregon 1, no. 10; Melbourne 3, no. 3: 3; New South Wales 4, no. 2: 4; London 3, no. 2: 4/3, no. 7/8: 3; West Berlin 2, no. 7/8: 3.

74 Joseph Russo, "Dick and Jane Revisited," *Gay Teachers Association Newsletter* 1, no. 10 (December 1, 1978): 3, NYPL LGB Periodicals Collection, box 147, New York Public Library Manuscript Division.

75 Pat Griffin described this tension as existing between "public accusation v. wish for personal integrity." Pat Griffin, "From Hiding to Coming Out, Empowering Lesbian and Gay Educators," in Harbeck, *Coming Out*, 167–196.

76 For a discussion of these LGBT youth groups in the early 1970s, see Stephan Cohen, *The Gay Liberation Youth Movement in New York: An Army of Lovers Cannot Fail* (New York: Routledge, 2007), chap. 4. Cohen points out that one of the goals of Gay Youth was to include youth as "full-fledged independent actors" in the gay liberation movement (p. 43). This demand for recognition as equals was revolutionary and a rejection of both the age hierarchy but also the student–teacher hierarchy that in many ways serves as the bedrock of American education. It is unclear whether members of the GTA had any reaction to this stance. Cohen mentions the GTA only briefly (pp. 184–185) to make the claim that teachers "followed the lead of the GAA and students" and to note that the founding documents of the GTA stated a commitment to the needs of gay students. Cohen's claim that teachers followed the GAA and gay students is perhaps an overreach, but overall his research on LGBT youth groups in the early 1970s provides concrete evidence that LGB teachers had examples of out and empowered LGBT youth on which to base their optimism about the future.

77 "Gay Teachers Speak at NCTE Conference in NYC," *Gay Teachers Association Newsletter* 1, no. 1 (January 1, 1978): 4, NYPL LGB Periodicals Collection, box 147, New York Public Library Manuscript Division.

78 For early examinations of the impact of the "recruitment myth" on lesbian teachers see Sherry Wood and Karen M. Harbeck, "Living in Two Worlds: The Identity Management Strategies Utilized by Lesbian Educators," in Harbeck, *Coming Out*, 141. For gay male teachers, see Eric E. Rofes, *Socrates, Plato, and*

Guys Like Me: Confessions of a Gay Schoolteacher (Boston, MA: Alyson Books, 1985).

79 John Zogby, "Being a Gay Teenager Is Not Always Gay," *Gay Teachers Association Newsletter* 1, no. 3 (March 1, 1978): 2, NYPL LGB Periodicals Collection, box 147, New York Public Library Manuscript Division.

80 *Gay Teachers Association Newsletter* 1, no. 3/4 (March/April, 1978): 4, NYPL LGB Periodicals Collection, box 147, New York Public Library Manuscript Division.

81 Lugg, *US Public Schools*, 49–54.

82 Lugg, *US Public Schools*, 53.

83 This is not an exhaustive list of the committees or activities of the GTA regarding LGB students. The formal committees of the GTA varied between 1974 and 1985, but the overarching goals of the organization remained constant. For example, the first explicit mention of the Student Services Committee is found in the February 1982 edition of the GTA newsletter, but similar efforts are apparent throughout the newsletter during the preceding five years.

84 GTA of NYC, "Letter to Mayor Koch re: Passage of Executive Order, 2/15/1978" n.d., LGTA of NYC Collection, box 5, file 142, LGBT Community Center National Archives, New York.

85 Leonard Buder, "Champion of School Discipline: Howard Lawrence Hurwitz," *New York Times*, March 26, 1976.

86 Max H. Seigel, "Principal Draws a Court Penalty: To Be Confined for Resisting Ethnic Survey in School," *New York Times*, June 24, 1976; Leonard Buder, "Examiner Assails Principal Who Ousted Girl Student and Proposes $3,500 Fine," *New York Times*, August 20, 1976.

87 "Sandy Gold and Marc Rubin on Jeanne Parr Show," *Gay Teachers Association Newsletter* 1, no. 3 (January 1, 1978): 4, NYPL LGB Periodicals Collection, box 147, New York Public Library Manuscript Division.

88 Meryl Friedman, "Letter from GTA to Mark Markowitz re: Howard Hurwitz Board of Regents Appointment," March 1980, LGTA of NYC Collection, box 2, file 147, LGBT Community Center National Archives, New York.

89 Martin Connor, "Letter from State Senator Martin Connor to Meryl Friedman re: Resolution of Hurwitz Candidacy," March 19, 1980, LGTA of NYC Collection, box 2, file 147, LGBT Community Center National Archives, New York.

90 *Gay Teachers Association Newsletter* 2, no. 3 (March 1, 1979): 6, NYPL LGB Periodicals Collection, box 147, New York Public Library Manuscript Division.

91 For example, GTA cochair Marc Rubin debated Rev. Kenneth Jadoff, the assistant director of communication for the Archdiocese of New York on local radio. "Radio Schedule," *New York Times*, December 2, 1978, 47.

92 "GTA Committee Reports," *Gay Teachers Association Newsletter* 1, no. 4 (April 1, 1978): 3, NYPL LGB Periodicals Collection, box 147, New York Public Library Manuscript Division.

93 Friedman, interview.

94 Hechinger and Hechinger, "The Truth about Homosexual Teachers," *McCall's* 105, no. 6 (March 1978).

95 GTA of NYC, "Speakers Bureau Survey; 1981," n.d., LGTA of NYC Collection, box 1, file 8, LGBT Community Center National Archives, New York.

96 GTA of NYC, "Gay and Lesbian Students" (flyer), 1982, *ONE* Subject File Collection, box 3, file "GTA," *ONE* National Gay and Lesbian Archives, Los Angeles.

97 GTA of NYC, "Bill of Rights for Gay Teachers and Students" (flyer), 1976, *ONE* Subject File Collection, box 3, file "GTA," *ONE* National Gay and Lesbian Archives, Los Angeles.

98 David Zucker, "For Education about AIDS," *Gay Teachers Association Newsletter* 6, no. 1 (January 1, 1983): 1, NYPL LGB Periodicals Collection, box 147, New York Public Library Manuscript Division.

99 GTA of NYC, "AIDS Awareness at Teachers College" (flyer), *ONE* Subject File Collection, box 3, file "GTA," *ONE* National Gay and Lesbian Archives, Los Angeles.

100 GTA of NYC, "Joseph E. Zogby Memorial" (flyer), October 1984, Marc Rubin Collection, Box 8, LGBT Community Center National Archives, New York.

101 "Scholarship Announcement," *Gay Teachers Association Newsletter* 8, no. 3 (March 1, 1985): 1, NYPL LGB Periodicals Collection, box 147, New York Public Library Manuscript Division; GTA of NYC, "Essay Contest, Joseph E. Zogby Scholarship, 1987" (flyer), LGTA of NYC Collection, box 2, file 65, LGBT Community Center National Archives, New York.

102 Graves, *And They Were Wonderful Teachers*, xvii.

103 "Briggs Initiative Update," *Gay Teachers Association Newsletter* 1, no. 9 (November,1978): 1, NYPL LGB Periodicals Collection, box 147, New York Public Library Manuscript Division.

104 The GTA was extremely concerned with the election of Reagan and organized an educational seminar about "surviving in the Reagan years."

105 "NEA and AFT Vote to Oppose Briggs Initiative," *Gay Teachers Association Newsletter* 1, no. 7/8 (November 1978): 3, NYPL LGB Periodicals Collection, box 147, New York Public Library Manuscript Division.

Chapter 4   California and the Image of LGB Teachers

Epigraph: Norman McClelland, interview by author regarding Gay Teachers of Los Angeles, May 18, 2017, recording, author's collection.

1 The sodomy law was not repealed as such but, instead, amended to not include consenting adults defined legally as being at least eighteen years old. See "Statutes and Amendments to the Codes of California 1975," 131, chap. 71, enacted May 12, 1975, https://clerk.assembly.ca.gov/content/statutes-and-amendments-codes-1975; Gallo, *Different Daughters*, 192.

2 *California Voters Pamphlet: 1978* (California Secretary of State, 1978, 28–32), http://library.uchastings.edu/ballot_pdf/1978g.pdf.

3 There is extensive coverage of Briggs's political ambitions and unsuccessful run for governor, particularly in the *Los Angeles Times*. See Grover Sales, "Anita, John: Thunder on the Right," *Los Angeles Times (1923–current file)*, December 4, 1977; Bud Lembke, "Briggs: Out of the Race but Still Running: Senator Will Return to Fray in Support of 2 Initiatives" and "Briggs: Out of the Race but Still Running: Sen. Briggs Is Still Running," *Los Angeles Times (1923–current file)*, May 21, 1978, Orange County; Tracy Wood and Craig Turner, "John Briggs—the Controversial

Notes to Pages 128–133 • 205

Crusader: Tax Probe Touches Senator as He Launches Another Campaign," *Los Angeles Times (1923–current file)*, March 2, 1979.

4 The debate over homosexuality in America's schools fits neatly into the category of religious debate that historian of education John Zimmerman describes as perennial and without a readily discernable compromise that would allow for opposing parties to reach a mutually agreeable end to the conflict. Zimmerman discusses religious education in schools, prayer in schools, and sex education, respectively chapters 6, 7, and 8, as arenas that were, and remain, flashpoints of the so-called culture-wars. See Jonathan Zimmerman, *Whose America? Culture Wars in the Public Schools* (Cambridge, MA: Harvard University Press, 2002).

5 Bureau of the Census, *Historical Statistics of the United States Colonial Times to 1970* (Washington, DC: U.S. Department of Commerce, 1976), A 9–28, A 195–209.

6 Bureau of the Census, *1980 Census of Population and Housing* (Washington, DC: U.S. Department of Commerce, 1983), Table 56.

7 United States, *1980 Census*, 1–14 f. 14.

8 United States, *1980 Census*, 1–16.

9 Bureau of the Census, *Asian Pacific Islander Population in the United States: 1980* (Washington, DC: U.S. Department of Commerce, 1983), Table 2.

10 The controversy of Reagan's policies nationally and his impact on California in particular are especially partisan, with conservatives lionizing his political achievements and liberals demonizing them. Neither Reagan's supporters nor opponents would argue that he was not effective or that his impact was not long lasting. For a conservative analysis of Reagan, see Steven Hayward, *The Age of Reagan: The Fall of the Old Liberal Order: 1964–1980* (New York: Crown Forum, 2009). For a liberal narrative dealing with the early 1960s and juxtaposing the rise of Reagan against the fall of Lyndon Johnson, see Jonathan Darman, *Landslide: LBJ and Ronald Reagan at the Dawn of a New America* (New York: Random House, 2015).

11 Bureau of the Census, *1950 Census of Population and Housing* (Washington, DC: U.S. Department of Commerce, 1953), 2, 5–51; Bureau of the Census, *1980 Census*, Table 56.

12 In 1980, the population of the San Francisco/Oakland metropolitan area was 3,250,630, or 13.7 percent of the state population, and the population of the Los Angeles Metropolitan Area stood at 7,477,503, or 31.5 percent of state population. In 1980, residents of these two metropolitan areas comprised 45.2 percent of California's total population and 49.6 percent of the state's urban population. See Bureau of the Census, *1980 Census*, Table 56.

13 Faderman, *Gay Revolution*, 367.

14 Harbeck, *Gay and Lesbian Educators*, 62.

15 Louis Sheldon, *Letter with Instruction for Distribution of Petitions*, California Defend Our Children, Fullerton, CA, 1978, 1–3, Briggs Initiative Collection, box 1, file 8, *ONE* National Gay and Lesbian Archives, Los Angeles.

16 John Briggs, *Letter with Instruction for Distribution of Petitions*, Office of Senator John V. Briggs, Sacramento, CA, 1978, Briggs Initiative Collection, box 1, file 8, *ONE* National Gay and Lesbian Archives, Los Angeles CA.

17 Louis Sheldon, *Letter re: Fundraising on Proposition 6*, Fulerton, CA, 1977, Briggs Initiative Collection, box 1, file 8, *ONE* National Gay and Lesbian Archives, Los Angeles; Blount, *Fit to Teach*, 149.

206 • Notes to Pages 133–136

18 Sheldon, *Fundraising on Proposition 6.*
19 Sheldon, *Fundraising on Proposition 6.*
20 California Defend Our Children, "Homosexuals Are Raising Millions to Defeat Us" (mailer) Fullerton, CA, 1978, Briggs Initiative Collection, box 1, file 8, *ONE* National Gay and Lesbian Archives, Los Angeles.
21 California Defend Our Children, "Save Our Children from Homosexuality in Our Schools" (mailer), Fullerton, CA, 1978, Briggs Initiative Collection, box 1, file 8, *ONE* National Gay and Lesbian Archives, Los Angeles.
22 The recentness of this scholarship is not atypical. The earliest works of LGB history were efforts by community members with historical context from the broadest perspective in the late 1970s; the earliest of these works was by Jonathan Ned Katz, *Gay American History: Lesbians and Gay Men in the U.S.A.* (New York: Avon Books, 1978). These works were followed by the efforts of professional historians to focus on particular parts of the LGB community, such as Estelle Freedman's work on women and nineteenth century sexuality, John D'Emilio's work on the origins of the gay community as a political force, and Lillian Faderman's research on female relationships and the premodern period. For examples of foundational works of LGBT history from this period, see John D'Emilio, *Making Trouble: Essays on Gay History, Politics, and the University* (New York: Routledge, 1992); Lillian Faderman, *Surpassing the Love of Men: Romantic Friendship and Love between Women from the Renaissance to the Present* (New York: William Morrow, 1981); Estelle B. Freedman, *The Lesbian Issue: Essays from Signs* (Chicago: University of Chicago Press, 1985); Estelle B. Freedman, "Sexuality in Nineteenth-Century America: Behavior, Ideology, and Politics," *Reviews in American History* 10, no. 4 (1982): 196–215; Estelle B. Freedman and John D'Emilio, "Problems Encountered in Writing the History of Sexuality: Sources, Theory and Interpretation," *Journal of Sex Research* 27, no. 4 (1990): 481–95.
23 For an exhaustive defense of this position, and an argument for why the progress of the LGB community in Los Angeles is a better exemplar for the experiences of LGB people in New York or San Francisco, see Moira Kenney, *Mapping Gay L.A.: The Intersection of Place and Politics* (Philadelphia: Temple University Press, 2001), chap. 1.
24 For discussions of the LGBT community of Los Angeles in the 1950s, 1960s, and 1970s, see Will Fellows and Helen P. Branson, *Gay Bar: The Fabulous, True Story of a Daring Woman and Her Boys in the 1950s* (Madison: University of Wisconsin Press, 2010); Daniel Hurewitz, *Bohemian Los Angeles and the Making of Modern Politics* (Berkeley: University of California Press, 2007); Eric C. Wat, *The Making of a Gay Asian Community: An Oral History of Pre-AIDS Los Angeles* (Lanham, MD: Rowman & Littlefield, 2002).
25 For example, Faderman and Timmons thoroughly examine the connections between class and gay and lesbian space in the early twentieth century, the impact of gossip journalism on gay and lesbians in the 1950s, and the waxing and waning of targeted police activity against gay men throughout the twentieth century. Lillian Faderman and Stuart Timmons, *Gay L.A.: A History of Sexual Outlaws, Power Politics, and Lipstick Lesbians* (New York: Basic Books, 2006).
26 For the backgrounds of these publications and their broader impact see Craig M. Loftin, ed., *Letters to One: Gay and Lesbian Voices from the 1950s and 1960s*

(Albany: State University of New York Press, 2012); Loftin, *Masked Voices*; Mark Thompson and Randy Shilts, *Long Road to Freedom: The Advocate History of the Gay and Lesbian Movement* (New York: St Martins Press, 1994).

27 For an examination of the role of gay men in Hollywood over the course of most of the twentieth century, particularly the use of gay actors in heterosexual roles and the secrecy surrounding their sexuality, see David Ehrenstein, *Open Secret: Gay Hollywood, 1928–1998* (New York: William Morrow, 1998). This double standard was the subject of a decades-long study by activist and scholar Vito Russo, which culminated in his book *The Celluloid Closet: Homosexuality in the Movies*, rev. ed. (New York: Harper & Row, 1987). Russo's activism and contributions to the LGBT rights movement and the Los Angeles gay community are further discussed in Michael R. Schiavi, *Celluloid Activist: The Life and Times of Vito Russo* (Madison: University of Wisconsin Press, 2011).

28 The LGB community, like any other intergenerational community, served as a source of connections to possible jobs and economic opportunities for its members and had all the complexities of race and class present in any other group. An example of this patronage, and the class dynamics it entailed, can be found in Helen Branson's memoirs describing her gay bar in the 1950s and its patrons being an informal employment agency. See Fellows and Branson, *Gay Bar*, 27.

29 McClelland, interview; Smith, "Organizing for Social Justice," 432.

30 Jerry Burns, "The Move to Ban Gay Teachers," *San Francisco Chronicle*, January 12, 1978, Briggs Initiative Collection, box 3, file 1, *ONE* National Gay and Lesbian Archives, Los Angeles.

31 McClelland, interview.

32 *California Voters Pamphlet: 1978.*

33 As mentioned in the first chapter detailing LGB teacher activism in the NEA, members of the UTLA belonged to both the NEA and the AFT.

34 McClelland, interview.

35 McClelland, interview; Blount, *Fit to Teach*, 129–131.

36 Smith, "Organizing for Social Justice," 433–436.

37 McClelland, interview; Blount, *Fit to Teach*, 151.

38 Robert Scheer, "A Times Interview with . . . : Sen. John Briggs on Homosexuality Briggs' Views on Homosexuality Incomplete Source," *Los Angeles Times (1923–current file)*, October 6, 1978, A4.

39 Peter Englander, interview by author regarding Gay Teachers of Los Angeles, June 6, 2017, recording, author's collection.

40 McClelland, interview.

41 McClelland, interview.

42 In his interview for this study, when questioned about the racial composition of the GTLA, Peter Englander responded, "Yes there were people there that were African American and Hispanic, some Asians, I can't remember anyone at that time with Armenian last names so there was some sort of representative mix in GTLA." Given this statement and the small size of the GLTA, eighteen or nineteen people, having even two to four people of color was a degree of racial diversity that should be noted. This diversity is not reflected in documentary sources on LGB teachers' groups, which seldom if ever noted the racial composition of their groups and is likely now only accessible via oral history. Englander, interview; Smith, "Organizing for Social Justice," 432.

208 • Notes to Pages 139–142

43 The political constraints placed on K-12 teachers who are also people of color is an area of history that has been examined primarily in the context of the American South. For examples of this occurring in the South in the context of desegregation, see David S. Cecelski, *Along Freedom Road: Hyde County, North Carolina and the Fate of Black Schools in the South* (Chapel Hill: University of North Carolina Press, 1994). Examples of the impact of race on the political and labor activity by teachers can also be found in Podair's research on the Ocean Hill–Brownsville crisis of the late 1960s in New York City. Podair, *Strike.*

44 Englander, interview.

45 McClelland, interview.

46 Faderman, *Gay Revolution*, 383–384.

47 Faderman and Timmons, *Gay L.A.*, chap. 3.

48 Susan Littwin, *The Gay Political Elite, July 1979*, Los Angeles, CA, 169–173, LGTA of NY Collection, box 7, file "Gay Liberation," LGBT Community Center National Archives, New York.

49 Englander, interview; McClelland, interview.

50 As of the writing of this study, two members of the GTLA continue to meet once a month for dinner as part of a standing engagement that has lasted since the late 1970s. After the GTLA membership shifted into the suburbs, the archival evidence of the group's continued existence dwindles and so it is unclear how long the latter incarnation of the GTLA existed.

51 For example, Hank Wilson began his activism protesting the Vietnam War outside high schools in his hometown of Sacramento before moving to San Francisco and beginning his teaching career. Hank Wilson, interview by Miriam Frank, Part 1, April 12, 1995, Out in the Union: Gays and Lesbians in the Labor Movement, recording, Miriam Frank Oral History Collection, Tamiment Library and Robert F. Wagner Labor Archive, New York; "A Gay Activist Campaign," *Washington Post (1974–current file)*, April 8, 1977, STYLE People/Entertainment/Gardens.

52 David Lamble, "10th Anniversary; Gay Teachers Struggle for Right to Teach, Take on the City's School Board," *Coming Up!* 6, no. 9e (June 1985), Lesbian School Workers Collection, box 1, file 1, June Mazer Lesbian Collection, Los Angeles.

53 For the purposes of simplicity, this chapter will use GTSWC.

54 The name change occurred between late 1976 and the summer of 1977, but beyond this range the exact date is unclear. The earliest appearance of the new name can be found in the first issue of the GTSWC newsletter. See Gay Teachers and School Workers Coalition, *GTSWC Newsletter* 1, no. 1 (August/September 1977): 2–3, Lesbian School Workers Collection, box 1, file 2, June Mazer Lesbian Collection, Los Angeles.

55 Hank Wilson, interview by Miriam Frank, Part 2, April 12, 1995, recording, Out in the Union: Gays and Lesbians in the Labor Movement, Miriam Frank Oral History Collection, Tamiment Library and Robert F. Wagner Labor Archive, New York.

56 Wilson, interview, Part 2; Lamble, "10th Anniversary."

57 Tom Ammiano, interview by Miriam Frank, Part 1, April 7, 1995, Out in the Union: Gays and Lesbians in the Labor Movement, recording, Miriam Frank Oral History Collection, Tamiment Library and Robert F. Wagner Labor Archive, New York.

Notes to Pages 142–146 • 209

58 Blount, *Fit to Teach*, 126–128.
59 Ammiano, interview, Part 1.
60 "Obituary: Reed Thomas A., S.J.," *San Francisco Gate*, June 24, 2003, http://www
.sfgate.com/news/article/REED-Rev-Thomas-A-S-J-2568567.php.
61 Blount, *Fit to Teach*, 127.
62 Hank Wilson, interview by Miriam Frank, Part 3, April 12, 1995, recording, Out
in the Union: Gays and Lesbians in the Labor Movement, Miriam Frank Oral
History Collection, Tamiment Library and Robert F. Wagner Labor Archive,
New York; S. Mary Bernadette Giles, "Letter re: Gay Teachers Coalition
Representation on Board of Youth and Education," June 28, 1977, Lesbian School
Workers Collection, box 1, file 15, June Mazer Lesbian Collection, Los Angeles.
63 Wilson, interview, Part 3.
64 Wilson, interview, Part 3.
65 Wilson, interview, Part 3; Blount, *Fit to Teach*, 143.
66 Faderman, *Gay Revolution*, 371–380.
67 Wilson, interview, Part 3.
68 Ammiano, interview, Part 1.
69 Wilson, interview, Part 3.
70 Ammiano, interview, Part 1.
71 Rachel Gordon, "Hank Wilson Dies: Gay Liberation Activist," *SFGate*, November 13, 2008, https://www.sfgate.com/bayarea/article/Hank-Wilson-dies-gay
-liberation-activist-3185940.php.
72 Smith, "Organizing for Social Justice," 426.
73 Ammiano, interview, Part 1.
74 Lesbian School Workers, "1977 Vanguard Grant Application," Vanguard
Foundation, San Francisco, Lesbian School Workers Collection, box 1, file 3, June
Mazer Lesbian Collection, Los Angeles.
75 Gay Teachers and School Workers Coalition, *GTSWC Newsletter* 1, no. 1
(August/September 1977): d3, Lesbian School Workers Collection, box 1, file 2,
June Mazer Lesbian Collection, Los Angeles.
76 There is considerable ambiguity regarding leadership structure of the LSW. Sara
Smith conducted numerous interviews with former members of the LSW but does
not include the names of leaders in her study. Likewise, publications from the
GTSWC and the LSW do not detail "leaders" of the LSW but instead refer to
members of specific committees. See Smith, "Organizing for Social Justice,"
425–428.
77 Faderman and Timmons, *Gay L.A.*, 181–186.
78 The history described by Faderman and Timmons may explain the conspicuous
lack of women in the GTLA mentioned earlier in this chapter. The GTLA had its
origins as a gay male discussion group, three years after the "split" between gay
male activist and lesbian activists in Los Angeles. Attracting women to a male-
dominated group in the context of distinctly separate communities would have
been decidedly difficult. In 1979, well after the defeat of Proposition 6, the GTLA
published an open letter to lesbian teachers positing various reasons why the group
continued to be male dominated and seeking a dialogue with lesbian teachers; the
letter noted that, in 1979, the ratio of men to women was ten to one. It is unclear
from available archival resources whether these efforts were successful. See Gay
Teachers of Los Angeles, "An Open Letter to Lesbian Teachers," September 1979,

210 • Notes to Pages 146–150

Betty Berzon Papers, box 42, file 60, *ONE* National Gay and Lesbian Archives, Los Angeles.

79 The political climate in San Francisco among feminist lesbians working with gay men was described by one lesbian leader as, "Then she thanks her colleagues 'who put up with a lot of [expletive deleted] during the early days of the campaign. And I would like to thank all the lesbian feminists who put away their anger and worked with the men,'" during the celebration speeches after Proposition 6. See Robert Reiley, "Homosexuality and Nature's Laws," *Wall Street Journal (1923—current file)*, January 22, 1979, sec. 1.

80 Smith, "Organizing for Social Justice," 427–429.

81 For various flyers and pamphlets detailing the activities of the LSW, see Lesbian School Workers Collection, box 1, files 2 and 4, June Mazer Lesbian Collection, Los Angeles.

82 Lesbian School Workers, *Slide Show Script*, 1978, San Francisco, 1, Lesbian School Workers Collection, box 1, file 5, June Mazer Lesbian Collection, Los Angeles.

83 Lesbian School Workers, *Slide Show Script*, 1–2.

84 Lesbian School Workers, *Slide Show Script*, 2.

85 Lesbian School Workers, *Slide Show Script*, 4.

86 Lesbian School Workers, *Slide Show Script*, 5.

87 Lesbian School Workers, *Slide Show Script*, 6.

88 The Briggs Initiative enjoyed early support in polls, a ten-point lead in some cases, but, as time went on, it lost that support and was eventually defeated 58.4 percent to 41.6 percent, with even Briggs's constituency in Orange County voting against the proposition. See Faderman, *Gay Revolution*, 383. See also Merrin Field, "A Major Shift to 'No' on Prop. 6," *San Francisco Chronicle*, October 5, 1978, Briggs Initiative Collection. box 3, file 1, *ONE* National Gay and Lesbian Archives, Los Angeles.

89 *California Voters Pamphlet: 1978.*

90 Larry Berner, a teacher in the rural Northern California town of Healdsburg who sued Briggs successfully for defamation of character, corroborates the relative absence of highly visible LGB teachers in the opposition campaign during an interview detailing his activities during the Proposition 6 campaign. Burner recalled that he personally was asked to not speak on behalf of any of the opposition groups because they felt that he might, "say something wrong" and become a political liability. See Larry Berner, interview by John Mehring, upon announcement of the settlement of *Berner v. Briggs*, 1982, San Francisco, Lawrence Berner vs. John Briggs Collection, box 2, file 5, James C. Hormel LGBTQIA Center, San Francisco Public Library. Berner did not belong to any LGB teachers' group; he was, as far as he knew, the only gay teacher in his school district, but was supported by his local teachers' union and, to a lesser degree, the community he taught in. See Cookie, "The Teacher Briggs Made Famous," *Sentinel*, September 22, 1978, 14, Briggs Initiative Collection, box 3, file 4, *ONE* National Gay and Lesbian Archives, Los Angeles; Catherine Barnett, *Gay Teacher Finds No Foes in Audience*, October 15, 1978, Briggs Initiative Collection, box 3, file 4, *ONE* National Gay and Lesbian Archives, Los Angeles. For a detailed account of Berner's activities during the Proposition 6 campaign, including his debates with State Senator John Briggs and reasons for Briggs utilizing Berner as an example of gay teachers, see Smith, "Organizing for Social Justice," 410–414.

Notes to Pages 152–162 • 211

91 For example, in the LGB press Proposition 6 was called "The Briggs Initiative" seemingly as often as it was referred to by its legal designation.

92 "Out of the Closet," *Los Angeles Times*, September 22, 1978, Briggs Initiative Collection, box 3, file 3, *ONE* National Gay and Lesbian Archives, Los Angeles.

93 Carl Nolte, "Ken Alexander, Former SF Examiner Cartoonist, Dies." *SFGate*, May 28, 2012, http://www.sfgate.com/bayarea/article/Ken-Alexander-former-SF -Examiner-cartoonist-dies-3589741.php.

94 For example, the possibility of teachers being unable to do their jobs because of Briggs-Initiative-inspired chaos was serious enough that it caused Ronald Reagan to reconsider his support of Proposition 6. Lillian Faderman describes the remarkable pitch that David Mixner and Paul Scott, both leaders of the "No on 6" campaign and gay men, made to Reagan. Through a network of conservative gay men and closeted aides working for Reagan, Mixner and Scott arranged a brief meeting where they astutely told the former governor, "Well this proposition would create anarchy in the classroom." Reagan was asked to "Imagine a kid getting a failing grade or being disciplined by a teacher or facing expulsion. To get even, all he'd have to do is accuse the teacher of being a homosexual. Teachers will be afraid of giving a low grade. They won't be able to maintain order in the classroom." Faced with the possibility that "kids were going to run the school," Reagan replied, "That's not what we want for California schools" and, as the two gay activists were leaving, "this might be a good day for you boys." A few weeks later Reagan publicly opposed Proposition 6, saying, "What if an overwrought youngster disappointed by bad grades, imagined it was the teacher's fault and struck out by accusing the teacher of advocating homosexuality?" delivering a tremendous blow to California Defend Our Children and John Briggs. Faderman, *Gay Revolution*, 377–383.

95 LA Times Editorial Board, "Dignifying Rumor and Innuendo," *LA Times*, August 21, 1978, Part III, 6, Briggs Initiative Collection. box 3, file 1, *ONE* National Gay and Lesbian Archives, Los Angeles.

96 *California Voters Pamphlet: 1978.*

97 Blount, *Fit to Teach*, 153–154.

98 Sara Smith points out that the African American community in California overwhelmingly opposed Proposition 6 in the 1978 election. Many African American activists were disappointed by the reality that LGB organizations working for the defeat of Proposition 6 seemed unwilling to actively oppose Proposition 7, "The Death Penalty Act." Proposition 7, also proposed by Briggs, increased penalties for first- and second-degree murder and passed by a wide margin; 71.1 percent voting "yes" versus 28.9 percent voting "no." See Smith, "Organizing for Social Justice," 174, 428.

99 Jack Cheevers, "Gay Teacher Issue Divides California," *Boston Globe (1960–1986)*, October 31, 1978, 44; Blount, *Fit to Teach*, 152.

100 *California Voters Pamphlet: 1978*, 30–31.

101 *California Voters Pamphlet: 1978*, 30–31.

102 *California Voters Pamphlet: 1978*, 30–31.

103 Blount, *Fit to Teach*, 151. For an account of Harvey Milk's activities during the "No on 6" campaign, see Randy Shilts, *The Mayor of Castro Street: The Life and Times of Harvey Milk* (New York: St. Martin's Griffin, 2008), 228–231.

Conclusion

1 Friedman, interview.
2 This observation holds true for the other American LGB teachers' groups discussed in the introduction as well, which all formed in cities with historically strong teachers' unions.
3 Blount, *Fit to Teach*, 156–159.
4 Gay Teachers of Maryland, *Gay Teachers of Maryland Newsletter* 3, no. 1 (May 1, 1981), box 3, file "Gay Teachers of Maryland Newsletter," Miscellaneous Human Sexuality Periodicals, Division of Rare and Manuscript Collections, Cornell University Library, Ithaca, New York.
5 For GTA newsletter, see *Gay Teachers Association Newsletter*, NYPL LGB Periodicals Collection, box 147—Melbourne 3, no. 3: 3; New South Wales 4, no. 2: 4; London 3, no. 2: 4 and 3, no. 7/8: 3; West Berlin 2, no. 7/8: 3.
6 Randal C. Archibold, "Public Lives: A Gay Crusader Sees History on His Side," *New York Times*, October 27, 1999.
7 The estimates of specific numbers are based on the recollections of activists during interviews conducted for this study and, as such, involve a range rather than a specific number. For example, according to Carol Watchler, the LGB Caucus dinner for the NEA annual meeting in 1988 had "fifty or sixty" attendees. The number of those attendees who were members of the caucus is unclear. Watchler, interview.
8 Watchler, interview.
9 Watchler, interview.
10 NEA, Research Division, *Status*, 67, table 49.
11 See *Bostock v. Clayton County, GA*, 590 U.S. 140 S. Ct. 1731; 2020 WL 3146686; 2020 U.S. LEXIS 3252.

Bibliography

Archival Collections Cited

Adele Starr Collection on Parents and Friends of Lesbians and Gays. *ONE* National Gay and Lesbian Archives, Los Angeles.

Advocate Records Collection. *ONE* National Gay and Lesbian Archives, Los Angeles.

AFT Educational Issues Department Records. Walter P. Reuther Library, Wayne State University, Detroit.

AFT Human Rights and Communications Department. Walter P. Reuther Library, Wayne State University, Detroit.

AFT President's Office Albert Shanker Collection. Walter P. Reuther Library, Wayne State University, Detroit.

AFT Secretary Treasury Office Records. Walter P. Reuther Library, Wayne State University, Detroit.

AFT Series Part II. Walter P. Reuther Library, Wayne State University, Detroit.

Barbara Gittings and Kay Tobin Lahusen Gay History Papers and Photographs. Manuscripts and Archives Division, New York Public Library, New York.

California Proposition 6 Briggs Initiative Collection 1977–1980. *ONE* National Gay and Lesbian Archives, Los Angeles.

Daniel Curzon Papers, 1950s–2014. James C. Hormel LGBTQIA Center, San Francisco Public Library, San Francisco.

David R. King Gay Rights Collection, 1975–2010. James C. Hormel LGBTQIA Center, San Francisco Public Library, San Francisco.

Eric E. Rofes Papers. James C. Hormel LGBTQIA Center, San Francisco Public Library, San Francisco.

Gay Sunshine Records, 1955–2005. *ONE* National Gay and Lesbian Archives, Los Angeles.

Gittings (Barbara) and Kay Tobin Lahusen Collection. *ONE* National Gay and Lesbian Archives, Los Angeles.

Lawrence Berner vs. John Briggs Collection, 1940–2004. James C. Hormel LGBTQIA Center, San Francisco Public Library, San Francisco.

214 • Bibliography

Lesbian, Gay, Bisexual and Transgender Periodical Collection. Manuscripts and Archives Division, New York Public Library, New York.

Lesbian and Gay Network Records. Tamiment Library/Wagner Archives, New York University, New York.

Lesbian and Gay Teachers Association of New York Collection. LGBT Community Center National Archives, New York.

Lesbian School Workers Collection, June Mazer Lesbian Archives, Werle Building, West Hollywood.

Lesbian School Workers Records, 1977–1978. UCLA Library Special Collections, Charles E. Young Research Library, Los Angeles.

Marc Rubin Collection. LGBT Community Center National Archives, New York.

Miscellaneous Human Sexuality Periodicals. Division of Rare and Manuscript Collections, Cornell University Library, Ithaca, NY.

National Education Association—Committees Records 857–1996. Gelman Library, George Washington University, Washington, DC.

Non LGBT Cover Story Collection. *ONE* National Gay and Lesbian Archives, Los Angeles.

NYPL LGB Periodicals Collection. New York Public Library Manuscript Division, New York.

ONE Subject Files Collection. *ONE* National Gay and Lesbian Archives, Los Angeles.

Out in the Union Collection. Tamiment Library/Wagner Archives, New York University, New York.

Randy Alfred Subject Files and Sound Recordings. GLBT Historical Society, San Francisco.

United Educators of San Francisco Part II. Walter P. Reuther Library, Wayne State University, Detroit.

United Federation of Teachers Records 1916–2002. Tamiment Library and Robert F. Wagner Labor Archives, New York University, New York.

William B. Kelley Papers. Gerber/Hart Library and Archives, Chicago.

Interviews

Ammiano, Tom. Interview by Miriam Frank, April 7, 1995. Out in the Union: Gays and Lesbians in the Labor Movement, Recording, Miriam Frank Oral History Collection. Tamiment Library and Robert F. Wagner Labor Archive, New York University, New York.

Dressler, Joshua. Interview by Jason Mayernick, March 23, 2015. Early Legal Scholarship on LGBT Teachers. Recording, Author's Collection.

Englander, Peter. Interview by Jason Mayernick, June 6, 2017. Gay Teachers of Los Angeles. Recording, Author's Collection.

Friedman, Meryl. Interview by Jason Mayernick, August 29, 2016. LGBT Teacher Activism in New York City. Recording, Author's Collection.

Futrell, Mary. Interview by Jason Mayernick, November 17, 2014. LGBT teachers and the NEA. Recording, Author's Collection.

Gish, John. Interview by Jason Mayernick, August 12, 2015. LGBT Teacher Activism. Recording, Author's Collection.

Horton, Jeff. Interview by Jason Mayernick, February 15, 2015. Recording, Author's Collection.

Hoyt, Jeff. Interview by Jason Mayernick, February 15, 2015. LGBT Teacher Activism in Los Angeles. Recording, Author's Collection.

McClelland, Norman. Interview by Jason Mayernick, May 18, 2017. Gay Teachers of Los Angeles. Recording, Author's Collection.

Rubino, Richard. Interview by Jason Mayernick, November 3, 2013. NEA and LGBT Activism. Recording, Author's Collection.

Stern, Jane. Interview by Jason Mayernick, October 31, 2014. LGBT Activism and the NEA. Recording, Author's Collection.

Watchler, Carol. Interview by Jason Mayernick, June 19, 2015. LGBT Teacher Activism. Recording, Author's Collection.

Weiner, Louis. Interview by Jason Mayernick, January 17, 2015. LGBT Teacher Activism in the AFT. Recording, Author's Collection.

Wilson, Hank. Interview by Miriam Frank, April 12, 1995. Out in the Union: Gays and Lesbians in the Labor Movement, Recording, Miriam Frank Oral History Collection. Tamiment Library and Robert F. Wagner Labor Archive, New York University, New York.

Periodicals Cited

Advocate. Los Angeles, CA
Atlanta Daily World. Atlanta, GA
Baltimore Sun. Baltimore MD
Boston Globe. Boston, MA
Chicago Defender. Chicago, IL
Chicago Tribune. Chicago, IL
Los Angeles Times. Los Angeles, CA
McCall's. New York, NY
New York Times. New York, NY
Oklahoma Journal. Oklahoma City, OK
Phi Delta Kappan. Arlington, VA
Press Democrat. Santa Rosa, CA
Sacramento Bee. Sacramento, CA
San Francisco Chronicle. San Francisco, CA
San Francisco Examiner. San Francisco, CA
Sentinel. San Francisco, CA
Wall Street Journal. New York, NY
Washington Post. Washington, DC
Washington Times Herald. Washington, DC

Other Secondary Sources

Aldrich, Robert. "Homosexuality and the City: An Historical Overview." *Urban Studies* 41, no. 9 (2004): 1719–1737.

Ammiano, Tom. "My Adventures as a Gay Teacher." In *Smash the Church, Smash the State! The Early Years of Gay Liberation*, edited by Tommi Avicolli Mecca, 40–42. San Francisco: City Lights, 2019.

Atkins, Gary. *Gay Seattle: Stories of Exile and Belonging*. Seattle: University of Washington Press, 2011.

216 • Bibliography

Bailey, Beth L. *Sex in the Heartland*. Cambridge, MA: Harvard University Press, 1999.

Baim, Tracy. *Out and Proud in Chicago: An Overview of the City's Gay Community*. Evanston, IL: Agate, 2009.

Bascia, Nina, ed. *Teacher Unions in Public Education: Politics, History, and the Future*. New York: Palgrave Macmillan, 2015.

Bérubé, Allan. *Coming Out Under Fire: The History of Gay Men and Women in World War II*. Chapel Hill: University of North Carolina Press, 2010.

Biegel, Stuart. *The Right to Be Out: Sexual Orientation and Gender Identity in America's Public Schools*. Minneapolis: University of Minnesota Press, 2010.

Blount, Jackie M. *Destined to Rule the Schools: Women and the Superintendency, 1873–1995*. SUNY Series in Educational Leadership. Albany: State University of New York Press, 1998.

———. *Fit to Teach: Same-Sex Desire, Gender, and School Work in the Twentieth Century*. Albany: State University of New York Press, 2006.

———. "Spinsters, Bachelors, and Other Gender Transgressors in School Employment, 1850–1990." *Review of Educational Research* 70, no. 1 (March 1, 2000): 83–101.

Boag, Peter. *Same-Sex Affairs: Constructing and Controlling Homosexuality in the Pacific Northwest*. Berkeley: University of California Press, 2003.

Boyd, Nan Alamilla. *Wide-Open Town: A History of Queer San Francisco to 1965*. Berkeley: University of California Press, 2003.

Braukman, Stacy. "'Nothing Else Matters but Sex': Cold War Narratives of Deviance and the Search for Lesbian Teachers in Florida, 1959–1963." *Feminist Studies* 27, no. 3 (October 1, 2001): 553–575.

Braun, Robert J. *Teachers and Power: The Story of the American Federation of Teachers*. New York: Simon & Schuster, 1973.

Bureau of the Census. *Asian Pacific Islander Population in the United States: 1980*. Washington, DC: U.S. Department of Commerce, 1983.

———. *Historical Statistics of the United States Colonial Times to 1970*. Washington, DC: U.S. Department of Commerce, 1976.

———. *1950 Census of Population and Housing*. Washington, DC: U.S. Department of Commerce, 1953.

———. *1980 Census of Population and Housing*. Washington, DC: U.S. Department of Commerce, 1983.

Cameron, Don. *Educational Conflict in the Sunshine State: The Story of the 1968 Statewide Teacher Walkout in Florida*. Lanham, MD: R&L Education, 2008.

———. *The Inside Story of the Teacher Revolution in America*. Lanham, MD: R&L Education, 2005.

Canaday, Margot. *The Straight State: Sexuality and Citizenship in Twentieth-Century America*. Princeton, NJ: Princeton University Press, 2011.

———. "'Who Is a Homosexual?': The Consolidation of Sexual Identities in Mid-Twentieth-Century American Immigration Law." *Law & Social Inquiry* 28, no. 2 (April 1, 2003): 351–386.

Caruso, Michael P. *When the Sisters Said Farewell: The Transition of Leadership in Catholic Elementary Schools*. Lanham, MD: R&L Education, 2012.

Cecelski, David S. *Along Freedom Road: Hyde County, North Carolina and the Fate of Black Schools in the South*. Chapel Hill: University of North Carolina Press, 1994.

Chauncey, George. *Gay New York: Gender, Urban Culture, and the Making of the Gay Male World, 1890–1940*. New York: Basic Books, 1995.

Cobble, Dorothy. *Dishing It Out: Waitresses and Their Unions in the Twentieth Century*. Urbana: University of Illinois Press, 1991.

Cohen, Stephan. *The Gay Liberation Youth Movement in New York: An Army of Lovers Cannot Fail*. New York: Routledge, 2007.

Cowie, Jefferson R. *Stayin' Alive: The 1970s and the Last Days of the Working Class*. New York: New Press, 2012.

Croix, St Sukie de la. *Chicago Whispers: A History of LGBT Chicago before Stonewall*. With a foreword by John D'Emilio. Madison: University of Wisconsin Press, 2012.

Cvetkovich, Ann. *An Archive of Feelings: Trauma, Sexuality, and Lesbian Public Cultures*. Durham, NC: Duke University Press Books, 2003.

D'Amico Pawlewicz, Diana. *Blaming Teachers: Professionalization Policies and the Failure of Reform in American History*. New Brunswick, NJ: Rutgers University Press, 2020.

Darman, Jonathan. *Landslide: LBJ and Ronald Reagan at the Dawn of a New America*. New York: Random House, 2015.

D'Emilio, John. *Making Trouble: Essays on Gay History, Politics, and the University*. New York: Routledge, 1992.

Deslippe, Dennis A. *Rights, Not Roses: Unions and the Rise of Working-Class Feminism, 1945–80*. Urbana: University of Illinois Press, 1999.

Dilley, Patrick. *Queer Man on Campus: A History of Non-Heterosexual College Men, 1945 to 2000*. New York: RoutledgeFalmer, 2002.

Downs, Jim. *Stand by Me: The Forgotten History of Gay Liberation*. New York: Basic Books, 2016.

Drescher, Jac, and Joseph P. Merlino. *American Psychiatry and Homosexuality: An Oral History*. New York: Harrington Park Press, 2007.

Dressler, Joshua. "Gay Teachers: A Disesteemed Minority in an Overly Esteemed Profession." *Rutgers Camden Law Journal* 9, no. 3 (1978): 399–445.

Drury, Darrel W., and Justin D. Baer, eds. *The American Public School Teacher: Past, Present, & Future*. Cambridge, MA: Harvard Education Press, 2011.

Duberman, Martin B. *Stonewall*. New York: Plume, 1994.

Eaton, William Edward. *The American Federation of Teachers, 1916–1961: A History of the Movement*. Carbondale: Southern Illinois University Press, 1975.

Eckes, Suzanne E., and Martha M. McCarthy. "GLBT Teachers: The Evolving Legal Protections." *American Educational Research Journal* 45, no. 3 (September 1, 2008): 530–554.

Ehrenstein, David. *Open Secret: Gay Hollywood, 1928–1998*. New York: William Morrow, 1998.

Eisenbach, David. *Gay Power: An American Revolution*. Reprint, New York: Da Capo, 2007.

Evans, Sara M. *Tidal Wave: How Women Changed America at Century's End*. New York: Free Press, 2003.

Faderman, Lillian. *The Gay Revolution: The Story of the Struggle*. Reprint, New York: Simon & Schuster, 2016.

———. *Odd Girls and Twilight Lovers: A History of Lesbian Life in Twentieth-Century America*. Reprint, New York: Columbia University Press, 2012.

———. *Surpassing the Love of Men: Romantic Friendship and Love between Women from the Renaissance to the Present*. New York: William Morrow, 1981.

Faderman, Lillian, and Stuart Timmons. *Gay L.A.: A History of Sexual Outlaws, Power Politics, and Lipstick Lesbians*. New York: Basic Books, 2006.

218 • Bibliography

Fejes, F. *Gay Rights and Moral Panic: The Origins of America's Debate on Homosexuality.* New York: Palgrave Macmillan, 2011.

Fellows, Will, and Helen P. Branson. *Gay Bar: The Fabulous, True Story of a Daring Woman and Her Boys in the 1950s.* Madison: University of Wisconsin Press, 2010.

Frank, Miriam. *Out in the Union: A Labor History of Queer America.* Philadelphia: Temple University Press, 2014.

Freedman, Estelle B. *The Lesbian Issue: Essays from Signs.* Chicago: University of Chicago Press, 1985.

———. "Sexuality in Nineteenth-Century America: Behavior, Ideology, and Politics." *Reviews in American History* 10, no. 4 (1982): 196–215.

Freedman, Estelle B., and John D'Emilio. "Problems Encountered in Writing the History of Sexuality: Sources, Theory and Interpretation." *Journal of Sex Research* 27, no. 4 (1990): 481–495.

Freeman, Joshua Benjamin. *Working-Class New York: Life and Labor since World War II.* New York: New Press, 2000.

Gaffney, Dennis. *Teachers United: The Rise of New York State United Teachers.* Albany: State University of New York Press, 2007.

Gallo, Marcia M. *Different Daughters: A History of the Daughters of Bilitis and the Rise of the Lesbian Rights Movement.* New York: Carroll & Graf, 2006.

Goldstein, Dana. *The Teacher Wars: A History of America's Most Embattled Profession.* Reprint, New York: Anchor, 2015.

Golin, Steve. *The Newark Teacher Strikes: Hopes on the Line.* New Brunswick, NJ: Rutgers University Press, 2002.

Gordon, Jane Anna. *Why They Couldn't Wait: A Critique of the Jewish Conflict over Community Control in Ocean Hill-Brownsville, 1967–1971.* New York: RoutledgeFalmer, 2001.

Gould, Deborah B. *Moving Politics: Emotion and ACT UP's Fight against AIDS.* Chicago: University of Chicago Press, 2009.

———. "The Shame of Gay Pride in Early AIDS Activism." In *Gay Shame*, edited by David M. Halperin and Valerie Traub, 221–255. Chicago: University of Chicago Press, 2009.

Graves, Karen. "'So, You Think You Have a History?': Taking a Q from Lesbian and Gay Studies in Writing Education History." *History of Education Quarterly* 52, no. 4 (November 1, 2012): 465–487.

———. *And They Were Wonderful Teachers.* Urbana: University of Illinois Press, 2009.

Griffin, Pat. "From Hiding to Coming Out, Empowering Lesbian and Gay Educators." In *Coming Out of the Classroom Closet: Gay and Lesbian Students, Teachers, and Curricula*, edited by Karen M. Harbeck, 167–196. New York: Haworth Press, 1992.

Hanhardt, Christina B. *Safe Space: Gay Neighborhood History and the Politics of Violence.* Durham, NC: Duke University Press Books, 2013.

Harbeck, Karen M., ed. *Coming Out of the Classroom Closet: Gay and Lesbian Students, Teachers, and Curricula.* New York: Haworth Press, 1992.

———. *Gay and Lesbian Educators: Personal Freedoms, Public Constraints.* Malden, MA: Amethyst, 1997.

Hayward, Steven. *The Age of Reagan: The Fall of the Old Liberal Order: 1964–1980.* Reprint, New York: Crown Forum, 2009.

Hobson, Emily K. *Lavender and Red: Liberation and Solidarity in the Gay and Lesbian Left.* Oakland: University of California Press, 2016.

Howard, John. *Men Like That: A Southern Queer History*. Chicago: University of Chicago Press, 2001.

Hunt, Gerald, ed. *Laboring for Rights: Unions and Sexual Diversity across Nations*. Queer Politics, Queer Theories. Philadelphia: Temple University Press, 1999.

Hurewitz, Daniel. *Bohemian Los Angeles and the Making of Modern Politics*. Berkeley: University of California Press, 2007.

Johnson, David K. *The Lavender Scare: The Cold War Persecution of Gays and Lesbians in the Federal Government*. Chicago: University of Chicago Press, 2006.

Johnston, Paul. *Success While Others Fail: Social Movement Unionism and the Public Workplace*. Ithaca, NY: ILR Press, 1994.

Kahlenberg, Richard D. *Tough Liberal: Albert Shanker and the Battles over Schools, Unions, Race, and Democracy*. Columbia Studies in Contemporary American History. New York: Columbia University Press, 2007.

Kaiser, Charles. *The Gay Metropolis: The Landmark History of Gay Life in America*. New York: Grove Press, 2007.

Kalleberg, Arne L. *Good Jobs, Bad Jobs: The Rise of Polarized and Precarious Employment Systems in the United States, 1970s–2000s*. New York: Russell Sage Foundation, 2011.

Katz, Jonathan Ned. *Gay American History*. New York: Avon Books, 1978.

Kennedy, Elizabeth, and Madeline Davis. *Boots of Leather, Slippers of Gold: The History of a Lesbian Community*. New York: Penguin Books, 1994.

Kenney, Moira. *Mapping Gay L.A.: The Intersection of Place and Politics*. Philadelphia: Temple University Press, 2001.

Kessler-Harris, Alice. *Out to Work: A History of Wage-Earning Women in the United States*. New York: Oxford University Press, 1982.

Kink, Steve. *Class Wars: The Story of the Washington Education Association 1965–2001*. Federal Way: Washington Education Association, 2004.

Kissen, Rita M. *The Last Closet: The Real Lives of Lesbian and Gay Teachers*. Portsmouth, NH: Heinemann, 1996.

———. "Voices from the Glass Closet: Lesbian and Gay Teachers Talk about Their Lives." Presentation at the Annual Meeting of the American Educational Research Association, Atlanta, GA, April 12–16, 1993. https://files.eric.ed.gov/fulltext/ED363556.pdf1993.

Letts, William J., IV, and James T. Sears. *Queering Elementary Education: Advancing the Dialogue about Sexualities and Schooling*. Lanham, MD: Rowman & Littlefield, 1999.

Loftin, Craig M., ed. *Letters to One: Gay and Lesbian Voices from the 1950s and 1960s*. Albany: State University of New York Press, 2012.

———. *Masked Voices: Gay Men and Lesbians in Cold War America*. SUNY Series in Queer Politics and Cultures. Albany: State University of New York Press, 2012.

Lugg, Catherine. *US Public Schools and the Politics of Queer Erasure*. New York: Palgrave Pivot, 2015.

MacLean, Nancy. *Freedom Is Not Enough: The Opening of the American Work Place*. New York: Sage; Cambridge, MA: Harvard University Press, 2006.

Maier, Mark H. *City Unions: Managing Discontent in New York City*. New Brunswick, NJ: Rutgers University Press, 1987.

Marcus, Eric. *Making Gay History: The Half-Century Fight for Lesbian and Gay Equal Rights*. New York: HarperCollins Publishers, 2002.

Mayernick, Jason. "The Gay Teachers Association of NYC and LGB Students: 1974–1985." *Teachers College Record* 122, no. 9 (2020): 1–30.

McCartin, Joseph A. *Collision Course: Ronald Reagan, the Air Traffic Controllers, and the Strike That Changed America*. Reprint, New York: Oxford University Press, 2013.

Mecca, Tommi Avicolli. *Smash the Church, Smash the State! The Early Years of Gay Liberation*. San Francisco: City Lights, 2009.

Meeker, Martin. "Behind the Mask of Respectability: Reconsidering the Mattachine Society and Male Homophile Practice, 1950s and 1960s." *Journal of the History of Sexuality* 10, no. 1 (2001): 78–116.

———. *Contacts Desired: Gay and Lesbian Communications and Community, 1940s–1970s*. Chicago: University of Chicago Press, 2006.

Mumford, Kevin J. *Newark: A History of Race, Rights, and Riots in America*. New York: New York University Press, 2007.

Murdoch, Joyce, and Deb Price. *Courting Justice: Gay Men and Lesbians v. the Supreme Court*. New York: Basic Books, 2002.

Murphy, Marjorie. *Blackboard Unions: The AFT and the NEA, 1900–1980*. Ithaca, NY: Cornell University Press, 1992.

National Education Association. *A Voice for GLBT Educators,* National Education Association Archives, Gelman Library, George Washington University, Washington, DC.

National Education Association of the United States, Research Division. *Status of the American Public School Teacher, 1980–1981*. Washington, DC: NEA, Research Division, 1982.

———. *Status of the American Public School Teacher, 2000–2001*. Washington, DC: NEA, Research Division, 2003.

National Education Association Records of the Representative Assembly. Washington, DC: NEA, 1972.

Perlstein, Daniel H. *Justice, Justice: School Politics and the Eclipse of Liberalism*. New York: Peter Lang, 2004.

Perrillo, Jonna. *Uncivil Rights: Teachers, Unions, and Race in the Battle for School Equity*. Chicago: University of Chicago Press, 2012.

Perry, Thelma D. *History of the American Teachers Association*. Washington, DC: National Education Association, 1975.

Podair, Jerald. *The Strike That Changed New York: Blacks, Whites, and the Ocean Hill-Brownsville Crisis*. New Haven, CT: Yale University Press, 2004.

Rofes, Eric E. *Socrates, Plato, and Guys Like Me: Confessions of a Gay Schoolteacher*. Boston: Alyson Books, 1985.

Rubin, Marc. "History of the Gay Teachers Association." *Gay Teachers Association Newsletter* 1, no. 1 (January 1, 1978).

Russo, Vito. *The Celluloid Closet: Homosexuality in the Movies*. Revised edition. New York: Harper & Row, 1987.

Schiavi, Michael R. *Celluloid Activist: The Life and Times of Vito Russo*. Madison: University of Wisconsin Press, 2011.

Schultz, Michael John. *The National Education Association and the Teacher: The Integration of a Professional Organization*. Coral Gables, FL: University of Miami Press, 1970.

Seidman, Steven. *Beyond the Closet: The Transformation of Gay and Lesbian Life*. Reprint, New York: Routledge, 2003.

———. *The Social Construction of Sexuality.* 2nd ed. New York: W. W. Norton, 2009.

Selden, David. *The Teacher Rebellion.* Washington, DC: Howard University Press, 1985.

Shaw, Stephanie J. *What a Woman Ought to Be and to Do: Black Professional Women Workers during the Jim Crow Era.* Women in Culture and Society. Chicago: University of Chicago Press, 1996.

Shelton, Jon. *Teacher Strike! Public Education and the Making of a New American Political Order.* Urbana: University of Illinois Press, 2017.

Shilts, Randy. *And the Band Played On: Politics, People, and the AIDS Epidemic.* New York: St Martin's Griffin, 2007.

———. *The Mayor of Castro Street: The Life and Times of Harvey Milk.* New York: St. Martin's Griffin, 2008.

Smith, Sara R. "Organizing for Social Justice: Rank-and-File Teachers' Activism and Social Unionism in California, 1948–1978." PhD diss., University of California, Santa Cruz, 2014.

Stein, Marc. *City of Sisterly and Brotherly Loves: Lesbian and Gay Philadelphia, 1945–1972.* Temple University Press, 2004.

———. *Rethinking the Gay and Lesbian Movement.* New York: Routledge, 2012.

Stewart-Winter, Timothy. *Queer Clout: Chicago and the Rise of Gay Politics.* Philadelphia: University of Pennsylvania Press, 2016.

Taft, Philip. *United They Teach: The Story of the United Federation of Teachers.* Los Angeles: Nash Pub, 1974.

Taylor, Clarence. *Reds at the Blackboard: Communism, Civil Rights, and the New York City Teachers Union.* New York: Columbia University Press, 2011.

Thompson, Mark, and Randy Shilts. *Long Road to Freedom: The Advocate History of the Gay and Lesbian Movement.* New York: St Martin's Press, 1994.

Tiemeyer, Philip James. *Plane Queer: Labor, Sexuality, and AIDS in the History of Male Flight Attendants.* Berkeley: University of California Press, 2013.

Urban, Wayne J. "Courting the Woman Teacher: The National Education Association, 1917–1970." *History of Education Quarterly* 41, no. 2 (June 1, 2001): 139–166.

———. *Gender, Race, and the National Education Association: Professionalism and Its Limitations.* Studies in the History of Education. New York: Routledge Falmer, 2000.

———. *More Than the Facts: The Research Division of the National Education Association, 1922–1997.* Lanham, MD: University Press of America, 1998.

———. *Why Teachers Organized.* Detroit: Wayne State University Press, 1982.

Wat, Eric C. *The Making of a Gay Asian Community: An Oral History of Pre-AIDS Los Angeles.* Pacific Formations. Lanham, MD: Rowman & Littlefield, 2002.

Weiner, Lois. *The Future of Our Schools: Teachers Unions and Social Justice.* Chicago: Haymarket Books, 2012.

Weiner, Melissa. *Power, Protest, and the Public Schools: Jewish and African American Struggles in New York City.* Piscataway, NJ: Rutgers University Press, 2012.

West, Allan. *National Education Association and the Power Base.* New York: Free Press, 1980.

Weston, Kath. "Get Thee to a Big City: Sexual Imaginary and the Great Gay Migration." *GLQ: A Journal of Lesbian and Gay Studies* 2, no. 3 (January 1, 1995): 253–277.

Windham, Anna Lane. *Knocking on Labor's Door: Union Organizing in the 1970s and the Roots of a New Economic Divide.* Chapel Hill: University of North Carolina Press, 2019.

222 • Bibliography

Wood, Sherry E., and Karen M. Harbeck, "Living in Two Worlds: The Identity Management Strategies Utilized by Lesbian Educators." In *Coming Out of the Classroom Closet: Gay and Lesbian Students, Teachers, and Curricula*, edited by Karen M. Harbeck, 141–166. New York: Haworth Press, 1992.

Zimmerman, Jonathan. *Too Hot to Handle: A Global History of Sex Education*. Princeton, NJ: Princeton University Press, 2015.

———. *Whose America? Culture Wars in the Public Schools*. Cambridge, MA: Harvard University Press, 2002.

Index

Note: Page numbers in *italics* refer to figures and tables.

Acanfora, Joseph, 25, 83

ACLU (American Civil Liberties Union),
24–25, 85–86

AFL-CIO (American Federation of
Labor and Congress of Industrial
Organizations), 33, 81, 86, 101, 193n25

AFT (American Federation of Teachers),
11–12, 17–18, 33–34; Delegate Assembly,
63–65; failed LGB constitutional
amendment, 76; First LGB resolution,
65–69; growth, 62; leadership, 64; LGB
caucus, 63; official caucuses, 64; opposition
to Briggs Initiative, 74–76; organizational
limitations, 83, 88; size and scope, 89–90

AIDS Crisis, 14, 49–51, 183n25, 189nn96–
97, 190n102; education, 55–56; impact on
GTA, 122; testing of students for HIV,
50, 190n118

American Federation of Teachers. *See* AFT

American Teachers Association, 32

Ammiano, Tom, 141–144

ATA. *See* American Teachers Association

Bay Area Gay Liberation (BAGL), 141–142

Bennet, William J.: Secretary of Education, 56

Boston: Gay and Lesbian Schoolworkers,
170, 183n22

Bradshaw, Roxanne, 55

Briggs, John, 154, 162; comics against, *151,
152, 155*; number of LGB teachers in
schools, 138; personal beliefs, 130; political
opportunity, 127–128; portrayal of LGB
teachers, 160; Proposition 7, 149

Briggs Initiative, 19, 48, 52, 74–76, 124,
137–138; comics against, 150–158

Bryant, Anita, 73–75, 124, 140, 143

California: ballot initiatives, 131, 133;
demographic shifts, 128–129; Proposition 7, 128, 146, 211n98

California Defend Our Children, 130–135;
Anita Bryant Campaign, 75; Christian
rhetoric, 132; logo, 131, *132*; mass
mailings, *132*; threat posed by LGB
teachers, 160

California Federation of Teachers, 75, 159,
192n12

Catholic, 93, 142, 186n48

Cheery Chalkboard. *See* Gay Teachers of
Los Angeles: newsletter

Chicago Gay Teachers' Association,
98–99

civil rights movement, 11, 39, 103, 149, 170,
186n37

224 • Index

Daughters of Bilitis, 100
District of Columbia: 1972 nondiscrimination law, 29
Dressler, Joshua, 83–84, 202n70

Englander, Peter, 138
Executive Order 10988, 27–28

Feldman, Sandra, 104–105, 200n45, 279
Florida, 73, 143, 184n10
Friedman, Meryl, 107–111, 126–127, 166
Futrell, Mary, 48, 51, 53

Gay Activist Alliance: New Jersey, 23
Gay Activist Alliance (GAA), 23–25, 84, 104, 202n76
Gaylord, James, 25
gay male teachers: Cold War repression, 7, 181n5
Gay Teacher and School Workers Coalition, 141, 206; community outreach, 142; gender-based schism, 144–146; post Prop 6, 144
Gay Teachers Association of New York, 28; Advocacy for LGB students, 191–192; GTA newsletter, 162, 166, 167, 171, 172; LGB student advocacy, 164; parties, 162; political advocacy, 118–119; relationship with UFT, 93–95, 104–107; Speakers Bureau, 120
Gay Teachers of Los Angeles, 135; foundation of, 136; gender politics, 140, 209n78; legal actions, 137–138; membership numbers, 207n42; newsletter, 138; post Briggs Initiative, 208n50; union participation, 137–138
Gay Teachers of Maryland, 170–171, 197n10
Gish, John, 17, 23–28, 44, 57, 87, 113, 167; court cases, 31–32, 83; NEA Gay Teacher Caucus, 28; political goals, 29, 30
GLSEN (Gay, Lesbian, Straight, Education, Network), 116–117, 172
GTA. See Gay Teachers Association of New York
GTLA. See Gay Teachers of Los Angeles
GTSWC. See Gay Teacher and School Workers Coalition

Helm, Mary, 84
Helm's Bill, 84–88
Helm's Law, 90, 178, 196n69
Holden, Robert, 60, 77–78
Horton, Jeff, 47–48, 50–51
Hurwitz, Howard L., 118–120

Ichabod Crane Debating Society, 43–47, 48

labor: impact on LGBT organizing, 37–38
Labor Movement, 35–37, 48, 95, 101, 182n15, 192n17
Lesbian School Workers, 126, 170; commitment to racial/class activism, 146; community outreach, 149; critique of mainstream education, 146; feminism, 145–146; opposition to Proposition 7, 149; slide show, 147–149
LGB students, 3, 5, 53, 84, 95, 112, 121; education of, 122; impact of antigay campaigns on, 209; misinformation of, 116–117; portrayal by LGB teachers, 114–115
LGB teacher groups: city based, 13; job security as issue, 5, 55, 103, 123, 163; locations of, 13, 113; membership size, 3–4, 97; racial diversity, 207n42; union based. See also AFT, NEA
LGB teachers, as role models, 112, 118–120, 162; coming out, 58, 110–111, 138; concept of honesty, 113–114, 176; connection to Civil Rights movement (see civil rights movement); job security (see LGB teacher groups); negotiation, 167–168; novelty of, 6; paranoia, 108; political agency, 6–8, 58, 169; privacy, 17, 50–53, 69–71, 75, 109, 156; professionalism, 22, 27–28, 239; recruitment myth, 75, 99, 115, 202n78; risks of advocacy, 116; "safe space," 1990s, 111, 116; social space as activism, 35, 44, 46–47, 110–111, 188n76; teacher responsibility, 19, 95, 112–114
Los Angeles, 139; LGBT history of, 136
Los Angeles Times: opposition to Prop 6, 134, 154, 155
LSW. See Lesbian School Workers

Maryland. See Gay Teachers of Maryland
Mattachine Society, 100, 136

McClelland, Norman, 135–139
Morrison v. the State Board of Education, 69–70

National Education Association. *See* NEA
National Gay Task Force (NGTF), AFT correspondence, 84–86; Board of Education of Oklahoma City v. National Gay Task Force, 86, 89; GTA comembers, 104
NEA (National Education Association), 11–13, 16; annual meeting, 26; collective bargaining, 36–37; desegregation of state associations, 33–34; development of, 45; initial LGB protections, 38–43; legal support for LGB members, 41; membership increases, 185n16; position on sexual orientation, 52; professional staffers, 30–31; Representative Assembly, 39–40; Research Division, 28; response to AIDS crisis, 54–56; shift to union activism, 27–28; size and scope, 25–26; state associations, 24, 34, 85; teacher professionalism, 22, 56–59
NEA/AFT Merger, 33, 189n84, 193n24
NEA/ATA Mergers, 33–34
NEA Gay and Lesbian Caucus, 47–48; AIDS crisis resolutions, 54–56; proposal for LGBT student support, 54
New York City Board of Education, 93, 106
New York City Department of Education: interactions with GTA, 110
New York Gay Teachers Association. *See* Gay Teachers Association of New York: GTA newsletter
New York State Legislature, 102–103, 119
New York State Teachers' Union, 64
NGTF. *See* National Gay Task Force
No on 6 campaign: exclusion of LGB teachers, 211n94; goals, 144

Ocean Hill/Brownsville, 103
Oklahoma Federation of Teachers, 85, 90
Oklahoma State Education Association, 85
One Magazine: Mattachine Society, 146, 200n58

Proposition 6. *See* Briggs Initiative
Proposition 7, 128, 149, 211n98

queer space, 45–46

Reagan, Ronald, 55–56, 155, 204n104, 205n10, 211n94
Rubin, Marc, 92–93, 104–105, 107–108
Rubino, Richard, 43–46

San Francisco: Board of Education, 141; Youth and Education Committee, 142
San Francisco Gay Liberation Parade, 1
San Francisco State University, 65–66, 192n11
San Jose State University, 65–66, 99
Save Our Children, 43–74, 143
school principals: opinions on LGB teachers, 120
Shanker, Albert, 80, 84, 87, 89, 125; impact on AFT policy, 63–65, 101–105; UFT/AFT President, 64, 193n24
Springer, Hank: UTLA president, 137
Stern, Jane, 39
Stonewall Riots, 100
straight allies, 19; Los Angeles, 139; in the NEA, 39–43; San Francisco, 144
Supreme Court: Board of Education of Oklahoma City vs. National Gay Task Force, 86–89; Eisenstadt v. Baird, 84; Griswold v. Connecticut, 84

teachers: barriers to political activism, 58, 123; as civil servants, 27, 158; desexualization of, 23; expectations of, 4, 7, 13, 34, 36, 59; gender demographics, 34–35; gender discrimination, 34, 36; mandatory HIV testing, 190n118; moral turpitude laws, 69, 85, 127, 159; political agency, 11, 81–82, 123, 148, 169; professionalism, 56–59; right to privacy, 17, 69, 109, 193n22; value of, 2, 159–163
teachers unions, opposition to, 36; political limitations, 56, 84, 88–89. *See also* AFT, ATA, NEA, UFT

Transgender teachers, 14–15, 54–55, 170
Tribe, Lawrence, 87–88

UFT. *See* United Federation of Teachers
United Federation of Teachers (UFT), 101–104, 110, 199n29; position on LGB teachers, 105–107; role in AFT, 62–64, 199n32
United Teachers of Los Angeles, 137
UTLA. *See* United Teachers of Los Angeles

Vanguard Foundation, 145
Village Voice, The, 107

Washington D.C: School Board, 154
Watchler: Carol, 48–49, 172–173
Weiner, Louis, 64
White, Ryan: at NEA annual meeting, 54–56
Wilson, Hank, 141–144

Zogby, John, 115–116, 122

About the Author

JASON MAYERNICK is an assistant professor of social foundations and leadership education at the University of North Georgia. He researches the history of education in the United States and is especially interested in tracing how that history intersects with that of marginalized peoples. He lives north of Atlanta with his husband, a small dog named Latka, and far too many books.